Automatic Transmissions and Transaxles

Classroom Manual

Fourth Edition

Chek-Chart

Mark Hambaum, Revision Author

James D. Halderman, Series Author

PEARSON

Prentice
Hall

Upper Saddle River, New Jersey
Columbus, Ohio

Library of Congress Cataloging in Publication Data

Automatic transmissions and transaxles / Chek-Chart.— 4th ed.
  p. cm.
 ISBN 0-13-094341-X (classroom manual) — ISBN 0-13-0943242-8 (shop
manual)
 1. Automobiles—Transmission devices, Automatic—Maintenance and
repair. I. Check-Chart Publications (Firm)

 TL263.H36 2004
 629.2'446'0288—dc22

                                                    2003021911

Editor in Chief: Stephen Helba
Executive Editor: Ed Francis
Chek-Chart Series Editor: James D. Halderman
Editorial Assistant: Jennifer Day
Production Editor: Stephen C. Robb
Production Supervision: Stephanie Seifert, D&G Limited, LLC
Design Coordinator: Diane Y. Ernsberger
Cover Designer: Mark Schumaker
Cover photo: Mark Hambaum
Production Manager: Matthew Ottenweller
Marketing Manager: Mark Marsden

This book was set in Palatino by D&G Limited, LLC. It was printed and bound by Courier Kendallville, Inc.. The cover was
printed by The Lehigh Press, Inc.

Pearson Education Ltd.
Pearson Education Singapore Pte. Ltd.
Pearson Education Canada, Ltd.
Pearson Education—Japan

Pearson Education Australia Pty. Limited
Pearson Education North Asia Ltd.
Pearson Educación de Mexico, S.A. de C.V.
Pearson Education Malaysia Pte. Ltd.

10 9 8 7 6 5 4 3 2 1
ISBN: 0-13-094341-X

Preface

Automatic Transmissions and Transaxles is part of the Chek-Chart Automotive Series. The package for each course has two volumes, a *Classroom Manual* and a *Shop Manual*. Other titles in this series include

- *Automotive Electrical and Electronic Systems*
- *Fuel System and Emission Controls*
- *Automotive Brake Systems*
- *Automotive Engine Repair and Rebuilding*
- *Engine Performance Diagnosis and Tune-Up*
- *Automotive Steering, Suspension, and Wheel Alignment*
- *Automotive Heating, Ventilation, and Air Conditioning Systems*

Each book is written to help the instructor teach students how to become excellent professional automobile technicians. The two-manual sets are the core of a complete learning system that leads a student from basic theories to actual hands-on experience. The entire series is job-oriented and designed for students who intend to work in the automotive service profession. Learning the contents and techniques in these volumes is a big step toward a satisfying and rewarding career.

The *Classroom Manual* and the *Shop Manual* provide an improved presentation of the descriptive information and study lessons, along with practical testing, repair, and overhaul procedures. The descriptive chapters in the *Classroom Manual* correspond to the application chapters in the *Shop Manual*, and they should be used together. Each book is divided into several complete segments. Instructors will find the chapters to be complete, readable, and well thought-out. Students will benefit from the many learning aids, as well as from the thoroughness of the presentation.

For over 75 years, Chek-Chart has provided vehicle service specifications to the automotive repair industry. Because of the comprehensive material, the hundreds of high-quality illustrations, and the inclusion of the latest automotive technology, instructors and students alike will find that these books keep their value over the years and they form the core of a professional library for a master technician.

HOW TO USE THIS BOOK

Why Are There Two Manuals?

Automatic Transmissions and Transaxles is not like other textbooks. It is actually two books, a *Classroom Manual* and a *Shop Manual*. The *Classroom Manual* provides what you need to know about automatic transmission theory. The *Shop Manual* provides diagnostic, adjustment, and repair techniques associated with automatic transmissions and transaxles and their individual components. Both manuals are valuable study and reference resources at home, in class, and in the shop. Both manuals are highly illustrated, including many step-by-step photographic sequences. Use the two manuals together to fully understand how the components work and how to diagnose and repair them when they malfunction.

What Is in These Manuals?

The *Classroom Manual* contains the following learning aids:

- The text is broken into short sections with subheads for easier understanding and review.
- Each chapter is fully illustrated.
- Key words are printed in **boldface type** and are defined in the glossary at the end of the manual.
- Questions following each chapter provide a review of the material covered.
- A brief summary at the end of each chapter helps in reviewing for exams.
- Included are short blocks of "nice to know" information that supplement the main text.
- At the back of the *Classroom Manual* is a sample test similar to those given for Automotive Service Excellence (ASE) certification. Use it to study and prepare for ASE tests.

In addition to detailed instructions on overhaul, test, and service procedures, the *Shop Manual* provides

- Information on how to use and maintain shop tools and test equipment
- Detailed safety precautions
- Troubleshooting procedures, charts, and tables to help diagnose transmission and transaxle concerns
- Professional repair tips to perform repairs more rapidly and accurately
- A complete index to help find information

Where to Begin?

The instructor will design a course to take advantage of available facilities and equipment. As a result, you may be asked to study certain chapters of these manuals out of order. That is fine; the important thing is to fully understand each topic before moving on to the next.

Study the vocabulary words and use the review questions. While reading in the *Classroom Manual*, refer to the *Shop Manual* and relate the descriptive text to the service procedures. When working on actual transmissions and transaxles, look back at the *Classroom Manual* to keep basic information fresh in mind. Servicing or repairing a modern automatic transmission or transaxle is not always easy. Take advantage of the information in the *Classroom Manual*, the procedures of the *Shop Manual*, and the knowledge of the instructor.

Remember that the *Shop Manual* is a good book for work, not just a good workbook. Keep it on hand while working on transmissions. For ease of use, the *Shop Manual* will lie flat on the workbench and will withstand quite a bit of rough handling.

To perform many transmission and transaxle repair procedures, you also need an accurate source of specifications. Most shops have vehicle service information resources such as service manuals or electronic information systems.

Using the Parts of Each Manual

The *Classroom Manual* is divided into two parts: Part One is "Transmission and Transaxle Fundamentals"; Part Two is "Transmission and Transaxle Electronics." The *Shop Manual* is divided into three parts: Part One is "General Service and Diagnostic Operations"; Part Two is "Transmission and Transaxle Overhaul"; and Part Three is "Specific Overhaul Procedures." The first part of each manual contains general information that applies to all automatic transmissions and transaxles. Part Two of the *Classroom Manual* explains electronic control theory and how it applies to modern automatic transmissions and transaxles. Part Two of the *Shop Manual* provides general procedures for removing, overhauling, and installing automatic transmissions and transaxles. Part Three of the *Shop Manual* provides information on how specific units are put together, how they work, and how to overhaul them. There are many similarities in the descriptions and overhaul procedures for different transmissions and transaxles, because modern automatic transmissions and transaxles are more similar to each other than they are different.

Acknowledgments

In producing this series of textbooks for automobile technicians, Chek-Chart has drawn extensively on the technical and editorial knowledge of the automobile manufacturers and component suppliers. Automotive design is a technical, fast-changing field, and we gratefully acknowledge the help of the following companies in allowing us to present the most up-to-date information and illustrations possible:

- Automatic Transmission Rebuilders Association
- Axiline: Precision Products Company
- Saxco Torque Converters
- Uyeda Brothers Automotive, Inc.
- Lubrizol Corporation
- Texaco, Inc.
- Lincoln Automotive
- DaimlerChrysler Corporation
- General Motors Corporation
- Buick Motor Division
- Cadillac Motor Car Division
- Chevrolet Motor Division
- Hydra-matic Division
- Oldsmobile Division
- Pontiac Division
- Mazda Motor Corporation
- Toyota Motor Corporation

Contents

PART ONE

Transmission and Transaxle Fundamentals

Introduction to Automatic Transmissions and Transaxles

This *Classroom Manual* discusses the theory of operation, function, and construction of automatic transmissions and transaxles. Automatic transmissions have replaced manual transmissions in many modern automobiles, both import and domestic. Automatic transmissions use a hydraulic system to shift gears automatically in relation to road speed and engine load conditions. Late-model automatic transmissions incorporate electronic systems to control shift timing and feel.

Automatic transmissions are used in **rear-wheel drive (RWD)** vehicles, and automatic transaxles are used in **front-wheel drive (FWD)** vehicles and some mid- and rear-engine RWD applications. Transmissions and transaxles are similar in function and operation. However, a transaxle contains the final drive and differential gears within the transaxle housing, whereas a transmission keeps them separate.

In this *Classroom Manual*, the term "transmission" is used to refer to an automatic gearbox. The term "transaxle" is generally reserved for specific transaxle references and to discuss the operations or construction characteristics that are unique to transaxle assemblies.

HISTORY AND DEVELOPMENT

Automatic transmissions are not a recent development. Some vehicles built in the first decade of this century had transmissions with gear systems similar to those used in modern automatic transmissions. By the late 1930s, Chrysler, Ford, General Motors, and other manufacturers had automatic or semi-automatic transmissions in experimental stages or limited production. Mercedes-Benz built a limited number of vehicles with an automatic gearbox in 1914. However, General Motors introduced the first fully automatic transmission, the Hydra-Matic, in 1940. The Hydra-Matic, available on select Oldsmobile and Cadillac models, was based on a semi-automatic design used by Buick in 1938.

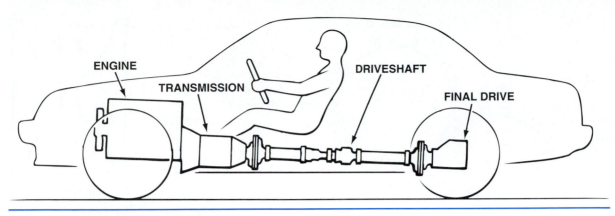

Figure 1-1. Typical vehicle powertrain.

Manufacturers began incorporating electronic controls into their automatic transmissions in the 1980s. Toyota introduced the first electronically shifted automatic transmission in 1983, and Ford followed in 1987 by adding electronic controls to some of their A4LD transmissions. Chrysler introduced the A604 Ultradrive transaxle in 1989, and General Motors followed in 1991 with the 4L60-E electronic transmission and the 4T60-E electronic transaxle.

POWERTRAIN COMPONENTS

The modern automatic transmission is no longer a stand-alone mechanical component but rather a part of the entire vehicle **powertrain**. The powertrain consists of all the components that generate, transmit, and distribute vehicle drive torque. It includes the engine, transmission, driveline, drive axles, wheels, final drive gears, and differential (see figure 1-1).

Many of these individual components are integrated into the vehicle electronic control system and can affect transmission operation. To service these transmissions, a technician must understand the functional and operational relationships between these individual components and the automatic transmission or transaxle.

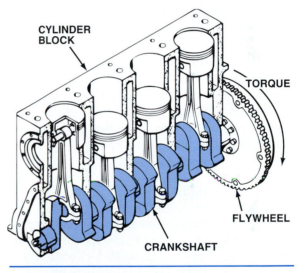

Figure 1-2. Engine drive torque.

Engine

The engine develops the drive **torque** used to operate the vehicle. Engine torque is the turning force generated by the rotation of the engine crankshaft and is a measure of the amount of work that can be done by the engine to drive the vehicle (figure 1-2). Torque is expressed in pound-feet (lb-ft) or inch-pounds (in-lb) in the U.S. Customary system or Newton-meters (Nm) in the metric system.

The engine develops drive torque by burning a regulated air-fuel mixture in its combustion chambers and translating the reciprocating motion of the pistons into the rotary motion of the crankshaft. The torque output of the engine becomes the input to

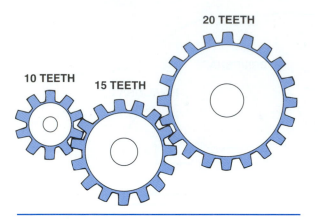

Figure 1-3. Gear ratios.

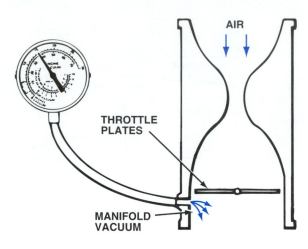

Figure 1-4. Engine load—vacuum, throttle opening.

the transmission and drivetrain, which in turn deliver it to the drive wheels to move the vehicle.

Engine Operation and Torque Curves

When the amount of torque produced by the engine is plotted against engine speed, it can be seen that the engine operates best within a certain speed range. This plot is known as a **torque curve**, and it graphically shows the torque output and efficiency of the engine for each gear.

When an engine is operating above or below the optimum range of its torque curve, it is working harder than necessary and less efficient. Varying the torque output directly by changing gears or indirectly by varying engine speed can optimize efficiency. An automatic transmission does this by upshifting or downshifting automatically.

Torque and Speed Modification

Vehicles vary engine torque and speed with a gearing system. The term **gear ratio** is a way of expressing the relationship between a drive gear (the input) and a driven gear (the output). The relationship may be the diameter of the gears, the number of teeth on the gears, or the number of revolutions one gear makes relative to the other (figure 1-3).

Usually, the gear ratio is calculated as the number of turns a drive gear requires to rotate a driven gear through one complete revolution. For example, if a drive gear with 12 teeth drives a second gear with 36 teeth, the gear with 12 teeth must rotate three times to turn the gear with 36 teeth one time.

This gear ratio is 3:1. Gear ratios do not have to be expressed as whole numbers, as is often the case with helical gears. For example, if a drive gear with 12 teeth drives a second gear with 32 teeth, the gear ratio is 2.67:1. Gear ratios provide an insight into the torque and speed relationship between gears or sets of gears. The difference in gear diameters, which allows the calculation of gear ratios, is based on the principle of leverage that is used to gain a mechanical advantage in a gear system. Gears can be combined in such a way that a driven gear provides more torque than its drive gear. Gear ratios are a measure of the torque multiplication in a transmission gearing system.

Torque and speed have a give-and-take relationship because of another physical principle. If torque increases, then speed decreases, and if speed increases, then torque decreases. For example, an output gear arranged to increase the torque of the input gear will also turn slower than the input gear. This is one reason there is a range of gears available in a transmission. Lower gears, such as first gear, produce more torque, but are not well suited to high-speed operation. The opposite is true for higher gears like third and fourth gear.

Engine Operating Load

Engine load can be measured by monitoring engine vacuum and/or throttle plate position (figure 1-4). Engine load is a basic oper-

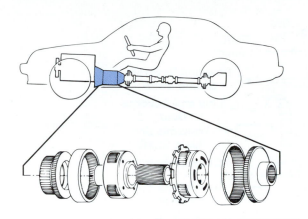

Figure 1-5. Transmission gearing.

ating consideration for all automatic transmissions, electronic and nonelectronic alike. On nonelectronic transmissions, engine load is monitored with a vacuum modulator or by mechanical linkage. Electronic applications use electrical sensors.

Transmission

The amount of torque generated by an engine is limited and inefficient at certain speeds. Therefore, it is desirable to increase the torque available to the drive wheels under certain vehicle operating conditions. By using different gear combinations, the transmission is able to provide extra torque when the need arises (figure 1-5). Different gear ratios also permit higher vehicle speeds. Transmission gearing must be able to reverse direction for backing up and have a neutral position for interrupting the power flow to the wheels.

Vehicle Gearing Needs
A vehicle does not require the same amount of torque under all driving conditions. For instance, it takes more effort (work) for an engine to move a vehicle from a standstill, to climb a steep hill, or to accelerate during a passing maneuver than it does to keep a vehicle moving at a constant speed on a level road.

Manual Transmission and Clutch
The essential function of any transmission, manual or automatic, is to provide the necessary gears to meet the changing needs of

the vehicle. With a manual transmission, this is done by direct action of the driver (figure 1-6). Shifting gears with a manual transmission requires the driver to depress the clutch pedal to mechanically separate the gears in mesh. This momentarily interrupts power flow through the drivetrain and allows the driver to move another set of gears into mesh.

Automatic Transmission

Automatic transmissions use **planetary gearsets** to provide different gear ratios. To select the appropriate gears, hydraulic clutches and bands hold or lock combinations of components together, providing different gear ratios (figure 1-7).

A planetary gearset allows the gears to remain in constant mesh. The transmission selects the proper gears automatically by monitoring the demands on the vehicle through engine load and vehicle speed, then initiating hydraulic action. The automatic shifting of gears does not interrupt power flow to the wheels.

Automatic transmissions use a fluid clutch assembly called a **torque converter** rather than a mechanical clutch assembly. The torque converter uses hydraulic automatic transmission fluid (ATF) to provide a fluid link between the engine and transmission. This results in a smooth, cushioned connection between the engine and transmission, and it permits them to remain engaged whether the vehicle is moving or at a standstill. Also, it allows a driver to start a stopped vehicle without using a clutch pedal.

An automatic transmission consists of several functional sections. Each section has a number of major components. To provide an overview of the basic operation of an automatic transmission, this chapter briefly examines each of these sections and their function. The main sections are as follows:

- Torque converter
- Geartrain
- Hydraulic system
- Control system

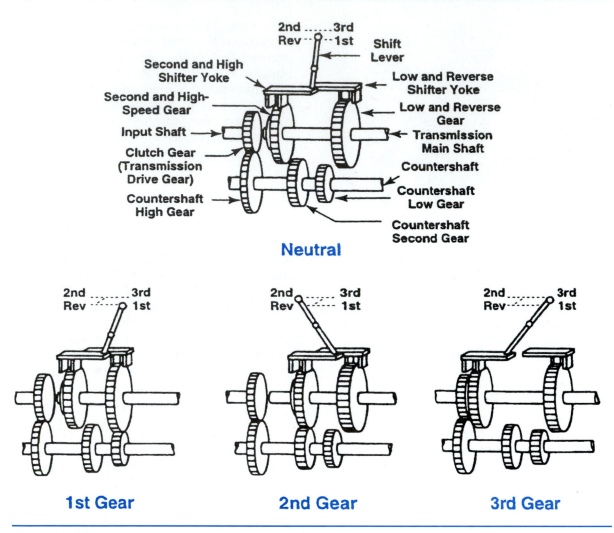

Figure 1-6. Manual transmission gearing.

Torque Converter

The torque converter assembly attaches to a flexplate, a flexible steel plate that serves as a flywheel. The flexplate bolts directly to the crankshaft-end flange. The torque converter receives the torque output of the engine and passes it to the transmission. The engine-to-transmission connection is made through a fluid clutch (figure 1-8). Early designs that transfer torque without modification are called fluid couplings. Later designs add an additional element that allows them to multiply engine torque under certain conditions. The later design is a true torque converter.

Most late-model torque converters also contain a **torque converter clutch (TCC)** assembly. The TCC provides a mechanical connection between the engine and transmission under certain operating conditions, such as cruising in high gear. This eliminates slippage from the fluid drive connection, increases drive efficiency, and improves fuel economy. The activation and control of a TCC can be any of the following:

- Hydraulic
- Mechanical
- Electronic

Each method is discussed in greater detail later in this *Classroom Manual*.

Geartrain

The majority of automatic transmissions use a planetary gearset in the **geartrain** to provide the different gear ratios that are needed. The geartrain consists of the plane-

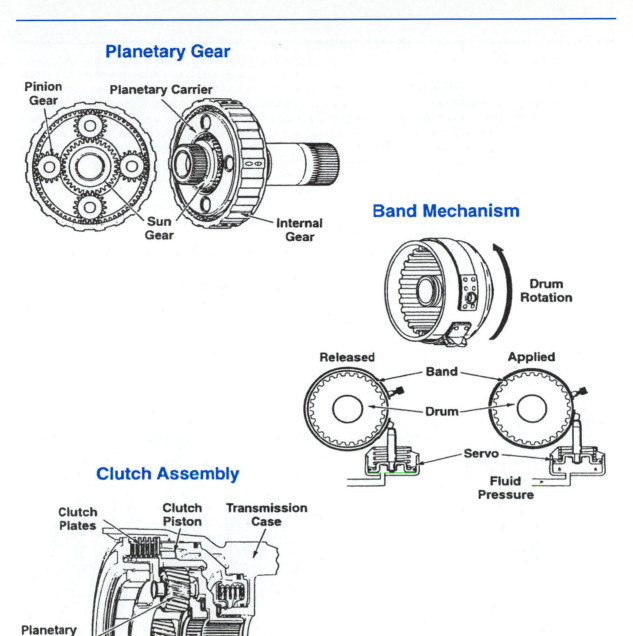

Figure 1-7. Planetary set, band mechanism, and clutch assembly.

tary gearset, shafts, drums, and hubs that connect the components together. Most automatic transmissions use either a Simpson or Ravigneaux compound planetary gearset design or some variation of these designs.

The Ford Motor Company might never have used sliding-gear manual transmissions in its vehicles if Henry Ford Sr. had had his way. The elder Ford never learned how to shift a manual transmission properly, and was opposed to using one in the vehicle that would replace the Model T. Ford wanted a planetary gear transmission that could shift automatically through the use of a hydraulic system.

After much argument, Edsel Ford Sr. and others convinced Henry to adopt a three-speed manual gearbox for the new Model A in 1928. When he finally consented to a manual transmission, or "crunch gears" as he called it, he reportedly said to one of his engineers, "If the public wants a sliding-gear transmission, let them have it. Let them find out what a contraption it is." Henry Ford never did understand why the Model A's transmission was so popular and continued experimenting with automatic planetary transmissions until 1941. By then, General Motors had launched the Hydra-Matic and beaten Ford to the marketplace with the first fully automatic transmission. It was not until 1951, four years after his death, that Ford introduced its first automatic transmission—the Ford-O-Matic.

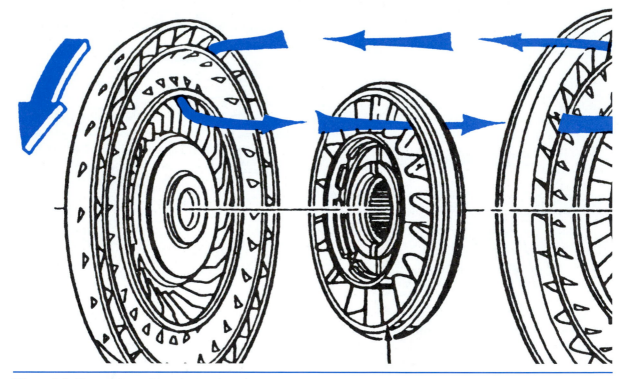

Figure 1-8. Torque converter cutaway view.

Hydraulic System

The basic operations of an automatic transmission involve the controlled use and application of pressurized hydraulic fluid (figure 1-9). An automatic transmission hydraulic system consists of all the parts and fluid circuits needed to create, regulate, and direct the hydraulic pressure and flow needed to control transmission operations. This includes the oil pump, apply devices, **valves, valve body**, and connecting passages. An electronically shifted transmission may also include electronic solenoids and motors to direct fluid flow.

The transmission hydraulic system transmits motion and converts fluid pressure into the mechanical force in order to apply the clutches and bands. The hydraulic system also lubricates and cools transmission components.

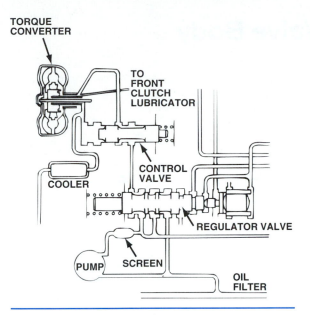

Figure 1-9. Hydraulic circuit.

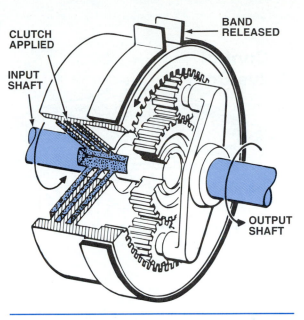

Figure 1-10. Typical clutch assembly.

Oil Pump

The oil pump is the source of fluid flow throughout the hydraulic system. Oil pumps are driven by the engine and connect to it in several ways. On most RWD transmissions, the torque converter drives the pump either through a drive hub or shaft. On an FWD transaxle, a chain-and-sprocket assembly often drives the pump.

The oil pump provides the amount of fluid flow needed to fill the hydraulic circuits and apply the control devices. All pumps are capable of creating an excessive amount of oil pressure, volume, and flow. Therefore, all transmissions and transaxles are equipped with a pressure regulator valve. This valve prevents damage to the system and provides a means of redirecting excess fluid back to the sump.

Apply Devices

Power flow through the gearset is controlled by applying clutches and bands. Clutches and bands are apply devices used to drive or hold various components of a planetary gearset to obtain the different gear ratios (figure 1-10). They are applied using the hydraulic pressure that is generated by the oil pump and pressure regulation system. The transmission hydraulic system is capable of converting this fluid pressure into the mechanical force needed to apply the clutches and bands.

Valve Body and Valves

For efficient operation, the transmission must apply and release clutches and bands at the correct time. This requires an automatic transmission to be capable of monitoring vehicle needs, timing shifts, and controlling the apply devices to select the different gear ratios. The valves, valve body, and fluid distribution system handle these functions (figure 1-11).

Shifts and Shift Timing

An automatic transmission determines the proper shift points by monitoring vehicle speed and engine load. When engine load is low in relation to vehicle speed, a higher gear ratio is more efficient, so the transmission upshifts. When engine load is high in relation to vehicle speed, a lower gear ratio is more efficient, so the transmission downshifts.

Hydraulic shift valves in the valve body initiate gear changes. These valves balance different hydraulic pressures to direct the fluid flow. **Throttle pressure**, which responds to engine load, pushes shift valves in one direction. **Governor pressure**, which

Valve Body

**Control
Valve Body**

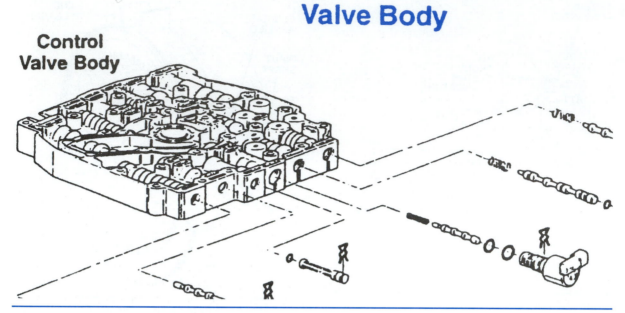

Figure 1-11. Typical valve body assembly.

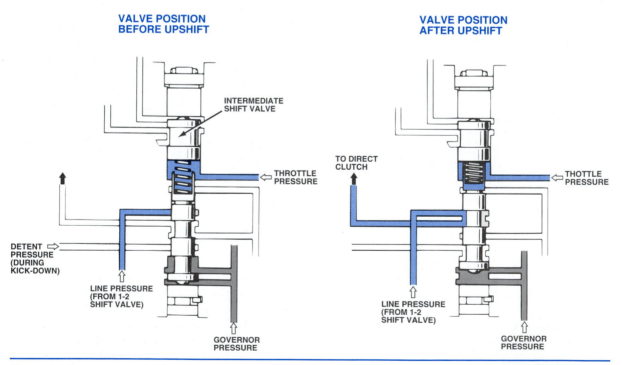

Figure 1-12. Hydraulic shift circuit.

responds to vehicle speed, pushes shift valves in the opposite direction (figure 1-12). When governor pressure exceeds throttle pressure, shift valves move to allow fluid under **mainline pressure** into the proper upshift circuit. When throttle pressure exceeds governor pressure, fluid is routed to the downshift circuit.

Pressure Signals

Governor pressure and throttle pressure are the two basic hydraulic pressure signals used in all automatic transmissions. Throttle pressure, an indicator of engine load, is measured through engine vacuum or throttle opening. Governor pressure, an indicator of vehicle speed, is usually measured by counting rotations of the output shaft.

Non-electronic transmissions generate governor pressure and throttle pressure indirectly using a **governor valve** and a **throttle valve**. Electronic transmissions can generate pressures directly using computer-controlled **solenoids** instead of governor or throttle valves. This allows the control system to regulate transmission shifts and shift timing.

Electronic Control System

Late-model automatic transmissions manage shift timing, regulate line pressure, and control converter clutch operation through an electronic control system. This system provides very precise control of operating conditions and vehicle components, resulting in better fuel economy, reduced emissions, and smoother shifts.

An electronic transmission is very similar in construction and operation to a non-electronic unit, and most internal components are identical. The main difference is that hydraulic pressure to the apply devices is controlled by an onboard computer system.

Electronic control systems have become increasingly sophisticated over the last several years. They receive input information from many vehicle functions. The latest versions integrate several systems to manage almost all system and component operations (figure 1-13).

GEARING AND GEARSETS

Most automatic transmission geartrains use compound planetary gearsets. These are combinations of two or more simple planetary gearsets. A compound planetary gearset provides more usable gear combinations

than a simple planetary gearset. However, both simple and compound gearsets have the same basic components and they function the same way (figure 1-14).

Generally, all automotive planetary gearsets allow the transmission to produce three or four forward gear ratios, a reverse gear, and neutral. The transmission gearing is augmented by further gear reduction at the final drive gear and torque multiplication within the torque converter.

Transmission Gearing

Some gear ratios are more advantageous to certain vehicle needs or operations than others. The gear ratios provided by the transmission geartrain allow the vehicle to be optimized for speed or torque. The lower gears allow more torque to the drive wheels but preclude high-speed operation. The higher gears allow the vehicle to operate well at high speeds but provide less torque.

Vehicle engineers select the exact gear ratios during the design stage. Gears are carefully selected to match the characteristics of other vehicle components in order to produce the most useful and efficient torque curves possible for that particular vehicle. An electronic transmission stores the torque curves and other design data in a reserved section of computer memory. The control system uses this information to determine shift points and to manage gear shifting for the vehicle.

Final Drive Gearing

Although the gearset in the transmission provides most of the gear ratio selection for the vehicle, other drivetrain components may further modify the gear ratio or the torque available to the drive wheels. These other components may include the final drive gears, differential, and transfer case.

Final Drives and Differentials

Final drive gears provide a means of transferring the output from the transmission to the differential gears. They are the final set of reduction gears in any transmission or transaxle. These gears provide gear reduc-

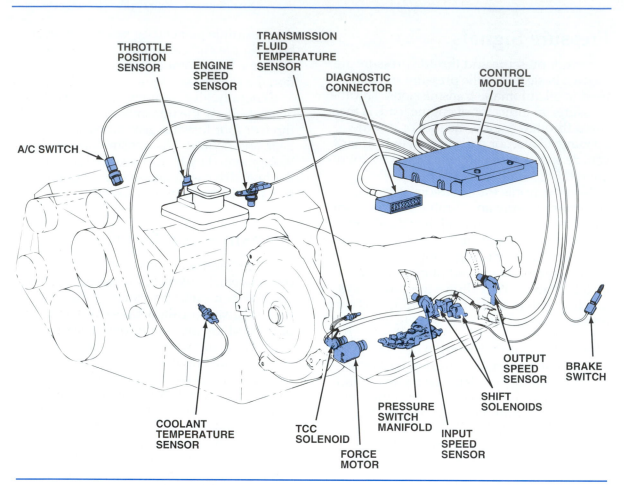

Figure 1-13. Common electronic input and output components.

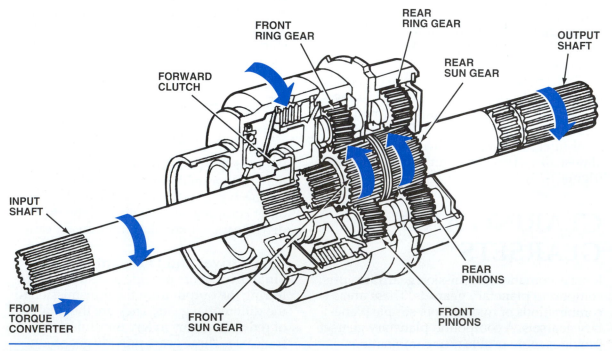

Figure 1-14. Compound planetary gearset.

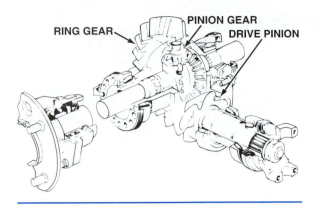

Figure 1-15. Final drive gears (RWD application).

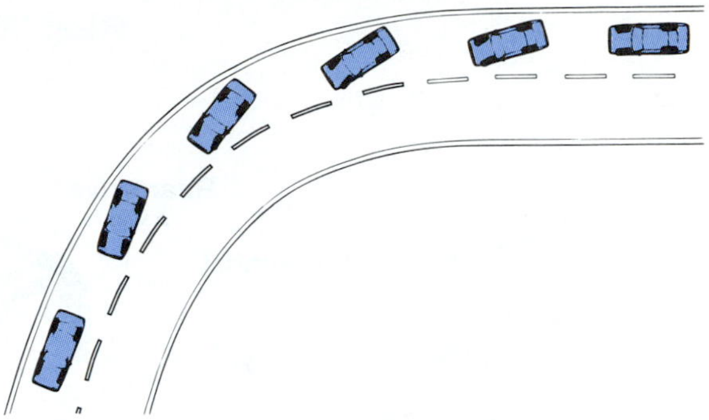

Figure 1-16. Turning radius.

tion when the vehicle requires an increase in drive torque (figure 1-15).

All of the torque output from the transmission passes through the same set of final drive gears, regardless of which transmission gear is selected. Final drive gears typically have a single, fixed gear ratio. Therefore, all torque output to the drive wheels is further modified by that same gear ratio.

The **differential** does not provide an actual change in gear ratio. It is used to distribute drive torque evenly to both drive wheels when the vehicle travels straight, and to compensate for the difference in wheel speed when the vehicle turns a corner.

When a vehicle travels in a straight line, both drive wheels travel the same distance at the same speed. However, when a vehicle turns a corner, the outer wheel must travel farther and turn faster than the inner wheel. The differential allows the outer wheel to rotate faster as the turn is made. It provides a momentary change in gear speed, but the primary purpose is to maintain vehicle control through a turn and to prevent excess tire wear, while not changing vehicle gearing (figure 1-16).

Final Drive Types and Designs

The type and location of the final drive and differential gears depends on the design and configuration of the vehicle and its powertrain. Most RWD vehicles use a longitudinally mounted transmission coupled inline to an engine at the front of the chassis. These vehicles transmit torque to the drive wheels through a driveshaft to the rear axle housing. The rear axle housing usually con-

tains the final drive and differential gears in this type of powertrain layout (figure 1-17).

RWD vehicles typically use a hypoid ring and pinion gear set to deliver transmission torque to the wheels. The gear set provides the final gear reduction ratio, changes the direction of the driveshaft power flow 90°, and transfers power to the drive wheels.

Most FWD vehicles use a transaxle coupled to a transverse-mounted engine. In these vehicles, the final drive gears are located within the transaxle housing. Because the crankshaft is parallel to the drive axles, these vehicles do not require a redirection of power flow to drive the front wheels (figure 1-18).

There are other final drive configurations; for example, some FWD vehicles use a longitudinally mounted engine. These applications may locate the final drive and differential gears in a separate case that bolts to the transaxle. Four-wheel drive (4WD) and all-wheel drive (AWD) vehicles generally use a transfer case to distribute the transmission output between two or four drive wheels. Transfer cases may be bolted directly to the transmission housing or they may be separate units mounted between the transmission and rear drive axle (figure 1-19).

There are some RWD vehicles that use mid- or rear-mounted engines. These configurations are often very similar to FWD vehicles with a transverse engine. Differential gearing and operation is substantially similar for all vehicles and is generally located with the final drive gearing. The most noteworthy differences are encountered with 4WD and

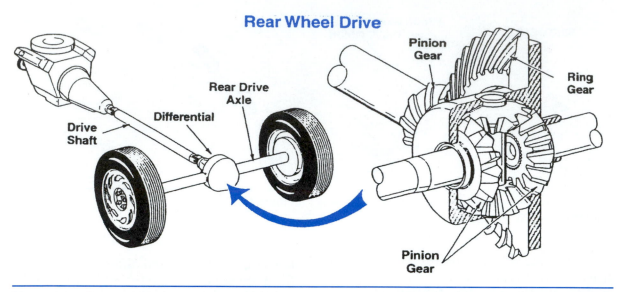

Figure 1-17. Final drive (RWD application).

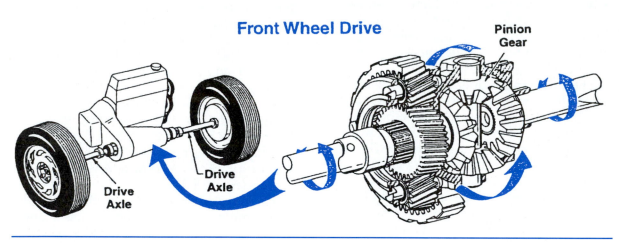

Figure 1-18. Final drive (FWD application).

AWD vehicles. These may allow independent differential gearing for all four wheels.

Overall Gear Ratio

The final torque output reaching the drive wheels may be modified by several drivetrain components and the final drive ratio. The total gear ratio, or overall gear ratio, is the cumulative result of all components. The output from one stage is the input to the next, so you can calculate the overall gear ratio quite easily by multiplying one gear ratio by the next ratio in line to produce a single, total figure.

ELECTRONIC AUTOMATIC TRANSMISSIONS

The use of automotive electronics has greatly increased since the mid-1980s. In the 1970s, most manufacturers switched to solid-state electronic ignition systems. In the 1980s, import and domestic manufacturers started to equip their production vehicles with electronic control systems. These systems were necessary to meet

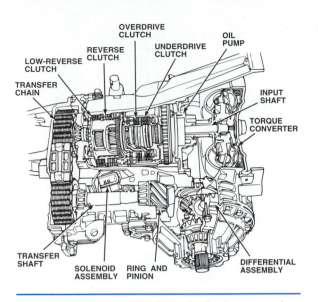

Figure 1-19. Chrysler 42LE longitudinally mounted transaxle.

increasingly stringent emissions and fuel economy standards.

Automotive electronic control systems have become more sophisticated over the years, and their use has expanded to include an increasing number of functions. The latest applications now integrate almost all vehicle functions into a single system. The electronic integration of engine, transmission, and other vehicle systems provides better control, faster response, and smoother operation for all systems.

The electronic controls added to a typical **electronic automatic transmission** have not changed the essential mechanical and hydraulic operations inside the transmission (figure 1-20). The internal components of electronic and nonelectronic transmissions are almost identical. Only the *control* has changed. An electronic control system enables the engine and transmission to share vehicle operating information from many sources and uses it to react quickly to changing vehicle operating conditions.

Transmission Operating Monitors

Automatic transmission operation requires constant monitoring of vehicle operating conditions and driver demands. This is true for both electronic and nonelectronic units, although electronic control systems are more flexible in what they can monitor.

As mentioned previously, the two basic operating parameters monitored by every automatic transmission are engine load and vehicle speed. Either engine vacuum or throttle position can be used as an indicator of engine load, while vehicle speed is usually measured by monitoring the rotation of the transmission output shaft. Non-electronic units typically measure engine vacuum with a vacuum diaphragm unit called a vacuum modulator, and they measure throttle position through mechanical linkage connected between the throttle plate at the intake manifold and the throttle valve lever at the transmission (figure 1-21). Electronic transmissions monitor the same signals using electronic sensors.

In addition, an electronically shifted transmission monitors engine load with a unit called a **manifold absolute pressure (MAP)** sensor. This device measures the air pressure or vacuum in the engine intake manifold and relays a vacuum-related electrical signal to the electronic control unit as an input. The control system also measures throttle position with a unit called the **throttle position sensor (TPS)**. However, this information is more often used to monitor driver demand than engine load.

The position of the gear selector is also an indicator of driver demand. For example, a sudden downshift from second to first gear is a demand for more drive torque. A common way to monitor gear selection is with a **manual valve lever position switch (MVLPS)**. Many units also monitor gear selection through pressure switches mounted on the valve body. The information from each source can be used to double-check the other.

Several methods are available for an electronically shifted transmission to measure vehicle speed. One method uses an LED device that mounts to the speedometer cable assembly. A more common method is to use a **permanent magnet (PM)** generator that attaches to the transmission housing (figure 1-22). The sensor uses projections on a trigger wheel that is mounted to the trans-

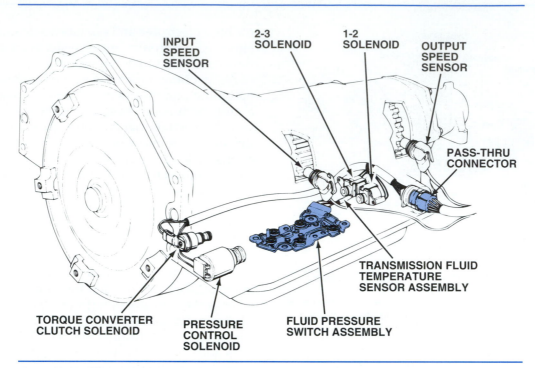

Figure 1-20. Electronic transmission controls (RWD application shown).

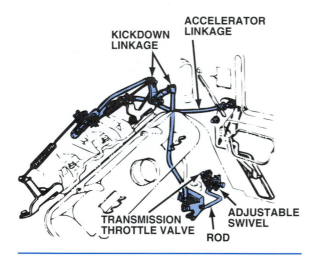

Figure 1-21. Mechanical throttle valve.

mission output shaft. This generates a speed-related electrical signal for the electronic control unit.

Automatic Transmission Control Methods

Until recently, automatic transmissions used a combination of mechanical and hydraulic methods to generate the funda-

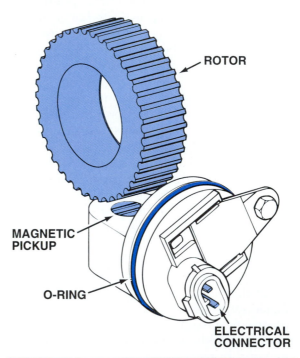

Figure 1-22. Magnetic speed sensor.

mental hydraulic pressures for controlling transmission operations. Nonelectronic transmissions use a throttle valve to generate and regulate the throttle pressure and a

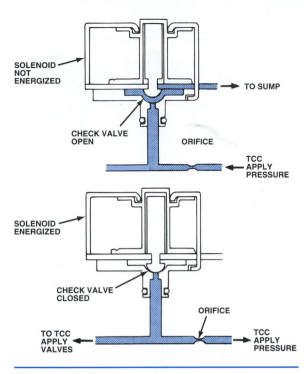

Figure 1-23. Electronic solenoid operation.

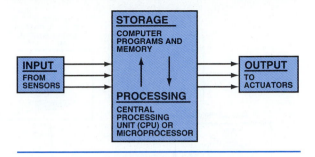

Figure 1-24. Input, processing, storage, and output relationship.

governor valve to do the same for governor pressure.

An electronically shifted transmission generally does not use a governor or throttle valve to generate and control fundamental hydraulic pressures. Instead, it manages pressure directly with electronic solenoids controlled by the onboard computer (figure 1-23). A solenoid is a small electric switching device that can rapidly switch on and off to open and close a hydraulic passage. This rapid on-off control has the effect of "feathering" the hydraulic pressure in the circuit, and it is capable of regulating the pressure very precisely.

Introduction to Control Systems

Automotive control systems are a combination of input sensors, onboard computer, output devices, and circuitry that links everything together. Sensors monitor mechanical actions and translate that infor-

mation into an electrical signal. The computer receives the information from the sensors, conditions it, and processes it together with information and programs stored in its own memory (figure 1-24).

Based on this data, the computer can make operating decisions for a single component or the entire vehicle. The computer then generates signals to carry out these decisions and to command the system actuators. Actuators transform these electrical signals into the appropriate mechanical actions.

Control System Operations

Control systems receive input information from sensors throughout the vehicle. They can adjust transmission operation to suit not only engine requirements but also requirements for all the other systems throughout the vehicle (figure 1-25).

Control systems are able to use vehicle sensor information as it occurs. The information stored in computer memory adjusts transmission performance to suit both short-term vehicle requirements (such as passing) and longer-term requirements (such as cruising). The latest-model control systems are able to manage very long-term vehicle requirements by compensating for factors such as wear in the transmission clutch packs.

An electronically shifted transmission with fully electronic control can use information to regulate transmission shift schedules and to modify hydraulic pressures to

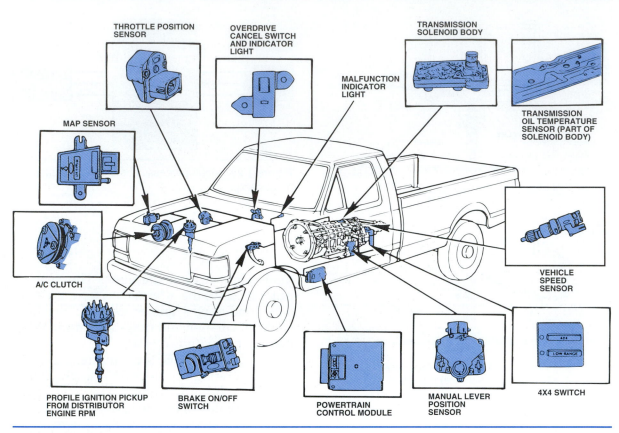

Figure 1-25. Electronic control system.

adjust shift quality and feel. Electronics also control TCC application and modify the control pressure to allow a limited slip under certain conditions.

Other operations and advantages include compensating for component wear through adaptive control, eliminating some band and mechanical linkage adjustments, limiting damaging operations when a vehicle requires servicing, and providing onboard test and diagnostic routines to aid the technician.

SUMMARY

Automatic transmissions and transaxles are replacing manually shifted units in many import and domestic vehicles. Automatic transmissions are used in RWD vehicles and automatic transaxles are more common in FWD vehicles. Unlike transmissions, transaxles have the differential and final drive gears located within the transaxle housing.

Automatic transmission operation depends on proper engine operation and characteristics such as torque curves and axle gear ratios that relate engine performance to transmission operation. Transmission and engine components are matched for maximum performance.

Engine performance is related to the load on the engine and requires different gearing to optimize performance. A transmission provides the different gear ratios to maximize engine torque and minimize engine wear. Engine operating load and vehicle speed are the two most important operating signals for both electronic and non-electronic automatic transmissions. The operating signals produce throttle and governor pressure and manage transmission shifts and converter clutch operation.

Most automatic transmissions use a planetary gearset to produce the different gear ratios. The planetary gearset is the mechanical heart of the transmission. It modifies and transmits engine torque through the rest of the drivetrain to the drive wheels. It is used in combination with the apply devices of the hydraulic system. The gear ratio produced by the gearset is combined with the gear ratios of other geartrain components to produce the overall gear ratio. The overall gear ratio is what is available at the drive wheels of the vehicle.

The torque converter provides a fluid connection between the engine and transmission. Later models use a torque converter clutch (TCC) to provide a direct mechanical link between the engine and transmission under certain conditions.

Nonelectronic automatic transmissions monitor vehicle operating conditions mechanically and control functions hydraulically. Electronic automatic transmissions monitor the same signals and manage hydraulic control directly by computer-controlled components.

Nonelectronic transmissions and electronic automatic transmissions are very similar internally. However, an electronic transmission allows greater flexibility and offers many service advantages.

Review Questions

Choose the single most correct answer. Compare your answers to the correct answers on page 213.

1. A vehicle powertrain consists of
   a. Engine, transmission, and driveline
   b. Drive axles and wheels
   c. Final drive gears and differential
   d. All of the above

2. Technician A says the engine develops vehicle drive torque. Technician B says the transmission can modify engine torque and pass it to the drive wheels.
   Who is right?
   a. A only
   b. B only
   c. Both A and B
   d. Neither A nor B

3. Technician A says that torque and speed can be modified by using gears. Technician B says that as gear ratio increases, torque and speed increase.
   Who is right?
   a. A only
   b. B only
   c. Both A and B
   d. Neither A nor B

4. Technician A says that gear ratio can be calculated from the number of teeth on the gears. Technician B says that gear ratio is a measure of how fast one gear rotates in relation to another.
   Who is right?
   a. A only
   b. B only
   c. Both A and B
   d. Neither A nor B

5. Technician A says gear ratio is a way to express the torque relationship between a drive and driven gear. Technician B says gear ratio is a way to express the speed relationship between a drive and driven gear.
   Who is right?
   a. A only
   b. B only
   c. Both A and B
   d. Neither A nor B

6. Technician A says engine vacuum is determined by how fast the engine clears the cylinders on the exhaust stroke. Technician B says engine operating load can be monitored by engine vacuum or throttle plate position.
   Who is right?
   a. A only
   b. B only
   c. Both A and B
   d. Neither A nor B

7. Technician A says that as torque increases, vehicle speed will increase. Technician B says that as torque decreases, vehicle speed increases.
   Who is right?
   a. A only
   b. B only
   c. Both A and B
   d. Neither A nor B

8. Technician A says that all automatic transmissions monitor engine operating load in some manner. Technician B says that electronic automatic transmissions use electronic sensors and do not need to monitor engine operating load.
    Who is right?
    a. A only
    b. B only
    c. Both A and B
    d. Neither A nor B

9. A transmission is used to
    a. Increase drive torque for heavy engine loads
    b. Increase drive speed for light engine loads
    c. Provide a neutral power flow path
    d. All of the above

10. Technician A says that shifting a manual transmission requires operating a clutch to separate the gears in mesh. Technician B says that automatic transmissions separate the meshed gears automatically when shifting and do not require a clutch.
    Who is right?
    a. A only
    b. B only
    c. Both A and B
    d. Neither A nor B

11. Technician A says that automatic transmissions use planetary gearsets to provide the different gear ratios. Technician B says that automatic transmissions use a torque converter instead of a mechanical clutch.
    Who is right?
    a. A only
    b. B only
    c. Both A and B
    d. Neither A nor B

12. Technician A says the torque converter uses engine oil to provide a fluid link between the engine and transmission. Technician B says the torque converter is attached to the engine crankshaft and receives the engine torque output.
    Who is right?
    a. A only
    b. B only
    c. Both A and B
    d. Neither A nor B

13. Technician A says planetary gearsets allow gears to remain in constant mesh so shifts can be made without interrupting the power flow. Technician B says that automatic transmissions select gear ratios using hydraulic clutches and bands to drive or hold members of the planetary gearsets.
    Who is right?
    a. A only
    b. B only
    c. Both A and B
    d. Neither A nor B

14. Technician A says a torque converter allows engine torque multiplication under certain operating conditions. Technician B says a torque converter is attached to the engine crankshaft by bolting it to the engine flywheel or flexplate.
    Who is right?
    a. A only
    b. B only
    c. Both A and B
    d. Neither A nor B

15. The transmission hydraulic system
    a. Transmits hydraulic force and motion
    b. Converts fluid pressure into mechanical force
    c. Lubricates and cools transmission components
    d. All of the above

16. Technician A says an automatic transmission determines shift points by monitoring vehicle speed and engine load. Technician B says that gear shifts are made by hydraulic shift valves in the oil pump.
    Who is right?
    a. A only
    b. B only
    c. Both A and B
    d. Neither A nor B

17. Technician A says throttle pressure is an indicator of engine load and governor pressure is an indicator of vehicle speed. Technician B says an automatic transmission upshifts when governor pressure exceeds throttle pressure.
    Who is right?
    a. A only
    b. B only
    c. Both A and B
    d. Neither A nor B

18. Technician A says the final drive gears further modify the transmission gear ratio. Technician B says the final drive gears transmit the torque output of the transmission to the differential and the drive wheels.
    Who is right?
    a. A only
    b. B only
    c. Both A and B
    d. Neither A nor B

19. Technician A says the differential compensates for the difference in wheel speed when a vehicle makes a turn. Technician B says the differential is used to modify the final torque output to the drive wheels.
    Who is right?
    a. A only
    b. B only
    c. Both A and B
    d. Neither A nor B

20. Technician A says modern electronic automatic transmissions are now completely electronic and no longer use mechanical gears. Technician B says servicing a modern electronic automatic transmission no longer requires a knowledge of hydraulics.
    Who is right?
    a. A only
    b. B only
    c. Both A and B
    d. Neither A nor B

2

Gears and Gearsets

Gears are the heart of any automotive transmission. They provide the building blocks for the transmission gearsets and geartrain components that allow a vehicle to use different gear ratios to meet its operating needs. This chapter examines all aspects of transmission gears and gearing systems and places special emphasis on the unique designs used in automatic transmissions.

The text begins with a look at the theory and operation of simple gear systems and how they transmit and modify torque. It continues by discussing how single gears are assembled into more complex units and details the construction and operation of simple planetary gearsets. Also examined is how simple planetary gearsets are assembled into compound planetary gearsets that are used in most automatic transmissions. The chapter concludes with a discussion of gearset design variations found in modern automatic transmissions.

GEAR TYPES

Gear types can be identified by the design and shape of the gear teeth and by the location of the teeth on the gear.

Spur and Helical Gears

The simplest type of gear is the **spur gear**. A spur gear consists of a gear blank with straight-cut teeth around its entire circumference. All gear teeth are parallel to the centerline, or **axis**, of the gear and are shaped to mesh with a similar set of gear teeth on a second spur gear (figure 2-1).

This spur gear design permits only one pair of gear teeth, one tooth of each gear, to be in mesh at any given time. The gear teeth make contact with each other over their full width at the same instant. These factors limit the load-carrying capacity of spur gears and make their operation noisy. However, some transaxles do use spur gears in the final drive gearing.

A **helical gear** is similar to a spur gear, although its teeth are cut at an angle to the

Figure 2-1. Spur gear—straight teeth.

Figure 2-2. Helical gear—angled teeth.

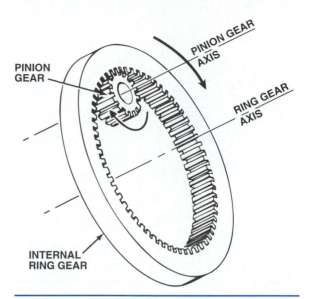

Figure 2-3. Pinion and internal ring gears.

Figure 2-4. External gear mesh.

axis of the gear (figure 2-2). This enables one and one-half gear teeth to be in contact at all times and allows the teeth to mesh gradually rather than all at once. As a result, helical gears are stronger and run quieter than spur gears. Most automatic transmission gears are helical gears.

External Gears and Internal Ring Gears

Both the spur gear in figure 2-1 and helical gear in figure 2-2 have gear teeth on their outside circumference. Gears with teeth on the outside are called **external gears**. External gears are the most commonly used type of gear.

When a gear has teeth on its inside circumference, as in figure 2-3, it is called an

internal ring gear. The teeth of an internal ring gear may be straight-cut spur or helical teeth. An internal ring gear may mesh with a smaller external gear designed to rotate as it travels around the inside of the internal ring gear. This type of external gear is called a **pinion gear** (figure 2-3).

When an external gear meshes with an internal ring gear, both gears rotate in the same direction (figure 2-3). When an external gear meshes with another external gear, the gears rotate in opposite directions (figure 2-4). In either case, both gears rotate along parallel axes.

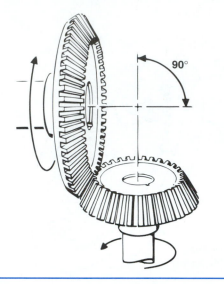

Figure 2-5. Bevel gears change rotation direction.

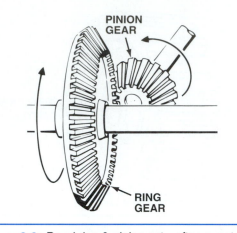

Figure 2-6. Bevel ring & pinion set—often a matched set.

Bevel, Worm, and Hypoid Gears

Unlike the gears discussed so far, bevel, worm, and hypoid gears change the axis of rotation. In most cases, the axis of rotation will change by 90°. However, other angles are possible depending upon the design of the gears.

Bevel Gears

Bevel gears change the direction of rotation in a drivetrain. The teeth of a bevel gear are cut at an angle to the outside gear surface. Simple bevel gears have straight-cut teeth similar to those on a spur gear (figure 2-5). Differential spider gears are a common example of the simple bevel gear.

Spiral bevel gears have curved teeth similar to those on a helical gear, which increase load-carrying ability and enable the gear to operate more quietly.

Spiral bevel gears are often supplied as a matched set (figure 2-6). With this combination, the larger gear is a ring gear and the smaller gear is the pinion. This combination of spiral bevel gears provides the final drive gearing in most RWD automotive differentials.

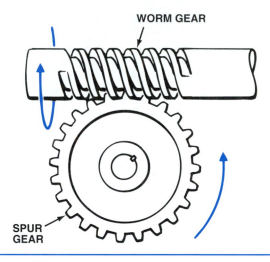

Figure 2-7. Worm and spur gears.

Worm Gear

A **worm gear** is essentially a threaded screw capable of driving a spur gear (figure 2-7). This gear configuration also changes the axis of rotation. The most common automotive uses of worm gears are in recirculating-ball steering boxes and speedometer cable drive mechanisms. A unique feature of a worm gear is that, although the worm gear can drive the spur gear, the spur gear cannot drive the worm gear.

Hypoid Gears

Hypoid gear teeth are curved much like the teeth of a spiral bevel gear (figure 2-8). This

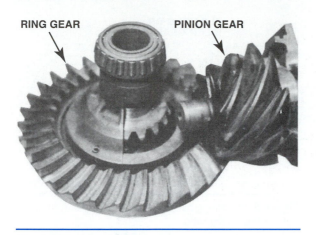

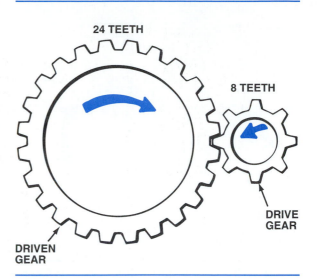

Figure 2-8. Hypoid gears.

Figure 2-9. Gear reduction—driven gear has more teeth than the drive gear.

design provides maximum gear tooth contact for strength and a gradual tooth engagement. This arrangement provides quiet operation because the pinion gear is offset below the centerline of the ring gear. Hypoid gears are generally available only as a matched set.

Hypoid gears are commonly used as final drive gears in rear axle differentials, where load-carrying ability and low noise are important. In addition, the offset pinion allows the driveshaft to be positioned lower in the vehicle, which allows the size of the hump in the vehicle interior to be reduced.

GEAR RATIOS

When one gear turns another, the speed the two gears turn in relation to each other is the gear ratio. Gear ratio is expressed as the number of rotations the drive gear must make in order to rotate the driven gear through one revolution. To obtain a gear ratio, simply divide the number of teeth on the driven gear by the number of teeth on the drive gear. Gear ratios, which are expressed relative to the number one, fall into the following three categories:

- Direct drive
- Gear reduction
- Overdrive

Direct Drive

If two meshed gears are the same size and have the same number of teeth, they will turn at the same speed. Since the drive gear turns once for each revolution of the driven gear, the gear ratio is 1:1; this is called a **direct drive**. When a transmission is in direct drive, the engine and transmission turn at the same speed.

Gear Reduction

If one gear drives a second gear that has three times the number of teeth, the smaller drive gear must travel three complete revolutions in order to drive the larger gear through one rotation (figure 2-9). Divide the number of teeth on the driven gear by the number of teeth on the drive gear and you get a 3:1 gear ratio. This type of gear arrangement, where driven gear speed is slower than drive gear speed, provides **gear reduction**. Gear reduction may also be called under-drive as drive speed is less than, or under, driven speed. Both terms mean the same thing and use is a matter of preference.

Gear reduction is used for the lower gears in a transmission. First gear in a transmission is called "low" gear because output

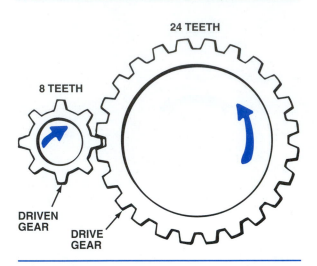

Figure 2-10. Overdrive ratio—driven gear with fewer teeth than the drive gear.

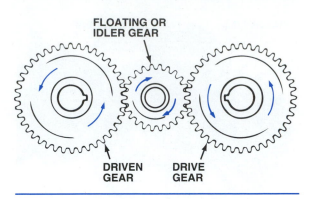

Figure 2-11. Idler gear—affects direction of rotation, not the final drive ratio.

speed, not gear ratio, is low. Low gears have numerically high gear ratios. That is, a 3:1 gear ratio is a lower gear than those with a 2:1 or 1:1 gear ratio. These three ratios taken in order represent a typical upshift pattern from low gear (3:1), to second gear (2:1), to drive gear (1:1).

Overdrive

Overdrive is the opposite of a gear reduction condition and occurs when a driven gear turns faster than its drive gear. For the gears shown in figure 2-10, the driven gear turns three times for each turn of the drive gear. The driven gear is said to overdrive the drive gear. For this example, the gear ratio is 0.33:1. Overdrive ratios of 0.65:1 and 0.70:1 are typical of those used in automotive applications.

Idler Gears

In a **geartrain**, a gear that operates between the drive and driven gears is called a floating gear or **idler gear** (figure 2-11). Idler gears do not affect the speed relationship between the drive and driven gears, although they do affect the direction of rotation. Reverse gear on an automatic transmission often uses an idler gear to change the direction of rotation.

When a drive and driven gear mesh directly, they rotate in opposite directions, (figure 2-4). When an idler gear is installed between the drive and driven gears, both gears rotate in the same direction, figure 2-11. The presence of idler gears in the geartrain does not affect the gear ratio.

TORQUE, SPEED, AND POWER

Gears have two primary purposes in a transmission: increase or decrease torque and raise or lower speed. Torque is a twisting force commonly expressed in pound-feet (lb-ft), inch-pounds (in-lb), or Newton-meters (Nm). Torque is calculated by multiplying the magnitude, or strength, of the force by the distance of the force from a center or pivot point.

For example, applying 10 pounds of force to a wrench at a distance of 1 foot from the center of a bolt exerts 10 pounds × 1 foot = 10 lb-ft of torque on the center of the bolt (figure 2-12). Gears apply torque much like a wrench does; each tooth of a gear is actually a lever. On a gear with a 2-foot radius, applying a force of 10 pounds to one gear tooth exerts 20 lb-ft of torque on the center of the shaft to which the gear attaches (figure 2-13). Torque is not the same as power, though the two terms are often incorrectly used as such. Torque is a force, which can perform **work** such as turning a shaft. **Power** is the rate, or speed, at which torque

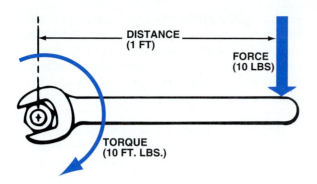

Figure 2-12. Torque—a twisting force.

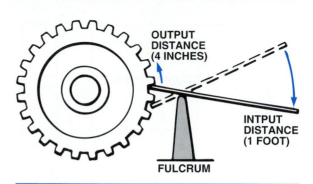

Figure 2-14. Lever and fulcrum provides torque multiplication.

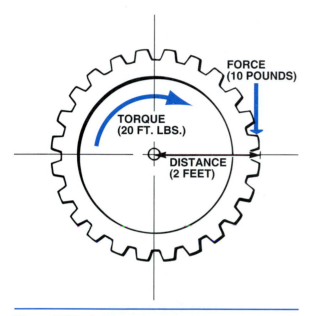

Figure 2-13. Gears apply torque.

can perform this work. Power is commonly expressed in horsepower, kilowatts, or foot-pounds per second. You can calculate engine horsepower by multiplying engine torque by the crankshaft rotation speed.

Torque and Speed Relationship

Torque and speed have an inverse relationship: as one goes up, the other goes down. With a constant input speed, transmission torque decreases as output speed increases; conversely, as transmission torque increases, output speed decreases.

Torque Multiplication

Levers can be used to increase or multiply torque. For example, a wheel that is too heavy for a person to turn by muscle power alone turns easily when that same person uses a lever and fulcrum to multiply the applied force (figure 2-14). The force, or torque, increases at one end, but the lever must be moved a greater distance at the opposite end to obtain the increase in force. Either distance or speed must always be given up in order to increase, or multiply, torque.

Gears can be used in the same way as levers to multiply torque. When two gears of the same diameter are meshed, the driven gear will turn at the same speed as the drive gear. Because there is no difference in speed, there is no difference in torque between the two gears.

If the drive gear is one-third the diameter of the driven gear, as in figure 2-9, it must rotate three times for each rotation of the larger gear. This means that the larger gear will turn three times slower than the smaller gear. At the same time the larger gear will exert three times the torque of the smaller gear. Remember, when speed decreases torque increases. In the example in figure 2-9, 10 lb-ft (1.1 Nm) of torque from the drive gear produces 30 lb-ft (3.4 Nm) of torque at the driven gear. The torque multiplying power of this system is 3:1, which is the same as the gear ratio.

Torque multiplication and gear ratios are directly related. When a gear system is in reduction, there is more torque available at

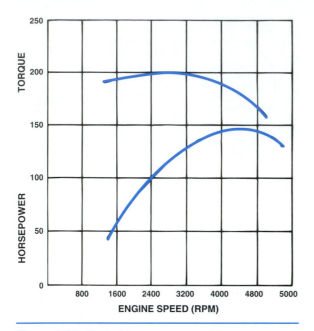

Figure 2-15. Typical torque curve and horsepower curve.

the driven gear, but less speed. When the gear system is in overdrive, there is less torque available at the driven gear, but greater speed. In designing mechanical devices such as transmissions, engineers choose gear ratios that provide the torque output to do the work.

Engine Torque Characteristics

The torque curve of an engine shows how much torque is available at different points within a range of engine speeds (figure 2-15). Note that over most of the range shown, the horsepower curve increases, while the torque curve stays relatively flat. This is because power equals torque multiplied by speed. As long as the speed increase is greater than the torque decrease power will increase as well. At the upper end of the range, the torque drops off far enough that higher engine speeds can no longer compensate and the power output begins to drop as well.

An internal combustion engine has a fairly limited torque range. High torque output is only available over a part of the

engine speed range. At low engine speeds, the engine does not produce enough torque at the crankshaft to move the vehicle. As engine speed increases it quickly exceeds the point where the torque curve peaks and the amount of power available to perform work drops off.

Because of these characteristics, torque multiplication must be provided between the crankshaft and drive axles to enable a vehicle to begin moving from a standstill and to accelerate at low speeds. Once engine rpm rises beyond the torque peak, a change in gear ratio brings engine speed back within the most efficient torque-producing range.

POWERTRAIN GEAR RATIOS

A transmission enables a vehicle to move more efficiently by maximizing engine torque. The transmission is aided in this task by the final drive gearing. These components work together to provide select gear ratios that take maximum advantage of engine torque available through various speed ranges.

Final Drive Gearing

The final drive is the last set of reduction gears the power flow passes through on its way to the drive axles. On most FWD vehicles, the final drive is located within the transaxle housing. On most RWD vehicles, the final drive is located apart from the transmission in the rear axle housing. Although an RWD axle assembly that contains the final drive is loosely called a differential, the term "differential" refers specifically to the gearing that allows the wheels to turn at different speeds as the vehicle negotiates a corner. A transaxle also uses a differential, however, it is within the transaxle housing along with the final drive gearing.

As mentioned earlier, an RWD vehicle generally uses hypoid gears for the final drive because the direction of rotation must make a 90-degree turn to transfer power flow from the driveshaft to the axles. Hypoid final drive gears are also used on some FWD vehicles if the engine mounts longitudinally. On a transverse-mounted engine, power flow is parallel to the drive axles, so a simple set of helical gears can serve as the final drive.

The torque converter in an automatic transmission provides additional torque multiplication for certain operating conditions. Therefore, final drive gear ratios may be numerically lower for a vehicle with an automatic transmission than they would be for a similar model with a manual transmission. Typically, the final drive gear ratio ranges from about 2.2:1 to 4:1 for vehicles with automatic transmissions.

Transmission Gearing

Some gear ratios are more advantageous to certain vehicle needs and operations than others. These conditions will be discussed and illustrated here for first, second, third, and fourth gear ratios. Different gear ratios can improve vehicle economy and performance over a wide range of driving conditions.

First Gear

First gear, or low range, is responsible for moving the vehicle from a standstill. For the average vehicle, this requires an overall torque multiplication from the engine to the drive axles of about 12:1. Remember, torque multiplication matches gear ratio. The overall gear ratio of engine speed to drive axle speed can be calculated by multiplying the transmission gear ratio by the final drive gear ratio. So, if the final drive gear ratio is 4:1 and the low gear ratio is 3:1, the overall gear ratio is: 4:1 × 3:1 = 12:1

As torque is *multiplied* by twelve, speed is *divided* by twelve. Thus, if the crankshaft turns at 1200 rpm, the drive wheels turn at: 1200 ÷ 12 = 100 rpm

This is useful and necessary to initiate vehicle movement, but it is undesirable as speed increases. With a 12:1 overall gear ratio, by the time the vehicle reaches 40 mph, the engine will be turning about 5000 rpm.

Second Gear

Second, or intermediate, gear takes over once the vehicle is in motion and the engine load is somewhat reduced. Typically, this second set of transmission gears will have a gear ratio of approximately 2:1. This provides some torque multiplication, though not as much as low gear. Multiplying this ratio of 2:1 by the final drive ratio of 4:1 gives a new overall gear ratio of 8:1. The driver can use this gear ratio to increase speed, while continuing to operate in a favorable region of engine torque and horsepower curves.

Third Gear

For cruising speeds, a third gear, or direct drive with a 1:1 gear ratio is built into the transmission. With a final drive ratio of 4:1, this provides an overall gear ratio of 4:1. For a three-speed transmission, direct drive is the top gear. However, four-speed transmissions allow higher drive speeds through the use of overdrive gearing.

Fourth Gear

Fourth gear, or overdrive range, engages during cruise to lower engine speed, reduce wear, and improve fuel economy. With an overdrive gear ratio, the output speed of the transmission is faster than the input speed, which is engine rpm. Applying a typical 0.7:1 overdrive gear ratio to a 4:1 final drive ratio reduces the overall gear ratio to 2.8:1.

PLANETARY GEARSETS

In a manual transmission, different gear ratios are obtained by sliding the gears into mesh. However, power flow must be momentarily interrupted (by using a clutch) before the gears are shifted. With an automatic transmission there is no driver-operated clutch, so gear shifts are not made by sliding gears into mesh. Automatic transmissions use a planetary gearset system that does not require manual gear shifting or an

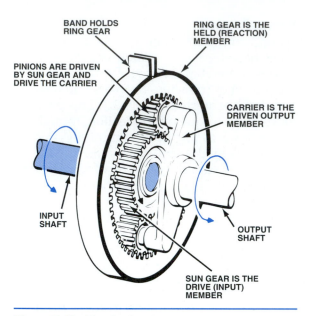

Figure 2-16. Simple planetary gearset.

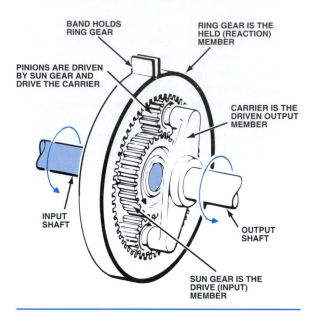

Figure 2-17. Transmitting torque through a planetary gearset.

interruption of powerflow to change gear ratios. A simple planetary gearset consists of the following three primary components:

- Sun gear
- Planet carrier assembly
- Ring gear

The **sun gear** gets its name from its position at the center of the gearset. The **planet carrier assembly** holds the pinion gears, also known as planet gears, which revolve around the sun gear. The outermost member of the gearset is the **ring gear,** which is the internal type with the teeth inside. The pinion gears are in simultaneous mesh with both the sun and ring gear.

The pinion gears are free to rotate on pins that are part of the carrier and the entire assembly rotates to direct power flow. The simple planetary gearset shown in figure 2-16 has only two planet pinions, but most transmission gearsets use three or four. The pinions are fully meshed with both the sun gear and internal ring gear *at all times*. The planetary gears never disengage to change gear ratios; power is simply redirected.

All gears in a planetary gearset are in constant mesh. The powerflow through a planetary gearset, both input and output, occurs along a single axis.

The parts in a planetary gear system may be known by several different names. The

internal ring gear is sometimes called an annulus gear or a ring gear. The planet pinion gears are often called planet gears or pinion gears. The planet carrier assembly is commonly referred to as the "carrier." In this *Classroom Manual*, the terms "sun gear," "ring gear," "pinions," and "carrier" are used when describing planetary gearset power flow and operation.

PLANETARY GEARSET POWER FLOW

In any planetary gearset, each gear always meshes with several other gears. Therefore, driving one gear will drive all of the other gears as well. This allows the gearset to provide different gear ratios, depending upon how power is distributed to transmit torque through the assembly. To transmit torque through a planetary gearset, a drive member rotates while a second member is held, which causes a third member to be driven (figure 2-17). Each member of a planetary gearset can play any one of these three roles to transmit torque. The various combinations of drive, held, and driven members result in the number of gear ratios available. Certain combinations of drive, hold, and driven can change the direction of rotation as well.

Power flows through a planetary gearset in several steps to get from the drive action of the first member to the driven action of the last member. The terms "drive" and "driven" simply describe how any two gears work together. When three or more gears are involved, the second gear is a *driven* gear in relation to the first, but a *drive* gear in relation to the third. For this reason, the drive member of a planetary gearset is known as the **input member**, the held member is the **reaction member**, and the driven member is the **output member**.

The terms "input member," "held member," and "output member" describe planetary gearset operations in this *Classroom Manual*. The text may also describe the actions of other members of the gearset to be turning, or serving, as a reaction member.

PLANETARY GEARSET OPERATIONS

The planetary gearsets used in automatic transmissions provide the following five basic gear operations:

- Gear Reduction
- Overdrive
- Reverse
- Direct drive
- Neutral

Driving and holding combinations of planetary gearset members will obtain all five basic gear operations.

Gear Reduction

When the carrier is the output, holding either one of the other members will result in a gear reduction. The output rotation will be in the same direction as the input rotation, but at a lower speed. Switching the

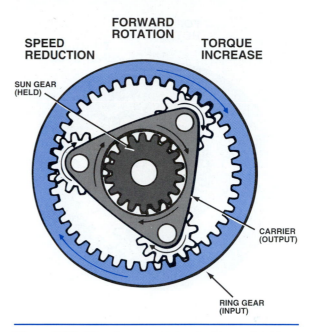

Figure 2-18. Planetary gearset reduction method 1.

input and held member provides two methods of obtaining gear reduction. Note that both methods use the carrier as the output member.

Method 1

To achieve gear reduction, the three planetary members are as follows:

- Ring gear—input
- Sun gear—held
- Carrier—output

In this configuration with the internal ring gear as the input member, the ring gear turns clockwise while the sun gear is held (figure 2-18). As the ring gear rotates clockwise, the pinions turn clockwise. Because the pinions are meshed with the stationary sun gear, they "walk" clockwise around it, moving the carrier clockwise with them, but at a reduced speed. The carrier is the output member.

Method 2

Switching the input and held members in the preceding example also results in a gear reduction, as follows:

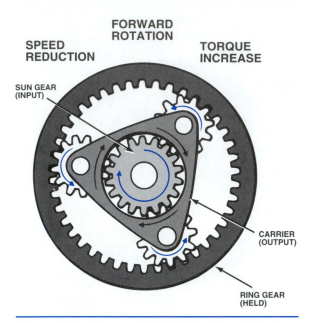

Figure 2-19. Planetary gearset reduction method 2.

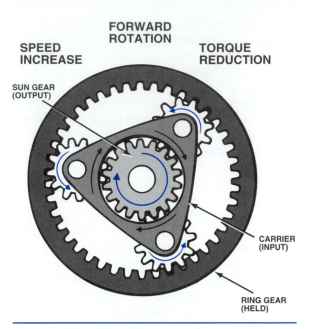

Figure 2-20. Planetary gearset overdrive method 1.

- Sun gear—input
- Ring gear—held
- Carrier—output

When the sun gear is the input member and turns clockwise, the pinions rotate counterclockwise (figure 2-19). If the ring gear is held, the pinions in mesh with the ring gear walk the carrier clockwise around the inside of the ring gear. The carrier is again the output member as it rotates in the same direction as the sun gear, at a lower speed.

Overdrive

When the carrier is the input member, and one of the other members is held, the remaining output member will rotate faster than the input member. The direction of rotation of the input and output shafts will be the same, but output speed is greater than input speed. As with gear reduction, there are two methods of obtaining overdrive. Note that both methods use the carrier as the input member.

Method 1

One way to achieve overdrive gearing is by using the following method:

- Carrier—input
- Ring gear—held
- Sun gear—output

The carrier, the input member, turns clockwise while the ring gear is held (figure 2-20). The pinions turn counterclockwise as they travel around the inside of the stationary ring gear, driving the sun gear clockwise. The sun gear is an overdrive output member, as it turns in the same direction as the input carrier but at a higher speed.

Method 2

Overdrive gearing is also available with the following method:

- Carrier—input
- Sun gear—held
- Ring gear—output

Again, the carrier is the input member and turns clockwise. However, this time the sun gear is held (figure 2-21). The pinions rotate clockwise along with the carrier and as a result the ring gear turns clockwise. The ring gear is the output member that rotates in the same direction as the input member, but at a higher speed.

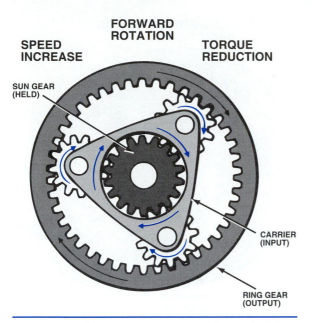

Figure 2-21. Planetary gearset overdrive method 2.

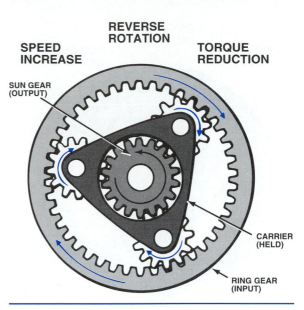

Figure 2-22. Planetary gearset reverse gear method 1.

Reverse

When the carrier is held, one of the other two members is the input and the remaining member will be the output. Under these conditions, the output member always turns in the opposite direction of the input member. The stationary carrier causes the pinions to act as idler gears to provide a reverse gear. There are two methods of obtaining reverse gear, in which the carrier is the held member for both.

Method 1
A simple planetary gearset provides reverse when the following is true:

- Ring gear—input
- Carrier—held
- Sun gear—output

The ring gear, the input member, turns clockwise. Because the carrier is held, input from the ring gear turns the pinions clockwise on their pins. The pinions then drive the sun gear counterclockwise as the output member (figure 2-22). With this arrangement, output speed is greater than input speed because the sun gear has fewer teeth than the ring gear. This type of reverse gearing is an overdrive condition with a directional change.

Method 2
Another way to obtain reverse is with the following arrangement:

- Sun gear—input
- Carrier—held
- Ring gear—output

When the sun gear is the input member and turns clockwise with the carrier held, the pinions rotate counterclockwise and drive the ring gear counterclockwise (figure 2-23). In this configuration, the output ring gear rotates slower than the input sun gear and they rotate in opposite directions. This arrangement produces a gear reduction with a directional reverse.

Direct Drive

When two members of a planetary gearset are locked together, they operate as a single member. If any two members of the gearset turn in the same direction and at the same speed, the gearset functions as a solid unit. The third member must lock with the other two and turn in the same direction and at the same speed. Two locked members result in a direct drive condition to deliver a 1:1 gear ratio.

There are three ways to obtain direct drive with a simple planetary gearset.

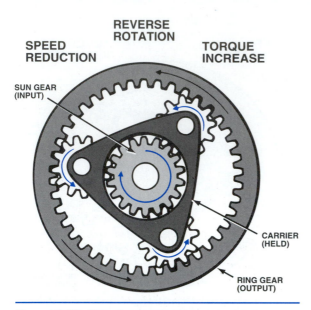

Figure 2-23. Planetary gearset reverse gear method 2.

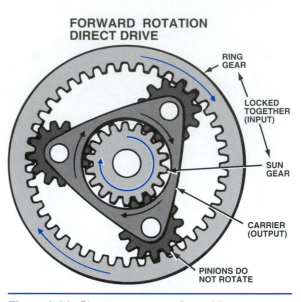

Figure 2-24. Planetary gearset direct drive gear method 1.

Notice that in all three methods, two members provide input while the third member provides output. The input member is locked to the output member because the pinions cannot rotate on the carrier pins. Therefore, output speed and direction match input speed and direction.

Method 1

This first method of obtaining direct drive is commonly used in modern automatic transmissions, as follows:

- Sun gear—input
- Ring gear—input
- Carrier—output

The sun and ring gear both provide input as they rotate clockwise at the same speed (figure 2-24). This prevents the pinions from rotating on their pins and drives the carrier clockwise. The carrier becomes the output and travels at the same speed as the input. As a result, the entire planetary assembly rotates as a single unit, providing a direct drive condition.

Method 2

An alternative direct drive method uses the ring gear as the output member, as follows:

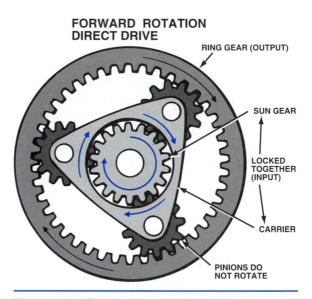

Figure 2-25. Planetary gearset direct drive gear method 2.

- Sun gear—input
- Carrier—input
- Ring gear—output

If you lock the sun gear and carrier together and turn them clockwise, the ring gear will also rotate clockwise at the same speed as the other two (figure 2-25). Locking the sun gear and carrier prevents the pinions from revolving around the sun gear or rotating on their pins. Therefore, the pinions hold

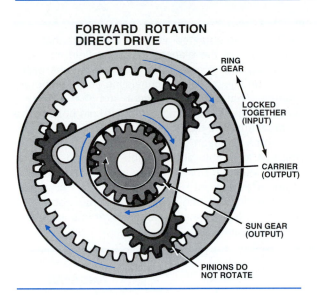

Figure 2-26. Planetary gearset direct drive gear method 3.

the ring gear and the entire assembly rotates clockwise as a unit.

Method 3
The sun gear can also function as the output member in a direct drive configuration, as follows:

- Ring gear—input
- Carrier—input
- Sun gear—output

If you lock the ring gear and carrier together and turn them clockwise, the result is the same as when the sun gear and carrier are locked (figure 2-26). The pinions cannot rotate, and the sun gear must move at the same speed and direction as the rest of the assembly. The planetary gearset rotates as a unit providing a direct 1:1 gear ratio.

Neutral
If any single member of a planetary gearset turns as an input but no member is held, there will be no output. This is a neutral power flow condition. For example, with the sun gear as the input member, if neither the carrier nor the ring gear is held, the pinions

	OPERATION								
	GEAR REDUCTION		OVERDRIVE		REVERSE		DIRECT DRIVE		
	1	2	1	2	1	2	1	2	3
SUN GEAR	H	I	O	H	O	I	I	I	O
RING GEAR	I	H	H	O	I	O	I	O	I
CARRIER	O	O	I	I	H	H	O	I	I

I = INPUT   O = OUTPUT   H = HELD

Figure 2-27. Planetary gearset operation summary.

are free to rotate on their pins. The pinions will move either the carrier or ring gear, depending on which has the least resistance, around the sun gear with them, but there is no transfer of torque. Regardless of which member moves with the pinions, there will be no output. The members of the gearset may turn, but the power flow is incomplete.

A similar result occurs if either the ring gear or carrier is the input member and neither of the other members are held. The pinions rotate and turn the remaining gearset member that offers the least resistance.

Figure 2-27 summarizes the methods for obtaining gear reduction, overdrive, reverse, and direct drive with a single planetary gearset. The operating status of the sun gear, ring gear, and carrier are identified as input (I), output (O), or held (H).

SIMPLE PLANETARY GEARSET SYSTEMS
A simple planetary gearset system consists of one sun gear, a carrier, and a ring gear. A single planetary gearset can provide all of the necessary gear ratios for a basic automatic transmission.

Using a simple planetary gearset along with a brake band and multiple-disc clutch as apply devices, you can design a two-speed automatic transmission. The transmission provides neutral and reverse gearing, and performs low to drive gear changes without any input from the driver.

Simple planetary gear systems like this were used in some early automatic transmissions. However, they are no longer used because they do not provide enough usable gear ratios for present-day applications. They also present design problems for the particular gearset members that must be driven or held. However, the simple planetary gearset remains the foundation upon which the compound planetary gearsets used in modern transmissions are built. In fact, a simple planetary gearset is often used together with a compound planetary gearset to provide additional overdrive gearing.

COMPOUND PLANETARY GEARSET SYSTEMS

A **compound planetary gearset** system is a configuration that contains more than just the three basic members of a simple planetary system. Compound planetary gearsets are capable of providing various combinations of gear reduction, direct drive, neutral, reverse, and overdrive.

The most popular compound planetary design is the **Simpson gearset**. Named for its inventor, the Simpson gearset consists of two simple planetary gearsets that share a common sun gear (figure 2-28). This combination is capable of providing three forward gears, as well as neutral and reverse. Basic operation, construction, and methods of obtaining various gear ratios with a simple planetary gearset also apply to the Simpson gearset. The main difference is the number of gear ratios.

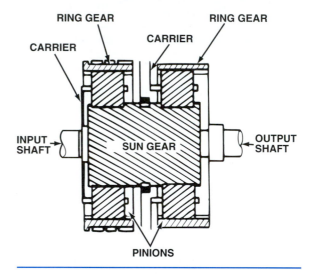

Figure 2-28. Simpson planetary gearset.

Another popular compound planetary design is the **Ravigneaux gearset**. The Ravigneaux system has two sun gears; two sets, one longer than the other, of planet pinions supported in one carrier; and a single ring gear (figure 2-29). This design provides four forward gears, two in reduction, one direct, and one overdrive, as well as neutral and reverse. Basic planetary gearset operation, construction, and control methods also apply to the Ravigneaux gearset.

Both of these compound planetary gearset designs have been used over the years by import and domestic manufacturers. Later chapters of this *Classroom Manual* detail the construction, operation, and control of these and other compound planetary gearset designs.

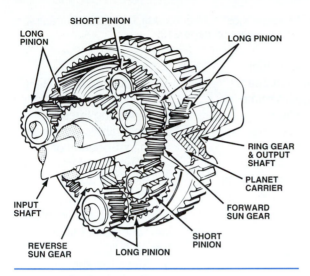

Figure 2-29. Ravigneaux gearset.

SUMMARY

Gears used in transmissions are classified by the shape and location of their teeth and by their relationship to other gears. Helical gears, with both internal and external teeth, are commonly used in automatic transmissions and hypoid gears are often used in rear axles.

A gear ratio expresses the torque-speed relationship between two gears and is based on the number of turns a drive gear must make to turn a driven gear one full revolution. When a driven gear turns slower than its drive gear, the gears provide a gear reduction. An example gear ratio for this condition would be 3:1. When a driven gear turns at the same speed as its drive gear, the gears provide direct drive, or 1:1 ratio. When a driven gear turns faster than its drive gear, the gears provide an overdrive ratio such as 0.7:1.

Transmission gears compensate for engine power output characteristics by regulating torque and speed. When gears increase torque, output speed decreases. When gears decrease torque, output speed increases.

Final drive gears provide torque multiplication in addition to that provided by the transmission gears. In front-engine RWD vehicles, the final drive is located in the rear axle assembly. In FWD vehicles and mid- or rear-engine RWD vehicles, the final drive is often located within the transaxle housing.

Automatic transmissions use planetary gearsets because they do not require manual gear shifting to change gear ratios. Gears of a planetary gearset are in constant mesh. Gear ratios are selected by driving or holding various combinations of planetary gearset members. A simple planetary gearset consists of sun, ring, and pinion gears that are mounted on a carrier assembly. Torque is transmitted through a planetary gearset by holding one member, driving a second, and taking output from a third.

A simple planetary gearset system uses one each of the three basic members. Simple planetary gearsets are rarely used alone in a modern automatic transmission but are often used with other gearsets to provide additional overdrive gearing. Most modern automatic transmissions use a compound planetary gearset assembly. Compound planetary gearsets are basically two simple gearsets combined into one assembly. The two most common compound planetary gearset designs are the Simpson gearset and the Ravigneaux gearset. Almost all automatic transmissions use some variation of these two planetary gearsets.

Review Questions

Choose the single most correct answer. Compare your answers to the correct answers on page 213.

1. Technician A says the teeth of a spur gear are cut parallel to the axis of the gear. Technician B says the teeth of a helical gear are cut at an angle to the axis of the gear.
   Who is right?
   a. A only
   b. B only
   c. Both A and B
   d. Neither A nor B

2. Technician A says helical gears are often used to change the direction of the axis of rotation. Technician B says bevel gears are often used to change the direction of the axis of rotation.
   Who is right?
   a. A only
   b. B only
   c. Both A and B
   d. Neither A nor B

3. Technician A says the centerline of the pinion gear is below the centerline of the ring gear in a hypoid gear set. Technician B says that manufacturers use hypoid-type final drive gears to reduce the hump in the passenger compartment.
   Who is right?
   a. A only
   b. B only
   c. Both A and B
   d. Neither A nor B

4. Technician A says that when two external gears mesh, both gears rotate in the same direction. Technician B says that when an external gear meshes with an internal ring gear, both gears rotate in the same direction.
   Who is right?
   a. A only
   b. B only
   c. Both A and B
   d. Neither A nor B

5. A gear ratio of 3:1 is an example of
   a. Overdrive
   b. Direct drive
   c. Gear reduction
   d. None of the above

6. Technician A says that gear reduction occurs when the drive gear turns faster than the driven gear. Technician B says that overdrive occurs when the driven gear turns faster than the drive gear.
   Who is right?
   a. A only
   b. B only
   c. Both A and B
   d. Neither A nor B

7. Technician A says that idler gears do not affect the gear ratio. Technician B says that idler gears are used to achieve an overdrive condition.
   Who is right?
   a. A only
   b. B only
   c. Both A and B
   d. Neither A nor B

8. Torque is
   a. Calculated by multiplying force times distance
   b. A twisting force
   c. Sometimes expressed in foot-pounds or Newton-meters
   d. All of the above

9. When gears are used to increase output speed, torque output
   a. Stays the same
   b. Fluctuates
   c. Increases
   d. Decreases

10. Technician A says gear ratio is calculated by dividing the number of teeth on the driven gear by the number of teeth on the drive gear. Technician B says gear ratio is calculated by multiplying the number of teeth on the drive gear by the number of teeth on the driven gear.
    Who is right?
    a. A only
    b. B only
    c. Both A and B
    d. Neither A nor B

11. If a driven gear has three times as many teeth as its drive gear, output torque will be
    a. Divided 3 times
    b. Divided 9 times
    c. Multiplied 3 times
    d. Multiplied 9 times

12. Power is
    a. Torque divided by speed
    b. Torque multiplied by speed
    c. The same as torque
    d. Torque plus speed

13. Technician A says that transmission gearing is used to increase engine torque to maximize efficiency at higher speeds. Technician B says that the final drive is the last set of reduction gears the power flow passes through on its way to the drive axles.
    Who is right?
    a. A only
    b. B only
    c. Both A and B
    d. Neither A nor B

14. The primary components of a simple planetary gearset are
    a. Sun and ring gears and carrier
    b. Sun, ring, and idler gears
    c. Sun, ring, and internal gears
    d. Sun, ring, and crescent gears

15. The member of a planetary gearset that is held in order to transmit torque is often called the
    a. Input member
    b. Output member
    c. Reaction member
    d. Turned member

16. To produce gear reduction with a simple planetary gearset, the carrier is always the
    a. Input member
    b. Reaction member
    c. Reversed member
    d. Output member

17. To produce overdrive with a simple planetary gearset, the carrier is always the
    a. Input member
    b. Reaction member
    c. Reversed member
    d. Output member

18. To produce reverse with a simple planetary gearset, the carrier is always the
    a. Input member
    b. Reaction member
    c. Reversed member
    d. Output member

19. Technician A says that when any two members of a planetary gearset are driven in the same direction at the same speed, the result is direct drive. Technician B says that when a planetary gearset is locked up, the result is direct drive.
    Who is right?
    a. A only
    b. B only
    c. Both A and B
    d. Neither A nor B

20. Technician A says most transmissions use compound planetary gearsets to provide the most usable gear combinations. Technician B says the most popular planetary gearset designs are the Simpson and Ravigneaux.
    Who is right?
    a. A only
    b. B only
    c. Both A and B
    d. Neither A nor B

3

Hydraulic
Fundamentals

An automatic transmission is a hydro-mechanical device that uses hydraulic pressure to activate and control a mechanical gearset. A specially blended fluid, automatic transmission fluid (ATF), transmits hydraulic pressure through the transmission.

A transmission hydraulic system generates fluid pressure to control the gearset apply devices and also distributes the ATF through a system of valves and passages. Transmission fluid performs four important tasks: It provides a fluid connection between the engine and transmission, transfers engine drive torque, lubricates the internal parts, and transfers heat away from the transmission. All of these functions are based on principles of hydraulics.

The first two chapters of this *Classroom Manual* discussed the mechanical gearing of an automatic transmission and how a gearset provides different gear ratios to meet the operating needs of the vehicle. Here, the hydraulic systems that control these mechanical gearsets will be discussed. This chapter begins with a discussion of hydraulic fundamentals and follows with an explanation of how they apply to an automatic transmission.

HYDRAULIC PRINCIPLES

To fully understand how an automatic transmission functions, it is necessary to be familiar with basic hydraulic principles. This segment discusses the fundamental hydraulic principles that govern the operation of all transmission hydraulic systems.

Hydraulics

Hydraulics is a branch of science that studies liquids and how they can apply pressure and transmit force and motion. The term hydraulics is a combination of two Greek root words: *hydror*—meaning water, and *aulos*—meaning a tube or pipe. In fact, water distribution systems are a common

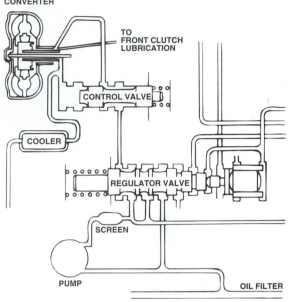

Figure 3-1. Hydraulic circuit diagram.

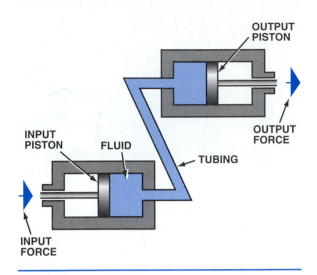

Figure 3-2. Hydraulic passages.

application of hydraulic principles. The hydraulic principles that govern the behavior of water systems apply to all liquids in motion, including transmission fluid. An understanding of these hydraulic principles is necessary to effectively diagnose and service automatic transmissions.

Hydraulic circuit diagrams, such as the one shown in figure 3-1, are effective tools for diagnosing many hydraulic-related automatic transmission concerns.

Fluids and Fluid Characteristics

The general term "fluid" refers to any matter that has the ability to move and change shape without separating when under pressure. Fluid matter can be either a liquid or gas. Gas is not suitable for use in a hydraulic system because it is compressible. This means the volume of gas in the system becomes smaller when the system is put under pressure. Hydraulic systems use liquids because a liquid is **incompressible**. Because a liquid does not compress, the volume of liquid remains the same when put

under pressure. Because of this property, a liquid can be used to apply force.

Liquids under pressure transmit force and motion similar to a mechanical lever. However, liquid has an advantage over a mechanical connection because it does not have a fixed shape. A liquid always assumes the shape of its container. This means it will fill all of the tubes and passageways within a system. Therefore, liquids can transmit pressure—which creates an apply force that is converted into motion—around corners and through bent passages in the transmission hydraulic circuits (figure 3-2).

Different transmission designs have unique fluid requirements, and several types of ATF are available. Using the correct fluid for a particular transmission is an important consideration. Each fluid is blended specifically to enhance certain fluid properties and perform certain functions within the transmission.

Pascal's Law

Blaise Pascal, a French scientist, discovered important facts about the behavior of liquids within a closed system. Through experimental observation, Pascal was able to determine that a liquid can be used to transmit force through a system to create motion (figure

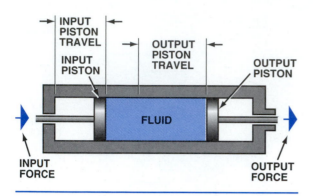

Figure 3-3. Fluid systems transmit pressure, force, and motion.

3-3). The laboratory experiments Pascal conducted on fluid systems made use of weights, pistons, and containers of various shapes and sizes. Pascal was able to summarize the results of his experiments into a single statement:

Pressure on a confined liquid is transmitted equally in all directions and acts with equal force on equal areas.

When further experimentation could not disprove this statement, this 17th-century theory eventually became known as *Pascal's Law.* In essence, this single statement provides the fundamental principle that covers the operation of all hydraulic systems (figure 3-4). To better understand Pascal's Law, it will be broken down into several smaller concepts and discussed individually.

Force

Force is a push or pull on an object that usually causes the object to move or change. There are different types of force as well as several ways to apply it. Some types of force and application methods are more useful than others.

The U.S. Customary system of measurement rates the application of force in pounds (lb) while the metric system rates force in Newtons (N). For simplicity, this *Classroom Manual* will not present the metric equivalent when discussing force. To convert pounds of force to Newtons, multiply by

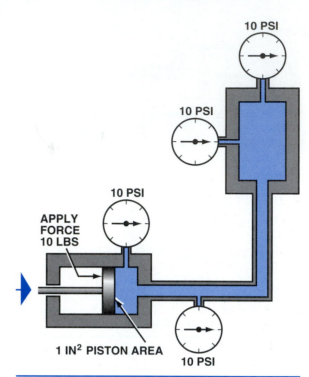

Figure 3-4. Hydraulic pressure is equal throughout the system.

4.448. Multiply Newtons by 0.2248 to convert to pounds.

Gravity is one type of force, although it is more commonly thought of as the weight of an object. For example, a vehicle weighs 2000 lb because gravity exerts a downward force of 2000 lb on it. Friction is another type of force, one which occurs when two objects move against each other. For example, if you push or pull this textbook across a desk top you will feel a slight drag that inhibits motion. This drag is the force of friction between the book and the desk top.

Friction is an important element in both hydraulic and mechanical systems. Transmission fluid must overcome fluid friction in order to fill and pressurize the hydraulic system. The pressurization of fluid is used to produce, apply, and hold force for the friction clutches and bands. Transmission fluid also has the additional job of removing the heat produced by the friction of gearset rotation, clutch and band application, and torque converter operation. An automatic transmission places transmission fluid under pressure to create the

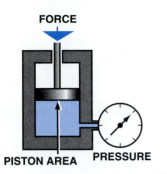

Figure 3-5. Determining pressure.

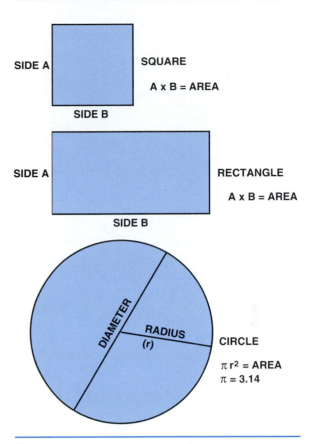

Figure 3-6. Surface area calculation.

mechanical force necessary to apply and hold gearset members.

Another type of force important in hydraulic systems is spring force, the force a spring produces when it compresses. Spring force is used to add (boost) or subtract (oppose) the effect of a hydraulic force. In an automatic transmission, a spring may work in combination with fluid pressure to reposition a valve, actuate a servo, or apply a clutch pack.

Pressure

Pressure is the amount of force applied to a certain area. Pressure is measured as the amount of force per unit of area and is expressed as either pounds-per-square inch (psi) in the U.S. Customary System, or kilopascal (kPa) in the metric system. This *Classroom Manual* displays pressure as psi only. Divide psi by 6.895 to convert to kPa.

To determine pressure, it is necessary to know the force with which it is being applied and the surface area upon which it acts. Calculate pressure by dividing force by area (figure 3-5).

$$\text{Force} \div \text{Area} = \text{Pressure}$$

Surface area is easy to calculate for standard geometric shapes (figure 3-6). To calculate the surface area of a square, simply multiply the length of one side by itself. The surface area of a rectangle is equal to the length of a short side multiplied by the length

of a long side. Determine the surface area of a circle using the formula πr^2. The symbol "π," or pi (pronounced "pie"), is the sixteenth letter of the Greek alphabet. In mathematics, π is a ratio of the circumference (length around) to the diameter (length across) of a circle. Regardless of the size of the circle, the value of π is always the same and can be rounded to 3.14. The symbol "r" in the equation is the radius of the circle. The radius is distance from the outer edge to the center of a circle, or half the diameter.

The cube in figure 3-7 measures 2 by 2 by 2 inches. To determine the surface area of one face of the cube, simply multiply 2×2. The result is 4, so the surface area is 4 square inches or 4 in^2. The volume of a cube equals the surface area (4) multiplied by the depth (2) and is expressed as cubic inches. In this case, volume is 8 cubic inches or 8 in^3. If 20 lb of force is applied to this cube, the force will act on the face of the cube to produce a pressure of 5 psi.

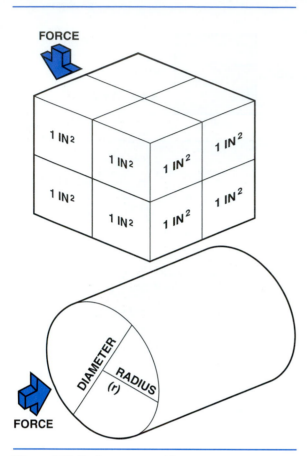

Figure 3-7. Surface area and force.

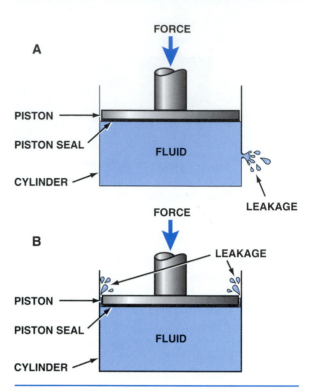

Figure 3-8. Pressure develops in a confined/closed system.

$$20 \text{ (lb)} \div 4 \text{ (in}^2) = 5 \text{ (psi)}$$

The diameter of the **piston** in figure 3-7 is 3 inches. To calculate surface area, multiply the radius by itself then multiply the result by π.

$$1.5 \times 1.5 = 2.25$$
$$2.25 \times 3.14 = 7.065$$

Rounding the answer to the nearest tenth, you get a surface area of 7.1 in². Apply a force of 20 lb to the face of this piston, and the result would be approximately 2.8 psi of pressure.

$$20 \text{ (lbs)} \div 7.1 \text{ (in}^2) = 2.8169014 \text{ (psi)}$$

Note: Pressure cannot develop in a hydraulic system unless the fluid is *confined* within a *closed system*. Neither hydraulic system in figure 3-8 is capable of developing pressure. Stroke the piston in illustration "A" and fluid flows out the opening at the side. The piston in system "B" does not seal against the cylinder wall and allows fluid to

flow past it as it moves down the bore. Neither of these systems can develop pressure, as they cannot confine the fluid.

Pressure develops in a hydraulic system as force is applied to the input piston. The amount of force applied and the surface area of the piston are the two major factors that determine system pressure. Remember, pressure equals force divided by area, so applying 10 lb of force to a 1-in² input piston will develop 10 psi of system pressure, as in figure 3-9.

$$10 \text{ (lb)} \div 1 \text{ (in}^2) = 10 \text{ (psi)}$$

In keeping with Pascal's Law, the same 10 psi of pressure exists throughout the entire system. When that pressure reaches the output piston, it acts on the surface area of the piston to produce an output force. Simply rearrange the system pressure equation to determine the amount of the output force: Force equals pressure multiplied by the surface area. Applying this equation to the example in figure 3-9 reveals 10 lb of output force.

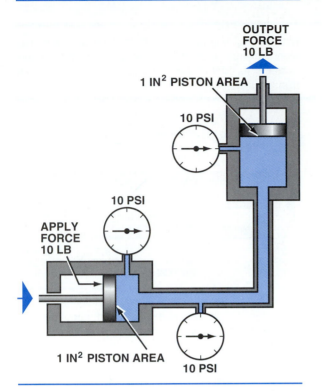

Figure 3-9. Force is determined by pressure and surface area.

$$10 \text{ (psi)} \times 1 \text{ (in}^2) = 10 \text{ (lb)}$$

Multiplication of Force

Pascal found he could use a hydraulic system to not only apply pressure and transmit force but to gain a mechanical advantage as well. Simply increasing either the piston size or apply force provides the advantage.

The basic relationship between force and distance in a hydraulic system is exactly the same as in a mechanical system. The discussion of gears in this *Classroom Manual* explained how a lever and fulcrum is used to increase force. However, a lever or gear can increase force only at the expense of distance traveled. The same holds true for a hydraulic system: a gain in mechanical advantage always requires a sacrifice. Applying 10 lbs of force to a 0.5-in^2 input piston will develop 20 psi of system pressure, as shown in figure 3-10.

$$10 \text{ (lb)} \div 0.5 \text{ (in}^2) = 20 \text{ (psi)}$$

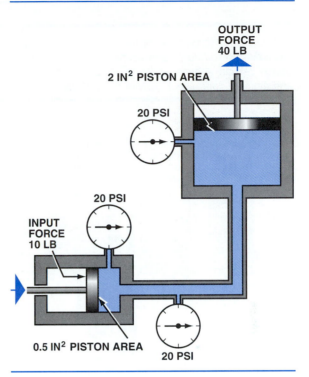

Figure 3-10. Hydraulic lever—multiplication of input force.

Remember, Pascal's Law says 20 psi of pressure exists throughout the system. However, apply this 20 psi of pressure to an output piston with greater surface area and the piston produces a greater output force. Again, to determine force, multiply pressure by area. Therefore, as figure 3-10 shows, applying 20 psi to a 2-in^2 piston delivers 40 lb of output force.

$$20 \text{ (psi)} \times 2 \text{ (in}^2) = 40 \text{ (lb)}$$

When a hydraulic system multiplies force in this manner, it is sometimes called a **hydraulic lever**. In practice, a hydraulic system will further multiply the force by using additional stages of mechanical leverage. Often, the final output force is many times greater than the initial input force.

A single hydraulic system is capable of developing different amounts of output force from a common system pressure. This might be the case in an actual automatic transmission when one hydraulic circuit must actuate several apply devices to control different gearset members. In figure 3-11, a single system pressure of 10 psi provides three different output forces.

The hydraulic systems of modern automatic transmissions provide automatic upshifts and downshifts to match vehicle speeds and engine torque for smooth and efficient operation. However, a hydraulic system is not the only way to control the shifting of a transmission. Several automakers used electric and vacuum systems to control the shifts in early semiautomatic transmissions.

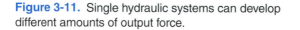

Figure 3-11. Single hydraulic systems can develop different amounts of output force.

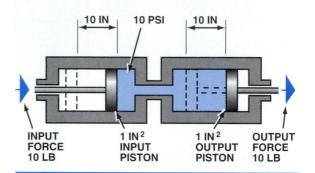

Figure 3-12. Surface area—travel relationship #1. When the surface area of the input and output pistons are equal, the distance the two pistons travel will be equal.

Transmission of Motion

Hydraulic systems can transmit and multiply force using hydraulic pressure, but what about motion? The size of the output piston in relation to the input piston can increase or decrease the output force, but the same change also affects output motion. This is due to a principle of physics that energy in a system is conserved. This means a system cannot create or destroy energy; it can only convert energy from one form into another. When one form of energy increases, another form of energy decreases to keep the system in balance.

A hydraulic system maintains balance by trading force and motion. Energy has the potential to do work. The work a hydraulic system performs uses force to move an output piston a certain distance. If energy is used to increase the output force, then output motion must decrease to keep the system in balance. If the output force decreases, then output motion must increase. In practical terms, if a hydraulic system increases output force over the input force, the output piston must travel a shorter distance than the input piston.

Applying a force of 10 lb to a 1-in² input piston develops a system pressure of 10 psi. Applying this pressure to a 1-in² output piston produces 10 lb of output force, figure 3-12. Because input force equals output force and the pistons have identical surface areas, the travel of the two pistons will also be equal. Similarly, if the input piston moves 10 inches, the output piston will move 10 inches; as long as the input and output pistons have the same area, input and output travel will be the same.

Now consider what happens if the system pressure is held constant at 10 psi and the surface area of the output piston is doubled. This will double the output force to 20 lb, but it will also reduce the output piston travel to half that of input to maintain balance in (figure 3-13). The same holds true for the opposite situation. With a constant system pressure of 10 psi, reducing the surface area of the output piston to half the size of the input piston will also cut output force by half. But, the output travel must double in order to keep the system in balance. A force of 10 lb moves an input piston with a surface area of 1-in² a distance of 10 inches, as shown in figure 3-14. Now, hydraulically link that piston to an output piston with a

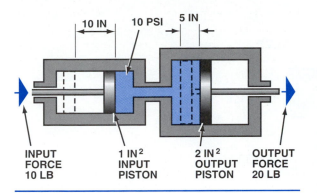

Figure 3-13. Surface area—travel relationship #2. When the output piston surface area is double that of the input piston, the output force also doubles. However, the output piston travel is half that of the input piston.

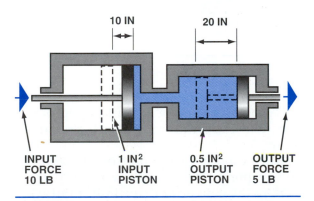

Figure 3-14. Surface area—travel relationship #3. When the output piston surface area is half that of the input piston, the output force is also reduced by half. However, the output piston travel is double that of the input piston.

0.5-in^2 surface area. The output piston will move 20 inches, but there will be only 5 lb of force from the output piston.

Hydraulics and Work

The work that goes into a hydraulic system can be reclaimed at the output, though in a slightly different form. Work is not simply due to the application of force; you must also consider the distance over which the force acts. This leads us to define work done by a hydraulic system as follows:

$$\text{Work} = \text{Force} \times \text{Distance}$$

Applying 100 lb of force to a 0.5-in^2 input piston creates a hydraulic system pressure of 200 psi, since pressure equals force divided by area. Apply the 200-psi pressure to an 8-in^2 output piston, and 100 lb of input force becomes 1600 lb of output force.

Assume that the 0.5-in^2 input piston attaches to the handle of a hydraulic jack. Pumping the handle moves the input piston through 8 inches of travel. Difference in piston sizes increases the output force 16 times over the input force. Therefore, the distance the output piston travels must also decrease by the same factor. Output piston travel is 1/16 of input piston travel, or 0.5 inch. The work put into this hydraulic system enables the jack to raise a 1600-lb load with a 100-lb input, but it does so at the expense of converting the 8-inch input piston travel into a 0.5-inch output piston travel.

SIMPLE HYDRAULIC SYSTEM

The hydraulic systems of all automatic transmissions are similar because they are built from the same basic components (figure 3-15). Even the most recent electronic transmission uses a hydraulic system that performs the same basic functions as a model without electronic controls. Here, the construction and function of a simple hydraulic system is examined. This system consists of a reservoir, pump, valves, passages, and output devices that control gearset members.

Reservoir

Every hydraulic system requires a reservoir to store fluid and make it available for use. The reservoir, also known as the **sump**, is the transmission oil pan. The reservoir is open to atmospheric pressure through the dipstick tube or a vent cap in the housing. This venting allows atmospheric pressure to act upon the fluid in the reservoir. As the oil pump turns, the gear action creates a low-pressure area (less than atmospheric pressure) on the suction side of the pump.

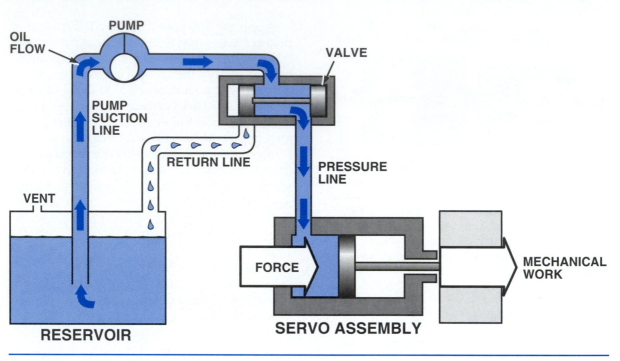

Figure 3-15. Basic hydraulic system.

Atmospheric pressure acting on the fluid actually pushes the fluid through the filter and into the hydraulic system.

The valve body is located on the side or top of the case on most transaxles. The valve body cover holds ATF (automatic transmission fluid) and serves as a secondary sump on these units. An additional oil pump is used on some models to ensure the valve body has an adequate supply of ATF. A thermostatic valve often controls fluid level between the cover and oil pan. Cold fluid level readings may be higher than hot readings. Refer to Chapter 12, "Transmission Fluid, Filter, and Cooler Service," for specific fluid level check procedures.

Pump

Every hydraulic system requires a **pump** to supply fluid flow and pressurize the system. However, the pump itself does not develop pressure. Pressure occurs only when there is a resistance to flow. Initially, fluid flows freely when a hydraulic circuit is empty or partially filled. Once the circuit is completely full, there is a resistance to further flow. At this

point pressure begins to build up in the circuit as the pump continues to create flow.

Most oil pumps mount directly behind the torque converter and are usually driven by the converter drive hub (figure 3-16). This connects the pump to the engine and allows it to respond quickly to engine demand. This type of oil pump operates whenever the engine is running.

Some transmissions place the oil pump in a different location and use alternate drive methods: Some pumps are driven directly by the torque converter hub, others are indirectly driven by a chain and sprocket assembly.

Three types of oil pumps are commonly used in automatic transmissions: gear, rotor, and vane. All three types operate similarly and are discussed in depth in later chapters of this *Classroom Manual*.

Pressure Regulation
Transmission oil pumps are capable of creating an excessive amount of pressure quickly, which could easily damage the transmission. Therefore, every transmission has at

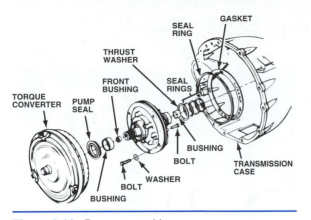

Figure 3-16. Pump assembly.

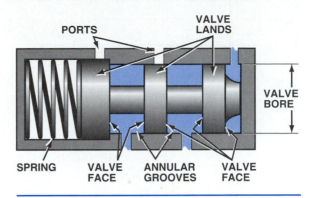

Figure 3-17. Typical spool valve.

least one valve that opens to relieve any excess pressure the pump generates. These pressure regulator valves maintain constant pressure within the system. Valves that regulate system pressure are directly in line with the oil pump output flow. Additional pressure valves may be located in other hydraulic circuits.

All transmission operating pressures derive from the regulated output flow of the oil pump. This regulated system pressure may be used directly, or it may be further modified to create other pressures. These additional hydraulic pressures control transmission shift points and tailor shift timing and feel.

Valves and Solenoids

Every transmission uses control valves to direct, regulate, or restrict the pressure and flow of transmission fluid. Transmission valves generally fall into the following two basic categories:

- Pressure-regulating valves
- Flow-directing valves

Some valves perform both functions at the same time. However, most are usually better suited to a particular job. Classify these dual-purpose valves by their primary operating function.

Electronic solenoid valves are used to direct fluid flow in modern electronic transmissions. Computer-controlled solenoids achieve precise control, allowing the transmission to compensate for a variety of conditions and simplify transmission and valve body design. Electronic controls are discussed in more detail in Chapter 10 of this *Classroom Manual*, "Electronic Control Systems."

Valve Operation

Most valves in an automatic transmission are **spool valves** that resemble the spools on which sewing thread is wound, as shown in figure 3-17. A spool valve generally has two or more **lands**, with an annular groove known as a valley between the lands.

The spool is a piston that slides back and forth inside a machined bore. The areas of a spool valve that seal to the bore are the lands, and the lands control the opening and closing of a number of hydraulic passages. Hydraulic pressures in the valley of the valve position the spool within the bore. There are many variations of the spool valve in a transmission. Some are simple, with only one valley to control one passage, while other valves may have four or five valleys and passages. A spring often installs at one end of a spool valve and spring force pushes the valve to the bottom of the bore.

The valleys of a spool valve are not always the same size, so there are different surface areas for the hydraulic pressure to

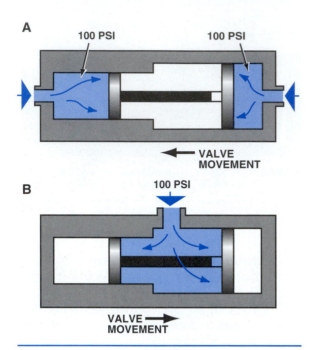

Figure 3-18. Spool valve movements.

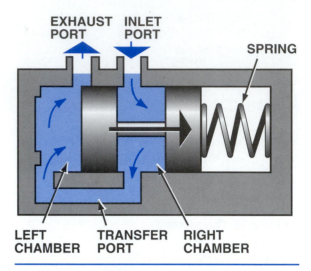

Figure 3-19. Pressure regulator valve operation.

act on. This controls the direction of valve movement when pressure is applied to the valve. According to basic hydraulic principle, increasing surface area increases force if pressure is constant. In the case of a spool valve, the largest surface receives the most force and determines the direction in which the valve will travel. Different-sized surfaces direct the movement of a spool valve, as shown in figure 3-18A.

In general, a spool valve that has equal pressure acting on unequal surface areas always moves in the direction of the greater force. The valve moves with a force equal to the greater force minus the lesser force. If the 100 psi acting on the spool valve in figure 3-18B creates 200 lb of force on the larger face and 100 lb of force on the smaller face, the spool will move to the left with 100 lb of force.

Springs are often used with valves to provide an additional force that can either add or oppose hydraulic pressure. In most instances, the spring helps to tailor valve operation for a specific application. This also allows production changes to be made in the field without physically changing the valve and allows the same valve body casting to be used in more than one vehicle.

Springs are often calibrated to work with a particular valve and cannot be used with other valves. Most *springs are not interchangeable* and must be kept with the valves they were designed for. In many cases, springs look very similar and can easily be switched during assembly; be careful.

Pressure-Regulating Valves

Pressure-regulating valves control the amount of pressure that the transmission hydraulic system, or a particular hydraulic circuit, develops. An automatic transmission uses two types of valves, pressure regulator and pressure relief, to control hydraulic pressure.

Pressure Regulator Valve

The **pressure regulator valve**, or pressure control valve, is usually a spool-valve-and-spring combination that regulates the main hydraulic system pressure. This pressure, commonly known as mainline pressure or simply line pressure, is the working pressure for the entire hydraulic system. The pressure regulator valve is directly in line with the output flow of the transmission oil pump.

Most pressure regulator valves balance pump pressure on one side of the valve against a preset spring force acting on the other side of the valve, as shown in figure 3-19. When hydraulic pressure is greater than spring force, the valve moves in its bore far enough to uncover an exhaust port. The exhaust port provides a low-pressure path to the sump. Excess pressurized fluid flowing through this port reduces system pressure. When hydraulic pressure drops below spring pressure, the regulator valve closes the port and pressure begins to build up again.

In operation, this sequence of events opening and closing the exhaust port occurs many times per second. This achieves a steady pressure as the forces working on each end of the valve hold it in balance. Because of this action, this type of valve is sometimes called a balanced valve.

Some pressure regulator valves use an additional mechanical or fluid force in combination with the fixed spring force acting on the valve. How much additional force is provided varies with operating conditions. These variations allow the pressure regulator valve to boost mainline pressure above its usual limit to meet the higher demands of a specific situation.

Pressure Relief Valve
A **pressure relief valve**, or pressure-limiting valve, allows fluid to escape through an outlet port once a preset level of pressure has built up in the system. Whereas a pressure regulator valve maintains steady pressure over a long period of time, a pressure relief valve tends to act suddenly to reduce excess pressure quickly.

A pressure relief valve generally prevents excess system pressure. However, there may be more than one pressure relief valve in a transmission. These additional valves protect critical hydraulic circuits from damaging buildup of pressure. A transmission hydraulic system always regulates system pressure with a pressure regulator valve and often uses a pressure relief valve as a safety mechanism in case the pressure regulator valve fails.

A common type of pressure relief valve is the **poppet valve** (figure 3-20). Poppet valves use a flat-faced piston valve and spring to prevent or allow fluid flow through an exhaust port. Under normal conditions, spring force keeps the poppet valve

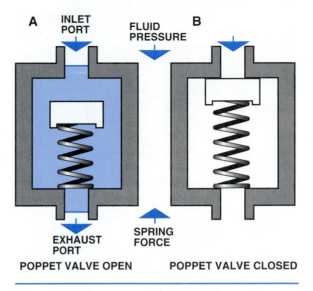

Figure 3-20. Pressure relief poppet valve.

seated to seal off the inlet port. When fluid flows into the inlet port, it develops a force against the face of the valve to oppose the spring force on the other side. When fluid force exceeds spring force, the poppet unseats, allowing fluid to flow through the exhaust port on the spring side of the valve.

Electronic Pressure Regulation
Electronic automatic transmissions often regulate hydraulic system pressure using computer-controlled solenoids. An onboard computer switches the solenoids on and off very quickly using pulse-width modulation (PWM). This pulsed switching positions an internal ball valve in the solenoid, which opens and closes the hydraulic circuit it regulates (figure 3-21). Electronic pressure control allows precise hydraulic system pressure regulation and can also be used to modify the timing and feel of transmission shifting. Electronic control will be covered in greater detail in Chapter 10 of this *Classroom Manual*.

Flow-Directing Valves
Flow-directing valves, or switching valves, control the direction and distribution of fluid flow in the hydraulic system. These valves may open or close passages, fill hydraulic circuits, apply or release clutches

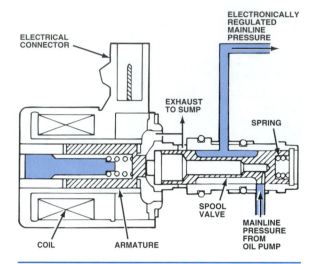

Figure 3-21. Fluid flow control using electronic solenoids.

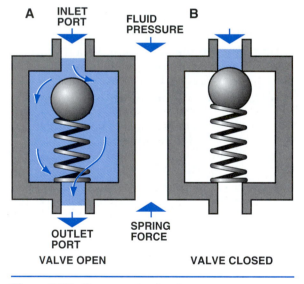

Figure 3-22. One-way check valve.

and bands, and control the direction of fluid flow from one passage or circuit to another. Several types of switching valves are used in automatic transmissions. The following is a description of the more common types.

One-Way Valves
As the name implies, a **one-way valve** allows fluid to flow in one direction. The spring-loaded ball check valve is an example of one type of one-way valve (figure 3-22). Valve operation is similar to that of a poppet

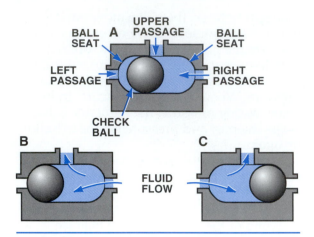

Figure 3-23. Two-way check valves.

valve. The spring holds the ball against its seat at the inlet port until fluid pressure overcomes spring force to push the ball from its seat. Fluid flows through the valve as long as hydraulic pressure exceeds the force of the spring.

Spring-loaded ball check valves are used as pressure-relief valves, and they work well on bypass circuits because they provide a fast apply rate with a slow release. A second type of one-way valve is a simple gravity valve. Operation is exactly the same as with the spring-loaded valves, except gravity replaces spring force. These are commonly used in transmission valve bodies.

Two-Way Valves
A two-way valve controls the fluid flow in two separate hydraulic circuits. The ball check valve is an example of a simple two-way check valve (figure 3-23A). The **check ball** moves in either direction to switch fluid flow between two hydraulic circuits. When fluid enters from the right passage, the ball moves to the left and seals off the left passage (figure 3-23B). Fluid pressure holds the ball against the left seat to block fluid flow in that direction and route fluid toward the upper passage. If fluid enters the ball check valve from the left passage, the ball moves to the right and seals off that passage (figure 3-23C). Again, fluid flow is directed toward the upper passage. The automatic sealing action of a two-way ball check valve allows two hydraulic circuits to share a common passage.

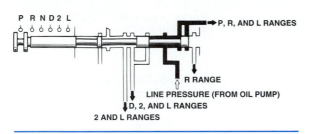

Figure 3-24. Manual valve.

The check balls in these valves are usually made of steel, but they can be nylon, rubber, or some composite material as well. Which material is used depends on the manufacturer and application. Steel balls generally hold up better but cause greater seat wear because of their hardness. The softer composite balls are easier on seats, and they cannot be magnetized.

Manual Valve

The **manual valve** (figure 3-24) is the primary flow-directing valve in an automatic transmission. This valve connects to a shift lever in the transmission, which in turn connects to the gear selector lever through a mechanical linkage. The driver controls manual valve position through the gear selector and shift linkage.

Mechanical linkage physically positions the manual valve in its bore for the particular gear range selected. This aligns the lands on the valve so they uncover ports feeding the correct hydraulic circuits. The manual valve receives mainline pressure from the pump output and distributes it to the hydraulic circuits uncovered by the valve lands.

Transmission Pressure Valves

These valves use mainline pressure to develop other hydraulic circuit pressures within the transmission. Pressure valves are normally spool valves that link to external components.

The throttle valve senses engine load and uses that operating signal to develop throttle pressure. Some throttle valves have linkage that connects them mechanically to the throttle plates on the intake manifold of the engine. Others use a vacuum servo that moves in response to changes in the engine manifold vacuum. In either case, the throttle

valve responds directly to engine load: A low engine load develops low throttle pressure while a higher load develops higher throttle pressure.

The governor valve monitors vehicle road speed and uses that operating signal to develop governor pressure. The governor valve normally follows transmission output shaft rotation speed, which increases with vehicle speed. As the output shaft speed increases, governor pressure also increases. Governor pressure opposes throttle pressure at the shift valves to control upshifts and downshifts in relation to vehicle speed.

Pressure valves *develop* rather than simply *route* hydraulic pressures. Electronic transmissions often replace these pressure valves with solenoids that can develop hydraulic pressure directly from electronic sensor signals. Additional information on pressure valves and solenoids is addressed in Chapter 10 of this *Classroom Manual*.

Shift Valves

A **shift valve** is a spring-loaded spool valve that controls the transmission upshift and downshift circuits (figure 3-25). Throttle pressure works against one side of the valve while governor pressure works against the other side. When one pressure is greater than the other, the valve moves to the upshift or downshift position and the valve lands uncover the ports to the relative circuits. A calibrated spring on one side of the valve assists throttle pressure to force the valve into the downshift position.

The combined spring force and throttle pressure acting on the right side of the valve in figure 3-26A is greater than the governor pressure that acts on the left side of the valve. This keeps the valve in the downshift position. In this position, the valve land blocks off the inlet port to prevent fluid from flowing to the outlet port and into the hydraulic circuit.

If governor pressure on the left side of the valve becomes greater than the combined spring force and throttle pressure on the right, the valve will move to the right, figure 3-26B. This opens the inlet port and allows the fluid to pass through the valley of the spool valve to the outlet port and into

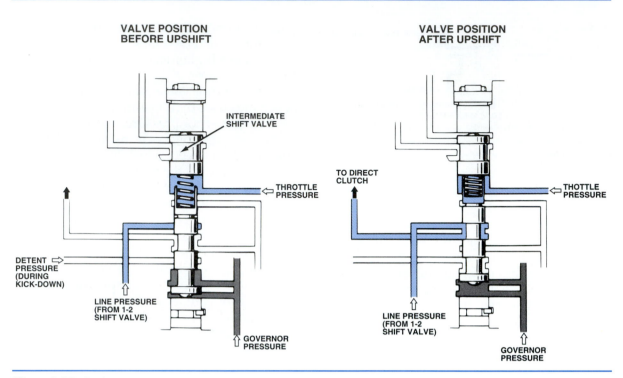

Figure 3-25. Shift valves balance governor pressure against throttle pressure.

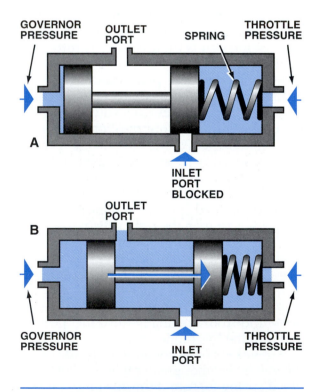

Figure 3-26. Shift valve movement—when governor pressure exceeds throttle pressure and spring forces.

the hydraulic circuit. Transmission shift valves may be referred to as "snap valves" because they shift almost instantly in response to pressure differential changes. Since these valves cause upshifts and downshifts, they are also known as "event-causing valves." There are only two positions for a shift valve: fully to the right or to the left. Otherwise, hydraulic pressure could apply control devices for two gears at once and damage the transmission.

Valve Body
Most of the valves in a transmission are located in the valve body (figure 3-27). Valve bodies can be either cast aluminum or cast iron and bolt up to the case. The valve body in most RWD transmissions is inside the oil pan at the bottom of the case. A transaxle valve body may be at the bottom of the case, on the back side of the torque converter housing, or the top or side of the transaxle housing, depending on the specific application.

Valve bodies have many fluid passages for the various transmission hydraulic circuits cast into them. These are sometimes called

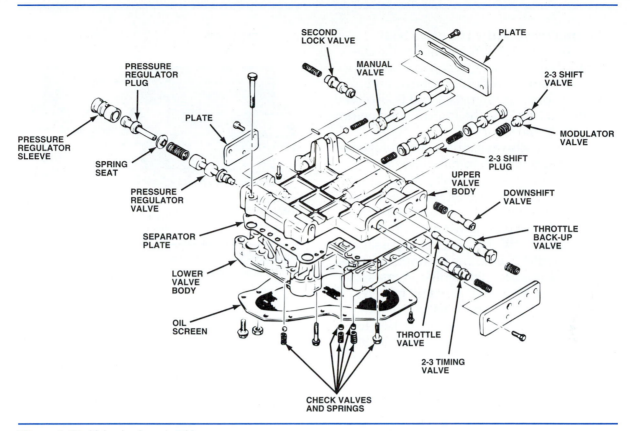

Figure 3-27. Valve body assembly.

worm holes or worm tracks. Some of these passages may be widened to form pockets that contain steel, nylon, or rubber check balls.

Most valve bodies consist of two or more cast sections that bolt together with a flat metal separator plate between them. The upper section of the valve body is part of the transmission case casting. The separator plate provides rigidity and contains calibrated drill holes and openings that help manage fluid flow. Valve bodies contain specialized valves and circuits that are particular to a specific transmission. Electronic solenoids are used in place of some valves on many modern transmissions (figure 3-28). This greatly reduces the complexity while improving the reliability of the valve body.

Shafts, Tubes, and Passages
The oil pump draws fluid from the sump and outputs it to the pressure regulator

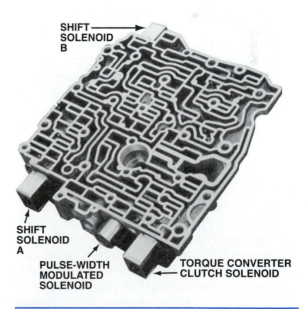

Figure 3-28. Solenoids direct fluid flow (4L80-E valve body shown).
General Motors Corporation, Service and Parts Operations

valve and valve body. The valve body directs fluid to the different hydraulic circuits to shift the transmission in response to driver demands, computer control, and hydraulic pressure signals. Fluid is also used to cool and lubricate the transmission before it returns to the sump.

All these pathways must connect together in some manner with minimal waste of space. Designers accomplish this using various combinations of tubes, shafts, holes, and drilled passageways to provide feed and return paths for each hydraulic circuit.

The valve body contains many passages that distribute fluid to the hydraulic circuits in the transmission. Transmission cases and pump bodies also have passages to transport fluid to the various internal components. Removable tubes are often used to link a circuit where parts may need to be removed for service. Drilled shafts are used to provide lubrication oil to the geartrain and apply fluid to the clutches. Together, these make up the fluid feed and return paths for each hydraulic circuit.

Actuators

Actuators are the output devices of the transmission hydraulic system. These pistons and servos convert hydraulic pressure into the mechanical force that applies the clutches and bands.

Once the fluid passes through all the lines and valves in the circuit it ends up at an actuator. At this point, fluid flow stops and pressure begins to build. Fluid pressure acts to create a force on the surface area of the actuator. This force then performs the mechanical work of moving the clutch piston or servo (figure 3-29). The amount of force the servo applies depends upon the surface area of the piston and the pressure of the fluid on the piston. Some solenoids in an electronic transmission may also be considered as actuators. Solenoids are actuators if they direct output pressure to a piston or servo to directly control transmission shifting.

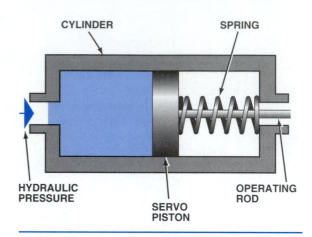

Figure 3-29. Actuator converts hydraulic pressure into mechanical movement.

Servos and Pistons

In mechanical terminology an actuator, or actuating mechanism, is generally called a **servo**. A servo is a device capable of converting energy into work. The clutch piston assemblies and band servos of an automatic transmission are all servos in the technical sense. However, for ease of identification they are usually designated as either a piston or servo according to the apply function.

In general, the term "servo" refers to the mechanism that applies bands and "piston" refers to the mechanism that applies clutches. The mechanism for applying bands is a hydraulic piston that connects to the brake band through mechanical linkage. The servo mechanism for applying clutches is a hydraulic piston that engages the clutch by squeezing the clutch plates together.

SUMMARY

Hydraulics is the study of liquids and how they are used to transmit force and motion and apply pressure. Hydraulic systems use liquids because liquids cannot be compressed. Hydraulic systems are governed by several well-defined principles that determine how fluid can transmit and multiply force. These principles are expressed in Pascal's Law. Two basic equations are commonly used to calculate hydraulic system pressure and force, as follows:

Force ÷ Area = Pressure

Pressure × Area = Force.

Many hydraulic system problems can be solved easily by remembering the following simple rules that apply to all hydraulic circuits:

- For any given input force, the hydraulic pressure is constant throughout the system.
- For any given input force, a small input piston develops more hydraulic system pressure than a large input piston.
- For any given hydraulic system pressure, a large output piston produces more force than a small output piston.
- An output piston that increases output force over input force will have less travel than the input piston.
- An output piston that reduces output force below input force will have more travel than the input piston.

The hydraulic system of an automatic transmission requires a fluid reservoir, a pump, and control valves to develop pressure and transmit force and motion to output devices or actuators. A hydraulic system does not develop pressure until there is a resistance to fluid flow.

Pressure relief and pressure regulator valves control and regulate hydraulic system pressure. Poppet, ball check, and shift valves are flow-directing valves. They direct the flow of hydraulic fluid from one passage or circuit to another without affecting pressure. Pressure valves, such as the throttle and governor valve, use mainline pressure to develop other hydraulic pressures that control upshifts and downshifts. Some valves perform both pressure regulation and switching functions, but they can be classified as one or the other by their primary function.

Solenoids are commonly used in late-model transmissions, and they are controlled by the computer under many conditions. Solenoids achieve precise control and simplify transmission and valve body designs.

Review Questions

Choose the single most correct answer. Compare your answers to the correct answers on page 213.

1. Technician A says that every transmission hydraulic system operates on the same basic principles of hydraulics. Technician B says the same principles of hydraulics that apply to a water system would also apply to a transmission fluid system.
   Who is right?
   a. A only
   b. B only
   c. Both A and B
   d. Neither A nor B

2. Technician A says that gas is not used in a transmission hydraulic system because gas is incompressible. Technician B says that liquids are used in a transmission hydraulic system because they expand in volume to fill the system.
   Who is right?
   a. A only
   b. B only
   c. Both A and B
   d. Neither A nor B

3. Technician A says force is a push or pull acting on an object. Technician B says pressure is force exerted on a given surface area.
   Who is right?
   a. A only
   b. B only
   c. Both A and B
   d. Neither A nor B

4. Technician A says force can be calculated by multiplying pressure times surface area. Technician B says force is usually measured in foot-pounds or Newton-meters.
   Who is right?
   a. A only
   b. B only
   c. Both A and B
   d. Neither A nor B

5. Technician A says pressure can be calculated by multiplying force times surface area. Technician B says pressure is usually measured in pounds-per-square inch or kilopascals.
Who is right?
   a. A only
   b. B only
   c. Both A and B
   d. Neither A nor B

6. If a force of 200 pounds is applied to a 4-in² input piston, the resulting system pressure is
   a. 80 psi
   b. 50 psi
   c. 20 psi
   d. 10 psi

7. If a hydraulic pressure of 100 psi is applied to a 10-in² output piston, the resulting output force is
   a. 100 lb
   b. 10 lb
   c. 1000 lb
   d. 10,000 lb

8. Technician A says the output force of a hydraulic system is dependent on pressure and area. Technician B says the output force of a hydraulic system is dependent on pressure only.
Who is right?
   a. A only
   b. B only
   c. Both A and B
   d. Neither A nor B

9. Technician A says a hydraulic system can be used to multiply force. Technician B says a hydraulic system can be used to multiply distance.
Who is right?
   a. A only
   b. B only
   c. Both A and B
   d. Neither A nor B

10. If the output piston of a hydraulic system is larger than the input piston, then the output motion will
   a. Be greater than the input motion
   b. Be less than the input motion
   c. Be the same as the input motion
   d. Depend on the system pressure

11. If pressure is uniform in a hydraulic system, then a large output piston will develop _____ output force than a small output piston.
   a. Less
   b. More
   c. Equal
   d. It depends on what type of fluid is used.

12. A complete hydraulic system must have
   a. Control valves and connecting passages
   b. A reservoir and pump
   c. An output device
   d. All of the above

13. Technician A says that pressure buildup can only occur when there is a resistance to fluid flow. Technician B says that pressure buildup can only occur when a hydraulic circuit is empty or partially filled.
Who is right?
   a. A only
   b. B only
   c. Both A and B
   d. Neither A nor B

14. Technician A says the pressure-regulating valves control the shift into high gear in a transmission hydraulic system. Technician B says the switching valves control the amount of hydraulic pressure developed in a transmission hydraulic system.
Who is right?
   a. A only
   b. B only
   c. Both A and B
   d. Neither A nor B

15. Technician A says that all transmission operating pressures are derived from the regulated output flow of the oil pump. Technician B says that every automatic transmission uses at least one pressure regulator valve.
Who is right?
   a. A only
   b. B only
   c. Both A and B
   d. Neither A nor B

16. Technician A says that most transmission valves are spool valves. Technician B says that springs are often used with valves to provide force against the valve.
    Who is right?
    a. A only
    b. B only
    c. Both A and B
    d. Neither A nor B

17. Technician A says that most pressure-regulating valves work by balancing hydraulic pressure against a spring force. Technician B says that many electronic transmissions may use solenoids to further regulate hydraulic pressure.
    Who is right?
    a. A only
    b. B only
    c. Both A and B
    d. Neither A nor B

18. Technician A says many automatic transmissions use a governor valve to monitor engine load and develop governor pressure. Technician B says many automatic transmissions use a throttle valve to monitor vehicle speed and develop mainline pressure.
    Who is right?
    a. A only
    b. B only
    c. Both A and B
    d. Neither A nor B

19. Technician A says that shift valves are generally spring-loaded balanced spool valves that control the transmission upshift and downshift circuits. Technician B says that when governor and throttle pressure are greater than spring force the transmission can upshift.
    Who is right?
    a. A only
    b. B only
    c. Both A and B
    d. Neither A nor B

20. Technician A says that solenoids may be considered as actuators. Technician B says that servos and pistons may be considered as actuators.
    Who is right?
    a. A only
    b. B only
    c. Both A and B
    d. Neither A nor B

4

Transmission Hydraulic Systems

This chapter begins with a look at how transmissions develop the different hydraulic pressures that are needed for operational control. It continues by examining how the transmission generates, regulates, and modifies these different pressures, and how upshifts and downshifts are controlled. This chapter also covers other functions essential to transmission operation, such as: lubrication, cooling, band and clutch application, and torque converter clutch control.

PRESSURE DEVELOPMENT AND CONTROL

Pressure development in an automatic transmission begins at the main, or front, oil pump. Typically driven by either a driveshaft or drive hub of the torque converter, the front pump delivers fluid to the transmission whenever the engine is turning over (figure 4-1). A transmission oil pump must be capable of monitoring the operating demands of the engine and meeting the fluid flow and pressure requirements of the transmission.

Pump Types

The following three major types of oil pumps are used in automatic transmissions:

- Gear
- Rotor
- Vane

Gear and rotor pumps are **positive-displacement pump** designs (figure 4-2). Positive, or constant, displacement pumps, displace, or deliver, the same amount of fluid for each revolution of the pump. The amount of fluid the pump delivers per revolution is *always* the same, regardless of the speed of pump rotation. However, as speed increases the total volume of fluid the pump delivers increases because the pump completes more revolutions.

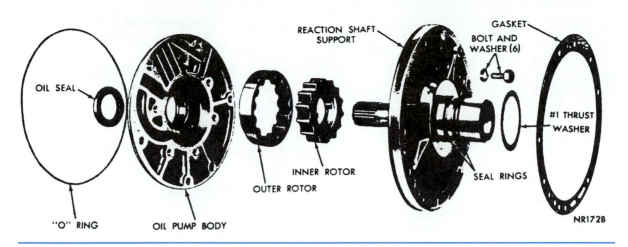

Figure 4-1. Transmission oil pump—driven by torque converter hub.

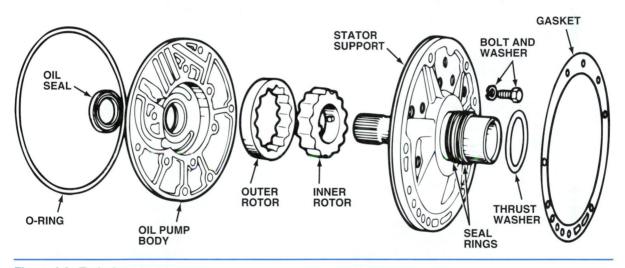

Figure 4-2. Typical rotor pump.

Even though transmission operation may not require all of the fluid flow a positive-displacement pump produces, the pump still delivers the same amount of fluid per revolution. As fluid flow increases past the capacity of the transmission circuit to store it, the fluid pressure in the circuit also increases. Therefore, all positive-displacement pumps require some form of pressure regulation.

In addition to creating excess pressure, a positive-displacement pump can be inefficient. As engine speed increases, an increasing amount of energy is needed to drive the pump. When the transmission cannot use all the fluid the pump flows, the energy used to drive the pump at a higher than necessary speed is wasted.

The vane pumps used in automatic transmissions are a **variable-displacement pump** design that can adjust the amount of fluid delivered per revolution (figure 4-3).

These pumps automatically regulate output volume based on the needs of the transmission. When pump speed is low, fluid requirements are high. For example, when engine and transmission first start up, the pump must deliver a high volume of fluid to fill the hydraulic system and lubricate the gears. As pump speed increases, the volume of fluid the pump delivers can decrease in response to a reduced demand from the

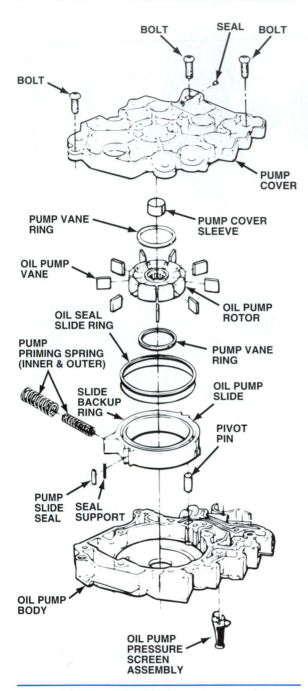

Figure 4-3. Typical vane pump.

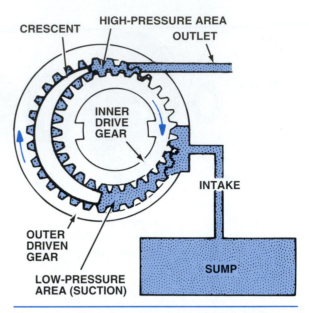

Figure 4-4. Typical gear pump assembly.

Gear Pump

A **gear pump** consists of two gears installed in a pump body, as shown in figure 4-4. The inner drive gear is powered by the torque converter and turns at engine speed. The gear connects to the converter by engaging flats, slots, or gear teeth on the hub of the converter. The inner gear drives the outer gear whenever the engine is turning. Both gears are in full mesh on one side of the pump body but separated by a crescent-shaped section of the pump body on the opposite side. Because of this, gear pumps are sometimes called gear-and-crescent pumps.

As the gears rotate, they create a low-pressure area at the point where they separate. This is called the suction side of the pump. The pressure developed at the suction side is lower than the atmospheric pressure acting on the fluid in the sump. The greater atmospheric pressure in the sump actually pushes the fluid into the pump inlet.

As the pump gears continue to rotate, they carry the fluid along in the spaces between the gear teeth, past the crescent, toward the pump outlet. Near the outlet, the clearance between the gears decreases to force the fluid out of the pump. The pump gears rotate and deliver fluid whenever the engine is turning over.

transmission. One advantage of variable-displacement pumps is they are self-regulating and do not require a pressure-regulating device. Variable-displacement pumps are also energy-efficient, as they do not flow more fluid than is required to operate the transmission.

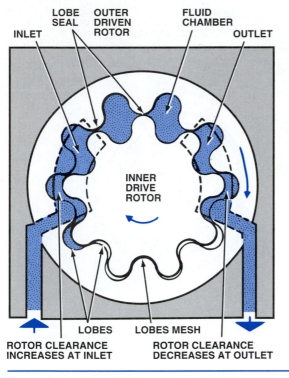

Figure 4-5. Typical rotor pump assembly.

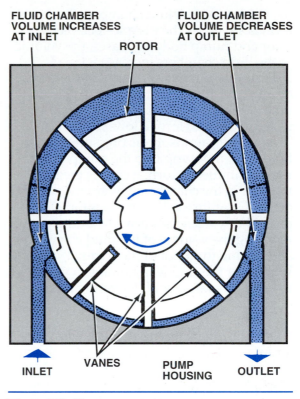

Figure 4-6. Simple vane pump.

Rotor Pump

A **rotor pump** operates on the same principle as a gear pump, but it uses inner and outer rotors rather than inner and outer gears, as shown in figure 4-5. The inner rotor is driven at engine speed by the torque converter hub, and it drives the outer rotor in turn. Unlike gears, which have teeth, rotors have lobes that mesh with one another. In a rotor pump, the unique meshing action of the lobes eliminates the need for a crescent to separate the rotors.

The lobes of the two rotors are in full mesh on one side of the pump, but separate slightly at the opposite side. As the rotors turn, the rounded lobes maintain a tight seal and carry small chambers of fluid as they rotate. The fluid volume is small where the rotors mesh, but it increases as the rotors begin to separate. As the volume of the fluid chambers increases, a low-pressure area develops, allowing fluid to flow from the sump into the pump inlet, as in a gear pump.

As the pump rotors continue to rotate, they carry the fluid around in the chambers formed between the lobes. Near the pump

outlet the clearance between the rotors decreases to force fluid out of the pump. Like a gear pump, a rotor pump also operates and delivers fluid whenever the engine is turning.

Vane Pump

In its simplest form, a **vane pump** consists of a rotor, vanes, and the pump housing, as shown in figure 4-6. Slots machined into the rotor around its circumference hold and position the vanes. The vanes fit loosely into the rotor slots so they are free to slide in and out as the pump rotates.

Typically, the torque converter hub drives the rotor so it rotates at engine speed. As the pump turns, **centrifugal force** moves the vanes outward in their slots to seal their outer edges against the inside of the pump housing. This forms fluid chambers between the vanes.

The rotor is positioned off center to the opening in the pump body. As a result, the rotor is closer to the pump body on one side of the housing than it is on the other. Where the rotor and pump body are close together, the volume of the fluid chambers the vanes form is small. As the distance between the rotor and pump body increases, the volume of the fluid chambers increase.

Basic operation is similar to that of a gear or rotor pump. As the rotor turns, the volume of the fluid chambers over the pump inlet increases to form a low-pressure area. This permits atmospheric pressure to push fluid from the sump into the pump. As the rotor continues to turn, it carries the fluid trapped in the chambers toward the pump outlet. Clearance between the rotor and pump body decreases near the pump outlet, reducing the volume of the fluid chambers, and forcing fluid out of the pump. Whenever the engine is running, a vane pump is operating and delivering fluid.

Variable-Displacement Vane Pump

Automatic transmissions use a refined version of the vane pump to make it variable displacement. The pump consists of a rotor, vanes, vane ring, slide, priming spring, and pump body. Rather than sealing against the pump body directly, the vanes seal against the inside of a slide. The rotor is located within the slide, and the slide mounts inside the pump body.

As with a simple vane pump, the rotor is positioned off center to the midpoint of the slide. In addition, the slide is able to pivot in relation to the rotor. This allows movement of the center point of the slide opening toward or away from the center point of the rotor. The pivoting slide is what gives the pump its variable displacement capability.

The vane ring fits inside the rotor and contacts the inner edges of the vanes. This limits the inward movement of the vanes and ensures they are always close to the surface of the slide. The ring also prevents the vanes from sticking in the rotor slots, and it minimizes the amount of fluid bypassing the vanes when pump speed is low and the amount of centrifugal force available to seal the vanes against the slide is limited.

When the engine is off, the priming spring holds the slide at its full offset against the left side of the pump body (figure 4-7). This position provides maximum pump output because it allows for the greatest variation in the sizes of the fluid chambers. It also

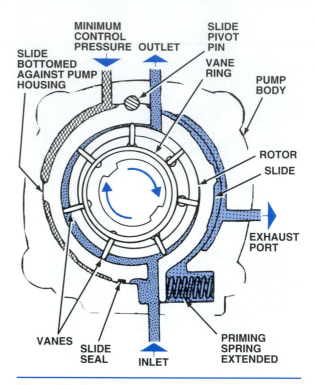

Figure 4-7. Variable-displacement pump—pump slide in maximum output position.

creates a large pressure differential between the atmospheric pressure acting on the fluid in the sump and the low-pressure area formed at the pump inlet. This primes the pump quickly during engine cranking and produces a large volume of fluid flow to fill the transmission hydraulic system within the first few moments of engine operation.

Once the engine starts, the variable-displacement vane pump operates much like a simple vane pump. The torque converter hub or pump driveshaft turns the rotor and vanes inside the slide. As the clearance between the rotor and slide increases on the inlet side and decreases on the outlet side, fluid is drawn into and forced out of the pump.

Most operating conditions do not require maximum output from the pump. Therefore, pump displacement must be reduced. Typically this is done by applying a control pressure to the back side of the slide (figure 4-8). Control pressure works against priming spring force and moves the slide toward the right to bring the center points of the slide opening and rotor closer together. As the center points align, the variation in the volume of the fluid chambers becomes

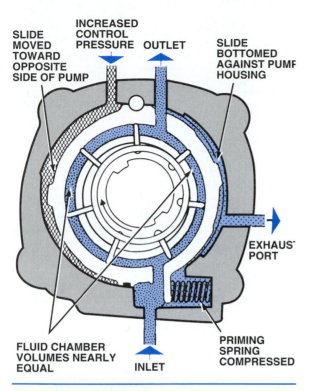

Figure 4-8. Variable-displacement pump—pump slide in minimum output position.

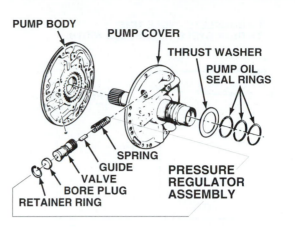

Figure 4-9. Pressure regulator valve.

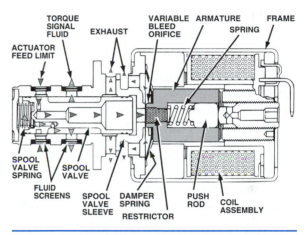

Figure 4-10. Typical electronically operated pressure control solenoid.

smaller, so the pump output flow decreases. Minimum pump output occurs when the slide is positioned fully against the right side of the pump housing.

During transmission operation, the pressure regulator valve continually varies the control pressure to adjust pump output to meet immediate operating needs. To ensure accurate regulation, pressure is never allowed to build behind the right side of the slide. Any fluid that does leak past the slide pivot pin or seal into this area escapes through an exhaust port.

Pressure Regulation

Because total pump delivery volume increases with speed, pressure will also increase with pump speed if left unchecked. In such a system, the pressure would quickly reach a level high enough to damage the transmission components. Therefore, a pressure regulator valve is used to monitor and control pressure.

A pressure regulator valve controls how much pressure develops within a circuit by varying the amount of restriction to fluid

flow (figure 4-9). Increasing the restriction increases the resistance to flow in the circuit, which subsequently reduces pressure. Reducing the restriction has the opposite effect of increasing flow and pressure.

Electronic Pressure Control

All automatic transmissions develop and regulate pressure from the pump outlet using a mechanical pressure regulator valve. However, there are times when it is necessary to further modify this mainline pressure in order to meet the needs of changing operating conditions. Electronic transmissions generally use a computer-controlled solenoid to modify system pressure (figure 4-10). Electronic pressure control allows

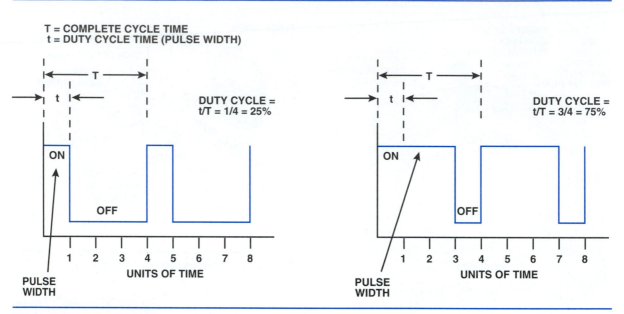

T = COMPLETE CYCLE TIME
t = DUTY CYCLE TIME (PULSE WIDTH)

DUTY CYCLE =
t/T = 1/4 = 25%

DUTY CYCLE =
t/T = 3/4 = 75%

Figure 4-11. Pulse-width modulation controls ON and OFF time.

hydraulic pressure to be fine-tuned to achieve precise regulation.

Solenoids that regulate mainline pressure generally adjust flow using a type of control known as pulse-width modulation (PWM). With PWM, the control module rapidly switches the solenoid on and off. Pulse width refers to the amount of time the solenoid is on, or energized, during each on-off-on cycle, as shown in figure 4-11. The percentage ratio of on-time to off-time during a cycle is known as the duty cycle. Modulation indicates that the computer can vary the pulse width to meet the changing demands of different operating conditions. This pulsed switching controls an internal ball valve in the solenoid, which opens and closes the hydraulic circuit it regulates, as shown in figure 4-12.

TRANSMISSION HYDRAULIC PRESSURES

Hydraulic pressures control all transmission shifting and shift operations. The principle control pressures are as follows:

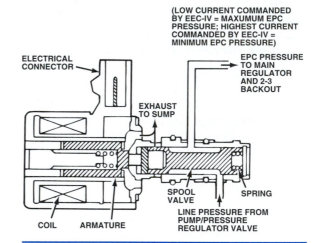

(LOW CURRENT COMMANDED BY EEC-IV = MAXUMUM EPC PRESSURE; HIGHEST CURRENT COMMANDED BY EEC-IV = MINIMUM EPC PRESSURE)

Figure 4-12. Internal ball valve controls fluid flow.

• Mainline
• Throttle
• Governor

To develop these pressures, the transmission requires a continuous source of fluid flow and a means of restricting flow according to operating conditions. In an automatic transmission, the pump is the source of all fluid flow. The valves, solenoids, and passages in the hydraulic circuits provide the restrictions that develop and modify transmission pressures.

Mainline Pressure

Mainline pressure is the source for all other hydraulic pressures used in the transmission. The pump develops mainline pressure, which is controlled by the pressure regulator valve at the pump output. Mainline pressure is used to apply the clutches and bands that control planetary gearset members and provide the hydraulic pressure used to upshift or downshift the transmission.

Mainline pressure is sometimes referred to as line pressure, control pressure, or drive oil. However, in this *Classroom Manual* the term "mainline pressure" refers to the regulated hydraulic pressure from the transmission pump output.

Regulated Mainline Pressure

Hydraulic systems have *fixed* restrictions to regulate pressure. Fixed restrictions do not change with operating conditions. For example, the pump has an outlet port, as well as lines and passages to and from the valves and control devices. These create constant, partial restrictions to fluid flow.

The pressure regulator valve that controls mainline pressure creates a *variable* restriction. A variable restriction is an opening in a hydraulic circuit that adjusts its size to alter the pressure developed in the circuit. The pressure regulator valve controls the high and low limits of mainline fluid pressure to meet various transmission operating conditions. Since the mainline pressure circuit is basically a single, closed system, the pressure regulator valve may be located anywhere in the circuit.

The pressure regulator valve begins to operate when the engine starts. Usually, pump output is routed to the other valves in the hydraulic system before passing through the regulator valve. As the output fluid passes through the regulator valve, it fills the torque converter and mainline circuits (figure 4-13). Pressure begins to build as the circuits fill. This pressure buildup acts on one end of the regulator valve to move the valve against the spring force at the opposite end. As long as pump pressure does not exceed spring force, full pump output is delivered to the transmission circuits.

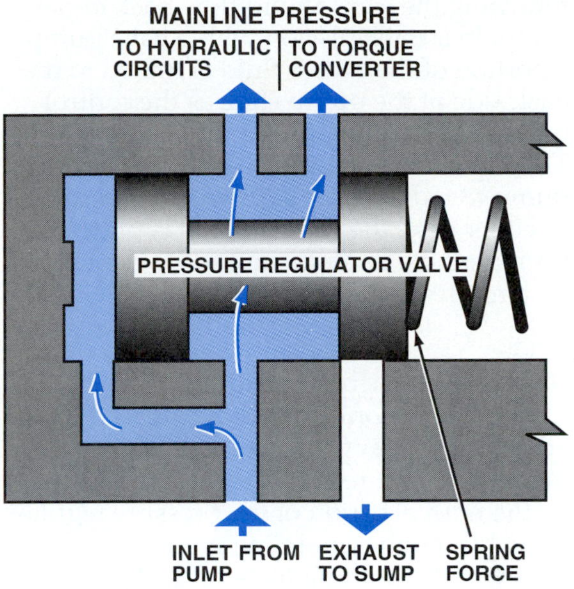

Figure 4-13. Pressure regulator valve forms variable restriction to control mainline pressure.

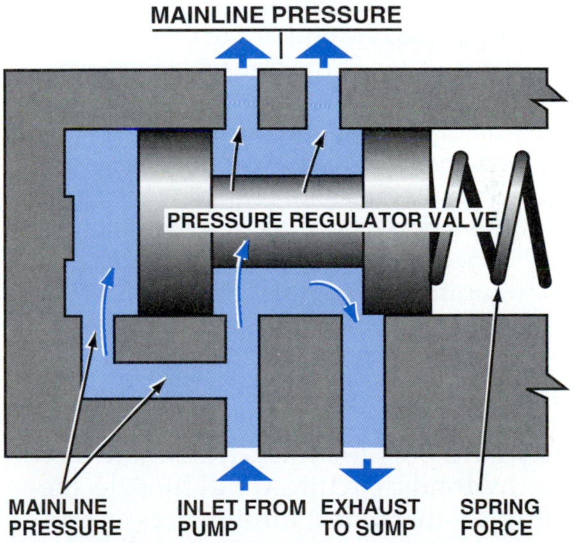

Figure 4-14. Open exhaust port—valve shifts position when system reaches maximum pressure.

As engine speed increases, the pump delivers more fluid to the regulator valve and increases pressure. The increased pressure on the valve overcomes the force of the spring, and the land moves to expose an exhaust port (figure 4-14).

In a transmission with a gear or rotor pump, excess pressure is relieved by returning the excess fluid flow back to the sump. In a transmission with a vane pump, a portion of the excess fluid is routed to the back side of the pump slide as the control pressure that offsets pump displacement. This equalizes the fluid chambers in the pump to reduce output flow and pressure. In either case, the transmission is protected from possible damage caused by excessive system pressure.

Boosted Mainline Pressure

Certain conditions, such as low-speed operation under heavy engine load, require a mainline pressure above the level delivered by the normal action of the pressure regulator valve. Higher mainline pressure increases the holding force of the apply devices. This prevents unwanted clutch and band slippage due to the increased torque output of the engine.

To increase mainline pressure, transmissions use several methods to apply additional force to one end of the pressure regulator valve. Some transmissions use mechanical linkage or auxiliary hydraulic pressure to reposition the regulator valve. Other transmissions use a **boost valve** located in the pressure regulator bore, or one or more independent boost valves in a separate bore of the valve body. Each of these configurations performs the same function: to increase mainline pressure on demand.

A typical boost valve acts against the spring end of the pressure regulator valve, as shown in figure 4-15. The boost valve may have pressure inlets from more than one hydraulic circuit. At full throttle, the throttle valve routes throttle pressure to the end of the pressure regulator boost valve. Throttle pressure and spring force combine to work against pump output pressure. The additional regulating force increases the mainline pressure that develops in the system.

A similar process occurs for reverse gear operation to help meet the additional torque needed for reverse. When the driver selects reverse gear, the reverse gear circuit feeds an auxiliary hydraulic pressure to the boost valve, as shown in figure 4-16. Valve opera-

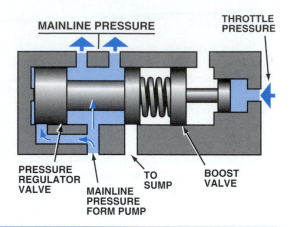

Figure 4-15. Boost valve uses throttle pressure and spring force to hold back the pressure regulator valve and increase mainline pressure.

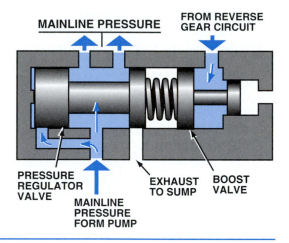

Figure 4-16. Reverse gear circuit pressure acts on boost valve to increase mainline pressure.

tion is similar to full throttle boost, and mainline pressure again increases.

Throttle Pressure

Throttle pressure is the hydraulic pressure signal that indicates engine operating load. It is derived from mainline pressure and increases with engine load or throttle opening. Throttle pressure works against governor pressure to control transmission shifting.

Automatic transmissions use throttle pressure as the primary shift control sig-

Shift Timing "Tuning"

Both mechanical and vacuum-operated throttle valves can be adjusted to fine-tune shift timing, causing the transmission shifts to occur at lower or higher vehicle speeds. This is done by increasing or decreasing the force that the mechanical linkage or vacuum modulator applies to the throttle valve.

As force on the throttle valve is increased, throttle pressure increases. Therefore, more governor pressure is required to overcome throttle pressure at the shift valve and shifts occur at a higher vehicle speed. As force on the throttle valve is decreased, throttle pressure decreases. Therefore, less governor pressure is required to overcome throttle pressure at the shift valve and shifts occur at lower road speeds.

To make this adjustment on a mechanically operated throttle valve, the linkage is shortened or lengthened. On a vacuum-operated throttle valve, the vacuum modulator is threaded farther into or out of the transmission case. Automakers provide adjustment specifications for the throttle-valve linkages and vacuum modulators on their vehicles to provide the best shift performance.

nal, and throttle pressure can be developed in a number of different ways. Some manufacturers refer to throttle pressure as "modulator pressure," especially on older units. However, the term "throttle pressure" is used throughout this *Classroom Manual*.

Transmissions without electronic shift controls develop throttle pressure through a throttle valve. The throttle valve is controlled either directly by mechanical linkage from the throttle plate, or indirectly by a vacuum diaphragm, or modulator. These move the valve in response to an engine manifold vacuum signal. In either case, mainline pressure is modified according to engine load, and throttle pressure develops.

Most electronic transmissions use a simpler method to develop throttle pressure: a computer-controlled solenoid instead of a throttle valve. These units respond to electrical signals from the electronic control system instead of direct mechanical connections. The solenoid contains an internal ball valve that can be opened and closed hundreds or thousands of times per second. The computer varies current to the ball valve to regulate how fast it cycles in order to develop and regulate throttle pressure. The control system monitors engine load through system sensors and processes the information to develop a throttle pressure that best meets vehicle needs.

Boosted Throttle Pressure

In many transmissions, throttle pressure is also used to regulate mainline pressure.

When engine torque output is high, the apply devices require a higher mainline pressure to hold the gearset members and prevent slippage. Throttle pressure increases mainline pressure by applying it to one end of a separate boost valve or to the pressure regulator valve itself. This increases force on the regulator valve, causing it to balance out at a higher pressure. Some transmissions also boost throttle pressure in manual low gear and sometimes manual second gear. Boosting the throttle pressure produces firmer transmission downshifts.

Governor Pressure

Governor pressure is a hydraulic pressure signal that indicates vehicle road speed. Like throttle pressure, governor pressure is derived from mainline pressure and increases with vehicle speed. Governor pressure and throttle pressure work together to control transmission shifting.

Hydraulically shifted transmissions develop governor pressure using a governor valve housed in a centrifugally operated mechanical **governor** assembly. The governor assembly is driven by the transmission output shaft and operates by the action of centrifugal force on a set of governor weights (figure 4-17). The weights either attach to a spool valve or they permit or prevent movement of check balls. As rotational speed increases, the weights are drawn out to reposition the spool valve or check balls and increase governor pressure.

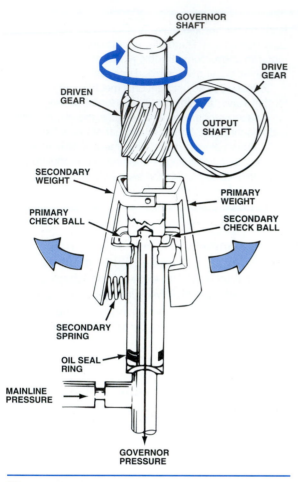

Figure 4-17. Mechanical governor valve uses weights and centrifugal force.

Most electronic transmissions use a computer-controlled solenoid instead of a governor valve to develop governor pressure. The operation is similar to that used in developing and regulating throttle pressure.

Torque Converter Pressure

A portion of the pump output flow is used immediately at start-up to fill the torque converter circuit. As we discussed, the torque converter is a type of fluid coupling that allows the transfer of torque from the engine through the drivetrain. The torque converter works best when completely full of slightly pressurized fluid. Torque converter pressure is generally regulated by a separate fill valve, or switch valve, that con-

trols the amount of mainline fluid into the converter. Some pressure is desirable, but full boosted mainline pressure would be excessive. We describe torque converter construction and operation in a later chapter of this *Classroom Manual.*

Torque Converter Clutch Apply Pressure

Most modern automatic transmissions use a hydraulic torque converter clutch. The torque converter clutch provides a direct mechanical connection between the engine and transmission (figure 4-18). This allows increased efficiency by eliminating the slippage that is unavoidable with a fluid coupling.

The torque converter clutch engages only under the following operating conditions:

- The engine is warm and can handle the extra load without stumbling.
- The vehicle speed is high enough to allow smooth power transmission.
- Engine and vehicle speed will not create a surge or shudder when the torque converter clutch is applied.
- The brake pedal is not depressed.
- The transmission is not shifting gears.

The hydraulic system provides mainline pressure to the converter clutch piston, locking the turbine shaft mechanically to the engine and allowing direct drive.

Many hydraulic and mechanical designs have been used to control the timing of converter clutch apply. However, the timing is usually controlled electronically by a solenoid in the computer system. Torque converter clutch design and operations are covered in later chapters of this *Classroom Manual.*

Oil Cooler Flow and Pressure

Automatic transmissions create a great deal of heat during normal operation, and the transmission fluid must be cooled to prevent overheating, excess component wear,

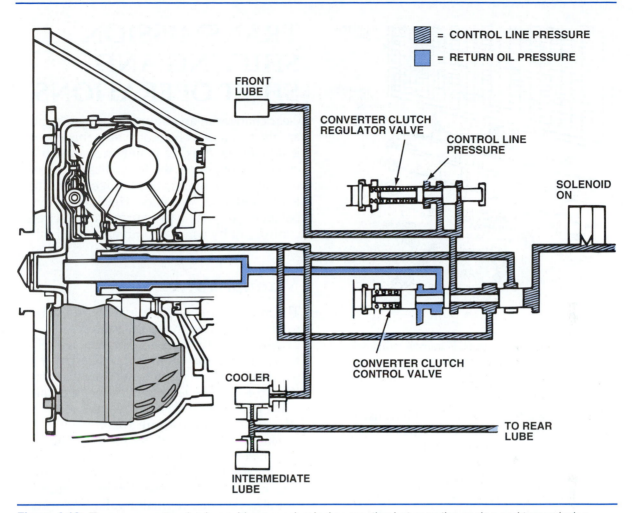

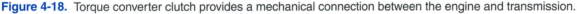

Figure 4-18. Torque converter clutch provides a mechanical connection between the engine and transmission.

and shortened fluid life. To cool the transmission, portions of the fluid are continuously passed through external tubing to the oil cooler. Fluid from the transmission is usually taken from the torque converter circuit because this is where the most heat is generated.

Vehicles with automatic transmissions use two types of oil cooler: internal or external. Most production vehicles use an internal oil cooler. These have a transmission fluid cooling tank that mounts inside of a radiator tank (figure 4-19). The oil cooler receives hot fluid from the transmission and transfers heat to the coolant in the radiator. The radiator then transfers heat to the outside air. An external transmission cooler is separate from the radiator and is generally for heavy-duty applications or installed as an

accessory. The external transmission cooler transfers heat directly to the outside air. This type of oil cooler looks and functions just like an engine cooling system radiator. Once the fluid passes through the cooler, external tubing returns it to the transmission. Fluid from the cooler flows either to the sump and mixes with fluid remaining in the pan or directly to the transmission lubrication circuit.

Lubrication Flow and Pressure

A portion of the pump output continuously flows through the circuits and passages in the case, valve body, and geartrain to

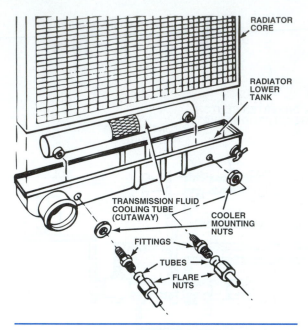

Figure 4-19. Internal oil coolers transfer heat from transmission fluid to engine coolant.

lubricate the moving parts of the transmission. Most transmissions also use the fluid returning from the oil cooler for lubrication. Fluid flows through orifices and drilled shafts to reach nested parts of the transmission. Fluid is also routed in this manner to operate certain transmission valves and apply devices (figure 4-20).

Band and Clutch Apply Pressure

The hydraulic control signals the operation of governor pressure and throttle pressure at the shift valves. The shift valves are calibrated to upshift and downshift at a preset balance of governor pressure and throttle pressure. To accomplish a gear change, the shift valves pass mainline fluid to the appropriate apply devices (clutches and bands), which apply or release gearset members and shift gears. By varying the pressure development and the sequence of fluid delivery, an automatic transmission can control the timing, quality, and feel of the shift.

TRANSMISSION SHIFTING AND SHIFT OPERATIONS

Gear changes in an automatic transmission are the result of a chain of events that occur inside the gearbox. To maintain a smooth, even flow of power, the transmission must respond to changing vehicle speeds, engine loads, and other variables. This is done by balancing opposing pressures with electronic controls, or by using a combination of both.

Manual Valve

The manual valve, or manual control valve, can be positioned manually with the gearshift selector linkage. This linkage relays the gear selection command of the driver to the manual valve lever at the transmission (figure 4-21). The lever moves the manual valve in its bore to one of several fixed "detent" positions (figure 4-22).

Manual valves are flow-directing valves that distribute fluid to the different hydraulic circuits needed for the selected gear range. The manual valve receives mainline fluid from the pressure regulator valve and routes this mainline fluid to charge the circuits of the correct shift valves and apply devices (figure 4-23). Lands and valleys of the spool-type manual valve direct fluid flow to some circuits and block flow to others.

Both electronic and nonelectronic transmissions use a manual valve to direct fluid to the hydraulic circuits. However, electronic transmissions use an electronic sensor at the manual valve linkage to perform an additional function. The sensor relays the position of the manual valve to the computer, which ensures that the transmission is in the correct gear.

Throttle Valve

The throttle valve senses engine load and develops throttle pressure from mainline pressure. The throttle valve may be controlled by mechanical linkage connected to

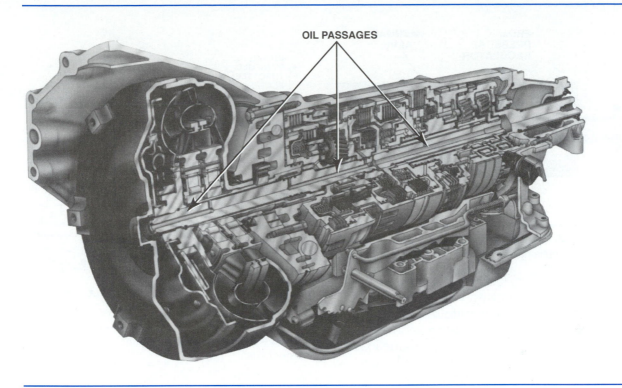

Figure 4-20. Transmission fluid is routed to clutches through drilled shafts in gearset. General Motors Corporation, Service and Parts Operations

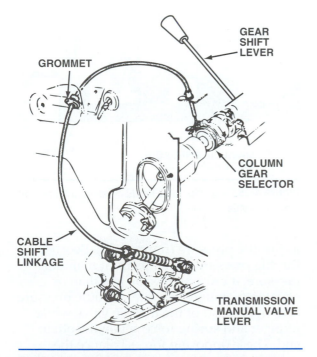

Figure 4-21. Manual valve connects gear selector and driver through shift linkage.

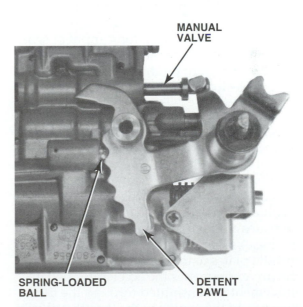

Figure 4-22. Manual valve lever positions the manual valve.

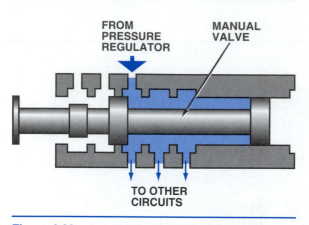

Figure 4-23. Manual valve distributes fluid to hydraulic circuits needed for gear range selection.

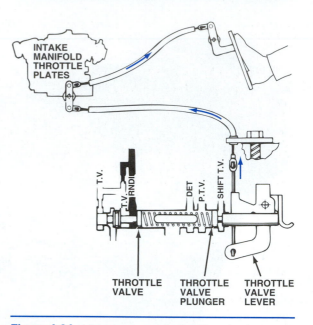

Figure 4-24. Linkage connects throttle valve to accelerator pedal.

the throttle plate or by a vacuum modulator that monitors intake manifold vacuum. In either case, the throttle valve responds directly to engine load. A light engine load develops a low throttle pressure; a higher load develops a higher throttle pressure.

Electronic transmissions use a computer-controlled solenoid in place of the throttle valve. The solenoid develops throttle pressure based on output signals from the computer. The computer calculates output signals based on the electronic input of sensors that monitor operating condition signals. Most current production transmissions feature electronic throttle pressure control.

Mechanically Operated Throttle Valve

A mechanical throttle valve assembly consists of the throttle valve, lever, and mechanical linkage. Linkage, which may be either the control rod or cable type, connects the throttle valve in the valve body to the throttle plates at the intake manifold on the engine. A separate linkage connects the throttle plates to the accelerator pedal. When the driver depresses the accelerator pedal, movement is transmitted through the throttle plate on the engine to the throttle valve in the transmission, as shown in figure 4-24.

When the throttle is closed, one land of the throttle valve blocks off the mainline pressure inlet port (figure 4-25). As the throttle opens, the linkage increases the force on the throttle valve and begins to uncover the inlet port allowing fluid to flow through the valve and exit at the outlet port

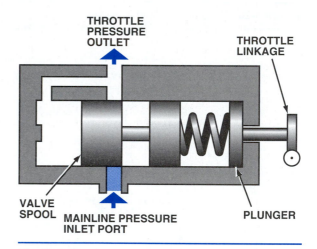

Figure 4-25. Throttle valve lands close off inlet port at closed throttle.

as throttle pressure (figure 4-26). Because throttle pressure develops from mainline pressure, it must always be less than or equal to mainline pressure. Throttle pressure acts on one end of the throttle valve while plunger and spring force act on the other end. These opposing forces balance the valve in its bore to provide a stable throttle pressure in relation to the position of the throttle plate opening. How much throttle pressure develops depends upon the opening of the inlet and outlet ports, which

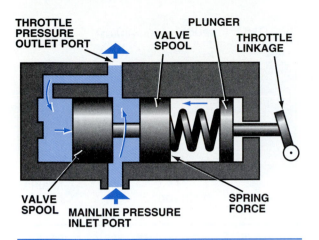

Figure 4-26. Throttle valve moves as throttle opens, allowing fluid through inlet port to develop throttle pressure.

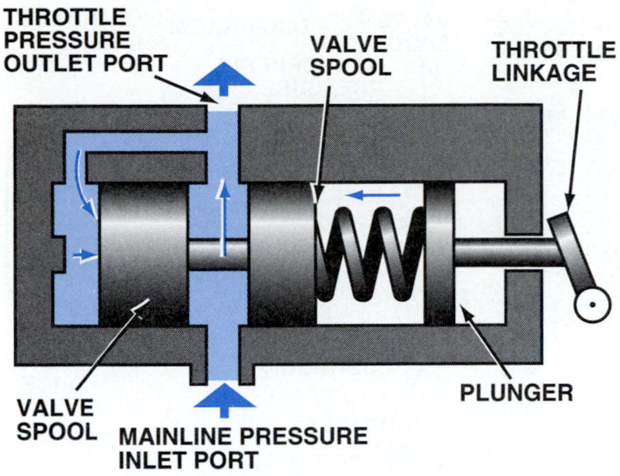

Figure 4-27. Throttle valve does not restrict flow at full throttle—throttle and mainline pressures are equal.

The Ford Foot Shifter

The Ford Model T was one of the most popular automobiles of all time. More than 15 million vehicles were built from October 1908 through May 1927, all of them with a planetary gear transmission. Henry Ford used a two-speed planetary gear transmission in his 1904 Model N and adapted it for the Model T in 1908. Everything was there in the Model T gearbox to make an automatic transmission, except a hydraulic system. Gears were kept from turning by bands, and gear combinations were turned simultaneously by a multiple-disc clutch. However, the driver had to do the shifting, which was done mostly with the feet.

The Model T had three foot pedals and a handbrake lever. When the handbrake lever was pulled back, it applied the drum brakes on the rear wheels and released the clutch. When the lever was pushed forward, it released the brakes and engaged the clutch. When the lever was between these two positions, it released both the brakes and the clutch. The clutch pedal, located on the left side of the floor panel, put the transmission in neutral when depressed half way. To get low gear, the driver pushed the clutch all the way down and held it. To get high gear, the driver released the clutch and let it come all the way out. The center pedal engaged reverse, and the right-hand pedal applied the transmission brake. Because the driver's feet were busy changing gears, the driver controlled the engine throttle by hand using a lever on the steering column.

depends on the opening of the throttle. The throttle valve inlet port opening increases as the drive depresses the accelerator pedal. At the wide-open throttle, the throttle valve is pushed into its bore as far as it can go and both the inlet and outlet ports are fully open. Under these conditions, throttle pressure equals mainline pressure (figure 4-27).

Vacuum-Operated Valve

A vacuum-operated throttle valve performs the same job as a mechanically operated one; the difference between the two valves is the method of applying control force.

Vacuum-operated throttle valves use a pushrod to connect the valve to a vacuum diaphragm. The diaphragm moves in response to changes in the intake manifold vacuum and moves the pushrod and throttle valve along with it. Manufacturers assign different names to their diaphragm assemblies, but the term "vacuum modulator" has gained acceptance for common usage.

A typical vacuum modulator has two airtight chambers separated by a flexible metal or rubber diaphragm, as shown in figure 4-28. The chamber on the valve side of the vacuum modulator is at atmospheric pressure while the other chamber receives

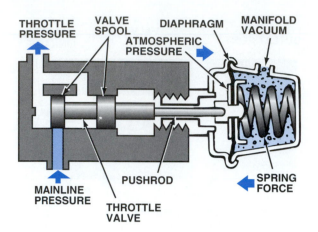

Figure 4-28. Vacuum modulator replaces mechanical linkage.

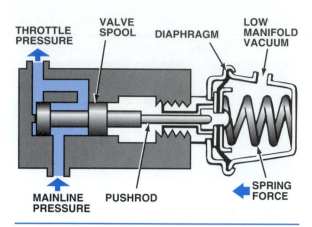

Figure 4-30. Spring force overcomes low manifold vacuum, holding throttle valve open and equalizing pressures.

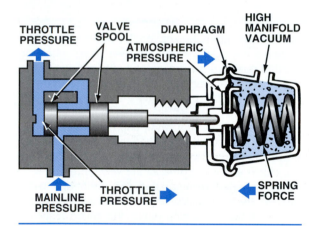

Figure 4-29. High manifold vacuum pulls throttle valve, partially blocking mainline pressure port.

manifold vacuum through a line or hose that connects it to the engine. The vacuum chamber also contains a spring that acts on the back side of the diaphragm to hold the valve in position when there is no vacuum signal.

With the engine idling or operating under a light load, manifold vacuum increases. A high vacuum signal, along with atmospheric pressure acting on the valve side of the diaphragm, overcomes the spring force, drawing the diaphragm away from the valve. Since the valve connects to the diaphragm by the pushrod, it moves to partially close off the mainline pressure inlet port, as shown in figure 4-29. As a result, throttle pressure is reduced and is less than mainline pressure.

When the engine operates under a heavy load and manifold vacuum is low, pressure is almost equal in both chambers of the vacuum modulator. The spring force pushes the spool valve into its bore, and fluid passes straight through the valve to equalize throttle and mainline pressures, as shown in figure 4-30.

Under most conditions, manifold vacuum does not allow atmospheric pressure and spring force to completely reduce throttle pressure. Instead, the throttle valve finds a balanced position that only partially obstructs the inlet port. This applies some throttle pressure to the end of the valve, which together with atmospheric pressure acts on the diaphragm. These two pressures oppose spring force to maintain a steady, regulated output.

Downshift Valves

At times, such as when passing another vehicle, a driver may require more torque during a light-load operating condition. To produce the extra torque, the transmission uses a valve to mechanically boost the throttle pressure and force a downshift. This valve may be called a kickdown, **detent**, or **downshift valve**.

In order to force a downshift, the driver depresses the accelerator pedal. This in turn opens the throttle plates past the detent point. How fast and how far the driver

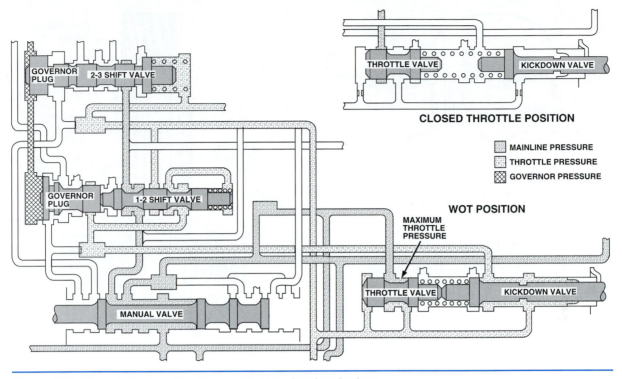

Figure 4-31. Downshift valve often incorporated into throttle valve bore.

depresses the pedal indicates how quickly torque is needed. The transmission sees sudden, full-throttle pedal application as a command to quickly develop maximum torque, and responds with a full throttle, also known as a hard or wide-open throttle, downshift. In response to a less sudden, partial depression of the accelerator pedal that demands less than maximum torque, the transmission responds with a part throttle or detent downshift.

Downshift valve configurations vary from vehicle to vehicle. Some downshift valves are incorporated into the throttle valve assembly where they work like a mechanical plunger in the throttle valve bore (figure 4-31). At wide-open throttle, the downshift valve forces the throttle valve to the end of its bore and throttle pressure rises to its maximum.

Downshift valves used with a vacuum modulator are usually operated by either mechanical linkage or electric switches and solenoids. In either case, when the throttle opens past its detent point, the downshift valve boosts throttle pressure or develops a higher auxiliary downshift pressure. Applying this pressure to the appropriate

shift valve overcomes governor pressure and forces a downshift. Some transmissions use a kickdown switch or solenoid to provide an electric signal that controls the downshift valve. The switch or solenoid attaches to the accelerator pedal and transmits a signal when the pedal travels past a predetermined point (figure 4-32). Electronic transmissions may monitor several electronic sensor signals, such as the throttle position sensor, brake switch, and manifold absolute pressure sensor, to get a complete picture of vehicle needs and driver demands.

Governor Valve

The governor valve develops governor pressure from mainline pressure based on the road speed of the vehicle. Governor pressure opposes throttle pressure at the shift valves to control shift points. Governor pressure increases as road speed increases.

The output shaft typically drives the governor valve on a RWD transmission. Either the final driveshaft or the intermediate shaft

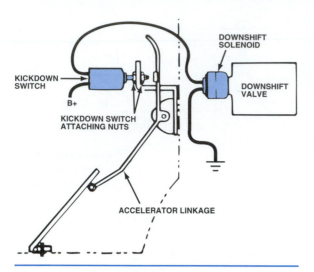

Figure 4-32. Electric kickdown switch and solenoid used to produce downshift.

provides drive for the governor on a transaxle. The two basic types of mechanical governor valve assemblies are as follows:

• Gear driven
• Shaft mounted

A mechanical assembly is not necessary on an electronic transmission, because a computer-controlled solenoid produces a variable governor pressure.

Gear-Driven Governors

A gear-driven governor uses a set of centrifugally operated weights to position either a spool valve or check balls. The position of the valve or check balls determine how much governor pressure the assembly produces by regulating a restriction to mainline fluid flow.

Gear-driven governors generally fit a machined bore in the rear of the transmission case and are held in place with a screw and bracket (figure 4-33). A drive gear on the transmission output shaft meshes with a driven gear on the governor shaft to drive the governor at a 1:1 ratio. Since the output shaft turns whenever the vehicle is moving, the governor also rotates at the same speed.

When the vehicle is at rest, the governor valve closes off the mainline pressure inlet. Both the governor pressure and exhaust ports are fully open so no governor pressure

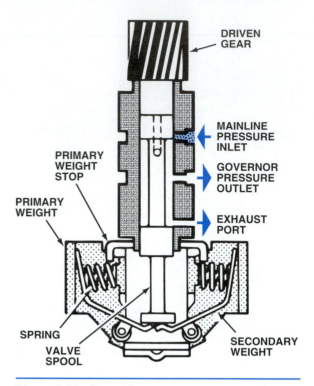

Figure 4-33. Gear-driven governor uses centrifugal force to develop governor pressure from mainline pressure.

develops. Any fluid that leaks past the valve land from the mainline pressure inlet flows through the exhaust port.

Spool Valve Designs
A spool-valve governor consists of two sets of weights and springs and one spool valve. Centrifugal force pushes the weights outward as the vehicle begins to move, and the weights act as levers to reposition the spool valve in its bore. Spool valve movement closes off the exhaust port and opens the mainline pressure inlet, allowing governor pressure to build (figure 4-34). When vehicle speed exceeds a certain point, the weights are at full extension and the mainline pressure inlet and governor pressure outlet ports are both fully open. Governor pressure will equal mainline pressure under these conditions.

Using two sets of weights increases the accuracy of pressure regulation at low speeds. This is important because even a slight offset of 2-3 psi of governor pressure may cause shift problems. The heavier,

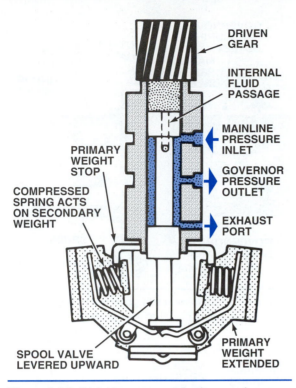

Figure 4-34. Weights move spool valve opening as speed increases, allowing governor pressure to build.

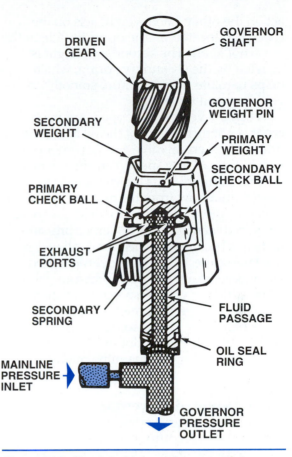

Figure 4-35. Check-ball type governor regulates governor pressure using ball valves.

primary weights move first and act through springs against the lighter secondary weights that actually move the valve spool. In some transmissions, the spring tensions for the two primary weights differ to provide even smoother regulation of governor pressure. As speed increases, the primary weights reach full travel and bottom out against their stops. Then, the secondary weights act alone to control the valve.

During operation, governor pressure is routed through an internal valve passage to act against the valve land at the driven gear end. This allows governor pressure to oppose the lever force applied to the other end of the valve. As a result, governor pressure will increase with vehicle speed. It then stabilizes as the speed becomes constant.

When vehicle speed exceeds a certain point, both sets of weights move out as far as possible. At this time, the secondary weights are bottomed on the primary weights, the exhaust port is fully closed, and both the mainline pressure inlet and the governor pressure outlet are fully open; therefore, governor pressure equals mainline pressure.

Check Ball Designs
Some transmissions use a gear-driven governor with check balls to regulate governor pressure (figure 4-35). This design is similar in placement and function to the spool-valve governor just described. A check-ball governor consists of two check balls, a governor shaft, a primary weight, a secondary weight, a governor weight pin, a secondary spring, and an oil seal ring.

In this governor, mainline fluid enters through a metered orifice at the inlet and flows through a fluid passage machined into the governor shaft. Two exhaust ports are drilled into the fluid passage, and governor pressure is determined by the amount of fluid allowed to flow out of these ports. The check balls provide a variable restriction to fluid flow through the exit ports.

As the governor valve rotates, centrifugal force causes the primary weight to act on one check ball and the secondary weight to act on the other. Each weight acts on the check ball located on the opposite side of the governor shaft. The secondary weight is assisted by the secondary spring, which helps regulate pressure more smoothly as vehicle speed increases.

When the vehicle is stopped and the governor is not turning, all of the oil is exhausted from the governor valve and governor pressure is zero. At low speed, centrifugal force transfer partially seats the check balls to restrict fluid flow from the exhaust ports and governor pressure begins to build. As governor speed increases, the governor pressure increases because the check balls allow less fluid to escape. When the governor speed remains constant, governor pressure stabilizes. At higher vehicle speeds, centrifugal force becomes great enough to hold both check balls fully seated so that no fluid escapes from the governor. At this point, governor pressure equals mainline pressure.

Shaft-Mounted Governors

Shaft-mounted governors attach directly to the transmission output shaft and rotate along with the shaft. Like a gear-driven governor, shaft-mounted units use centrifugal force acting on weights to control governor pressure. A shaft-mounted governor assembly consists of an inner weight, an outer weight, a valve spool, a spring, and a valve shaft that tie the components together.

With the vehicle at rest, one land of the governor valve spool blocks off the mainline pressure port. Any fluid that leaks past the valve land flows through the exhaust port, so governor pressure is zero (figure 4-36). As the vehicle begins to move, output shaft rotation develops centrifugal force that draws the governor weights outward. The weights pull the valve shaft along with them, moving the valve spool, which closes the exhaust port and opens the mainline pressure inlet (figure 4-37). Mainline pressure then enters the governor valve where it becomes governor pressure and exits through the governor pressure outlet.

As with the gear-driven governor valve, two weights regulate governor pressure more accurately. At low vehicle speeds, only the heavier outer weight moves. When the

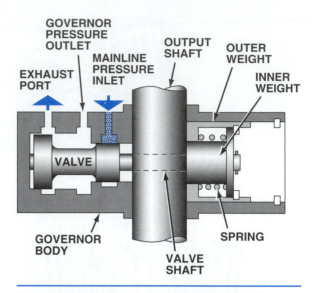

Figure 4-36. Shaft-mounted governor assembly closes off mainline pressure inlet at rest.

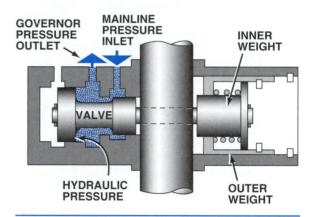

Figure 4-37. Weights move the valve to open inlet port and close exhaust port at speed.

outer weight travels far enough to fully compress the spring, the inner weight begins to move.

Governor pressure continues to increase as centrifugal force increases, but it is modulated by directing pressure against the larger land inside the governor valve. This creates a force that partially opposes the force created by the weights. As a result, governor pressure increases with vehicle speed and stabilizes when vehicle speed is constant. At high speeds, the governor valve is open as far as possible and governor pressure equals mainline pressure.

Shift Valve Operation

Shift valves are flow-directing or switching valves that react to governor pressure and throttle pressure to initiate gear changes. By monitoring engine load through throttle pressure and vehicle speed through governor pressure, upshifts and downshifts can be timed to meet the needs of many different driving conditions. For this reason, shift valves are sometimes called shift-timing valves. Most transmissions have several shift valves.

A shift valve directs fluid flow to upshift the transmission when governor pressure exceeds throttle pressure. Under these conditions, higher vehicle speed requires the greater efficiency of a high gear more than engine load requires the greater torque available from a lower gear.

Shift valves are spool-type valves with governor pressure acting on one end and throttle pressure acting on the opposite end. A calibrated spring on the throttle pressure side of the valve provides an additional force for governor pressure to overcome. The position of the valve in its bore either blocks mainline pressure or allows it to flow through the spool and into the apply passages.

When vehicle speed is low, throttle pressure and spring force are stronger than governor pressure. Under these conditions, one land of the shift valve blocks the mainline pressure inlet port, preventing fluid flow to the apply devices (figure 4-38). Governor pressure rises as vehicle speed increases, and at some point it will exceed the throttle pressure and spring force. As this happens, the valve moves sharply to open the inlet port (figure 4-39). This allows mainline pressure to pass through the shift valve and into the apply circuit to cause an upshift.

When a shift valve moves, it shifts to the other position almost instantly. There must be no hesitation or "hunting" between positions. Otherwise, several actuators may be applied at the same time. For this reason, shift valves are sometimes called snap valves.

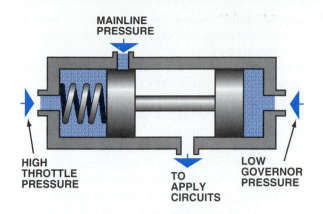

Figure 4-38. Shift valve blocks mainline pressure when throttle pressure and spring force are greater than governor pressure.

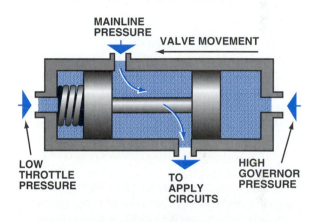

Figure 4-39. Shift valve snaps open to allow mainline pressure flow when governor pressure exceeds throttle pressure and spring force.

Shift Timing and Smoothing

Transmission shifts must be timed so that the gear ratio selected at that moment matches the needs of the vehicle, the torque produced by the engine, and the demands of the driver. This is necessary to provide a balance of performance and efficiency for all driving conditions.

If a vehicle is accelerating slowly and smoothly, the transmission calls for an upshift as soon as possible to achieve better fuel economy. Under these conditions, torque demand is low and the driver is not depressing hard on the accelerator. The throttle plates are only slightly open, so manifold vacuum remains fairly high. All this results in a low throttle pressure, which means a relatively low governor pressure can overcome the throttle pressure at the shift valve. As a result, upshifts occur while the car is traveling at low speed during light- or part-throttle operation. If the same vehicle is accelerating rapidly or climbing a hill, more torque is needed and the transmission must hold low gear longer for better performance. As the driver depresses the accelerator pedal farther the throttle plates open wider and intake manifold vacuum drops. This results in a higher throttle pressure that requires a higher governor pressure to upshift the transmission. As a result, upshifts are delayed until the vehicle reaches a higher road speed during heavy- or full-throttle acceleration.

Shift Valve Sequencing

Figure 4-40 shows a simplified hydraulic diagram for a three-speed automatic transmission in low gear. This simple design uses two shift valves. The 1-2 shift valve handles upshifts and downshifts between first and second gears, and the 2-3 shift valve handles upshifts and downshifts between second and third gears.

Fluid flows from the pump through the pressure regulator valve where it becomes mainline pressure. Mainline pressure then travels to the manual valve. With the vehicle at rest, the manual valve routes mainline pressure directly to the low gear apply circuit, as well as to the throttle valve, governor valve, and 1-2 shift valve. When vehicle speed is high enough, governor pressure overcomes throttle pressure at the 1-2 shift valve (figure 4-41). The valve snaps open and delivers mainline pressure to the intermediate apply circuit to fill and pressurize the actuator to engage second-gear. At the same time, pressure in the second-gear apply circuit fills the low-release circuit to release first gear. This prevents the transmission from being in two gears at once. Movement of the 1-2 shift valve also delivers mainline pressure to the inlet port of the 2-3 shift valve, which is closed by one of the valve lands.

The spring in the 2-3 shift valve is stronger than the spring in the 1-2 shift valve, in order to ensure the 1-2 shift valve

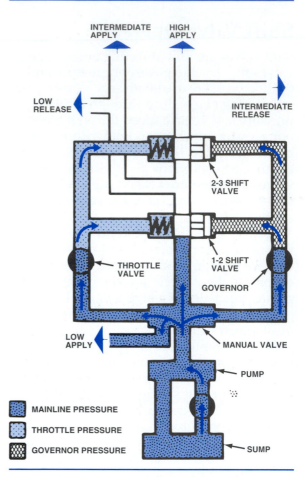

Figure 4-40. Simple hydraulic circuit—three-speed transmission in first or low gear.

opens first. Because higher governor pressure is required to overcome throttle pressure and spring force on the 2-3 shift valve, the shift from second to third occurs at a higher speed than the shift from first to second. When governor pressure is high enough, the 2-3 shift valve opens to route mainline pressure to the high apply circuit and the intermediate release circuit (figure 4-42). This upshifts the transmission into drive, while at the same time releasing the second gear apply devices.

Accumulators and Orifices

Care must be taken to apply the actuators precisely. If pressure applies too quickly, the resulting gear shift may be harsh or jarring. If pressure applies too slowly, clutches and bands may slip, causing soft shifts. Either condition causes premature wear.

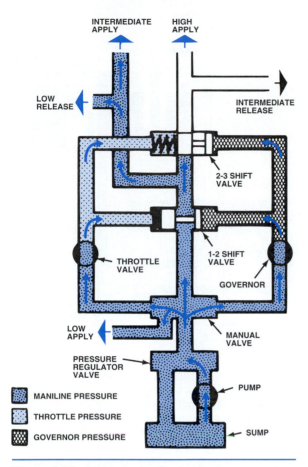

Figure 4-41. Simple hydraulic circuit—three-speed transmission in second gear.

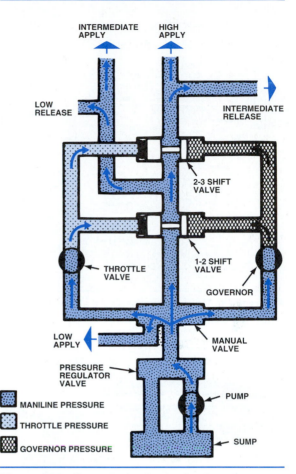

Figure 4-42. Simple hydraulic circuit—three-speed transmission in third or drive gear.

Gear shifting can be made smoother by timing the application and release of the clutches and bands so that one is beginning to apply just as the other is releasing. Electronic transmissions smooth shifting directly by varying the timing and applying pressure with computer-controlled solenoids, thus allowing precise control under most driving conditions. Without electronic control, the transmissions must accomplish smooth shifting indirectly with shift valves and fixed mechanical orifices and accumulators.

Orifices

An **orifice** is a small restriction in a fluid passage that functions as a simple type of pressure-regulating valve (figure 4-43). An orifice may be a restriction in the line or a hole between fluid chambers. Orifices delay pressure buildup temporarily until fluid fills

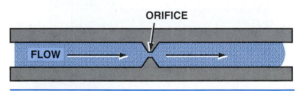

Figure 4-43. Orifice—small calibrated opening.

the next chamber beyond the restriction. Orifices can be cast into the valve body, drilled into separator plates, or cast into clutch drums (figure 4-44).

When fluid reaches an orifice, it meets a resistance to flow and pressure begins to build up. Pressure is highest on the side of the orifice with the greater amount of fluid, and pressure continues to increase until the other side also fills with fluid. When both chambers are full, fluid flow stops and pressure equalizes on both sides of the orifice.

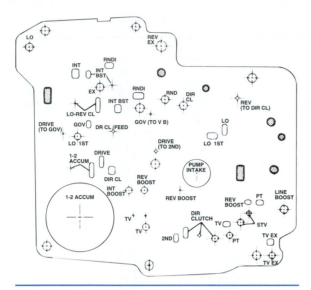

Figure 4-44. Valve body separator plate—some passages are calibrated orifices.

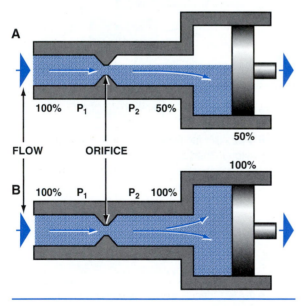

Figure 4-45. Orifice that momentarily delays fluid flow.

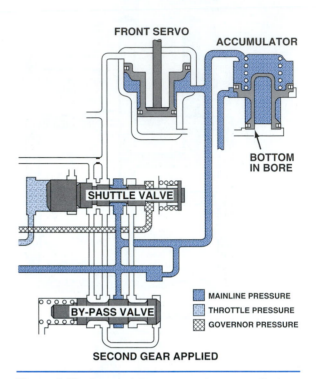

Figure 4-46. Accumulators even out pressure fluctuations to provide smooth shifts.

Figure 4-45 shows an orifice between two chambers of a hydraulic system. The size of the orifice reduces fluid pressure on one side (P1) by half as it passes through to the other side (P2). This makes it possible to begin applying the piston on the P2 side of the orifice with half the pressure that is normally available in the system. This low-pressure application moves the piston slower and with less force than usual, to take up any clearance. As pressure builds, the applying force of the piston begins to drive or hold the gearset member. Once both chambers are full and pressure is equal, full system pressure firmly applies the piston.

Accumulators

An **accumulator** is a device that cushions the application of an apply device for a smoother shift feel. Two designs, piston and valve, are commonly used.

A piston accumulator uses a spring-loaded piston operating in a bore to cushion the apply circuit to which it is hydraulically linked. When the shift valve directs mainline fluid to apply the servo, the fluid begins to flow to the accumulator (figure 4-46). Because the accumulator piston offers much less resistance than the apply piston, it moves first. As pressure builds, the accumulator piston continues moving in its bore until it bottoms out. Once the accumulator circuit is full, the servo piston begins moving to apply the band or clutch. The result is a slightly longer but smoother gear shift.

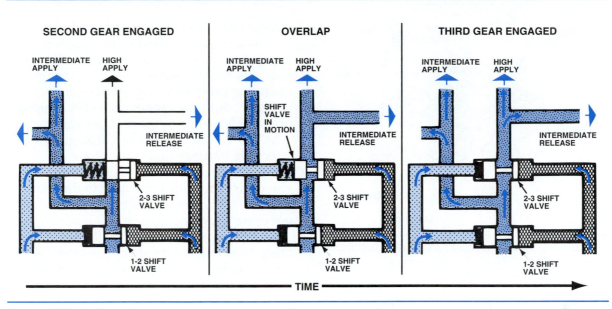

Figure 4-47. Shift overlap occurs when one gear applies as another releases.

Shift Overlap

Overlapping the shifts provides a smooth transition as the transmission changes gears. This is accomplished by applying the clutches and bands used to control the upcoming gear just as the clutches and bands used for the previous gear are released (figure 4-47). Shift overlap keeps the rotational speed of the gearset members constant and under control. However, the overlap must be carefully timed so that the transmission is not in two gears at once.

Shift overlap is usually managed either by using the hydraulic circuits of the apply side to release the previous actuators or by making the upcoming actuator apply dependent on the release of the previous actuators. As an example, consider a 2-3 upshift on a Ford A4LD transmission in which application of the direct clutch is dependent on the release of the intermediate band. Apply pressure to the direct clutch cannot build up until the intermediate servo piston is fully bottomed in its bore. This hydraulic circuit lockout prevents the transmission from being in both second and third gear simultaneously.

Automatic Transmission Fluid

Automatic transmissions use a special blend of transmission fluid. The type, width, pattern, and design of the clutch discs and bands have all been chosen to work with the friction properties of a particular ATF. Fluid properties affect how fast and freely transmission fluid can flow under different temperature and pressure conditions. Changing fluid types or adding shift additives to the fluid can result in problems ranging from slightly changing the shift points to allowing enough slippage to burn up the transmission completely.

Electronic Shift Control

For most automatic transmissions, throttle and governor pressure interact at mechanical shift valves to control transmission shifting. A mechanical shift occurs when the governor pressure acting on one side of the valve exceeds throttle pressure and spring force on the other side. This moves the shift valve and routes mainline pressure to the correct apply and release circuits. Most electronic transmissions use this shifting procedure. However, electronic transmissions develop and regulate governor and throttle pressure with computer-controlled solenoids. Solenoids also develop and regulate mainline pressure and route that pressure directly to the clutches and bands (figure 4-48).

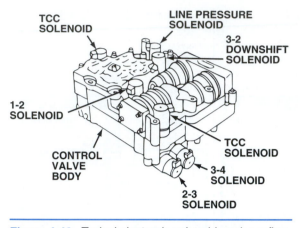

Figure 4-48. Typical electronic solenoid-pack configuration.

Some electronic transmission designs have completely eliminated shift valves and use solenoids to directly control transmission shifting. This simplifies the valve body and reduces the weight and complexity of the transmission. In addition, the control system is able to precisely tailor pressure and shift timing for maximum economy and performance.

SUMMARY

Most automatic transmissions use a gear, rotor, or vane pump to develop fluid flow and pressure. Gear action at the pump input creates a low-pressure area that allows atmospheric pressure to force fluid from the sump into the pump. Fluid is discharged at the pump outlet to fill and pressurize transmission hydraulic circuits.

Gear and rotor pumps are positive displacement pumps. Their output volume increases with pump speed. The vane pumps used in automatic transmissions are variable-displacement pumps. Variable-displacement pumps adjust output volume to meet operating demands.

The three basic control pressures used in every automatic transmission are mainline, throttle, and governor pressure. Mainline pressure is controlled by a pressure regulator valve. The pressure regulator valve controls pump output to prevent excessive

system pressure in the hydraulic circuits. Mainline pressure operates the gearset apply devices and is the source for all other transmission pressures. The other system operating pressures may equal mainline pressure, but they cannot exceed it. Mainline pressure is routed to the manual valve, which is moved by gearshift linkage to select the transmission drive range. Mainline pressure is also routed to the shift valves, which control the flow to the transmission apply devices based on throttle and governor pressure signals.

Mainline pressure is normally held at a fairly constant, fixed value. However, when operating loads are high, mainline pressure may be increased. Under these operating conditions, either boost valves or auxiliary hydraulic pressures assist the regulating force at the spring end of the pressure regulator valve. This increases mainline pressure to the transmission apply devices, which increases mechanical force and prevents the gearset members from slipping under increased torque loads.

A throttle valve controls throttle pressure. The throttle valve is operated by a mechanical linkage that attaches it to the throttle plate or by a vacuum modulator that responds to intake manifold vacuum. The throttle valve input pressure acts on a regulating spool valve that restricts fluid flow and develops throttle pressure. Throttle pressure increases with engine load and acts against governor pressure at the shift valves to time gear shifts. Throttle pressure may also assist in regulating mainline pressure. Electronic automatic transmissions use a computer-controlled solenoid instead of a throttle valve to develop throttle pressure.

When drive torque requirements are high, throttle pressure may be temporarily increased using a mechanical downshift or kickdown valve. This forces the transmission to downshift, allowing the engine to operate in a speed range where greater torque is available.

Governor pressure is mechanically controlled by a governor valve, which is driven from the transmission output shaft or final driveshaft. Mechanical governors rely on centrifugal force acting on weights to control a spool valve or check balls that restrict fluid flow. Governor pressure can also be produced electronically using a computer-controlled solenoid. In either case, governor pressure is a pressure signal that builds and increases as vehicle road speed increases. Governor pressure is used to oppose throttle pressure and regulate gear changes.

Throttle pressure and governor pressure interact at the shift valves to control transmission upshifts and downshifts. A mechanical shift occurs when governor pressure acting on one side of the shift valve exceeds the combined throttle pressure and spring force acting on the other side. Some transmission designs have eliminated the shift valves and use electronic solenoids to directly control transmission shifting.

ATF develops the primary hydraulic control pressures, operates the shift valves, and fills and pressurizes the torque converter. ATF is also used to lubricate gears and internal components and to operate the transmission apply devices. ATF is specially blended for particular transmissions: It has friction modifiers that enhance certain friction properties of the fluid and greatly affect shift timing and feel.

Review Questions

Choose the single most correct answer. Compare your answers to the correct answers on page 213.

1. The major types of oil pumps used in an automatic transmission are
   a. Gear, vane, rotor
   b. Gear, crescent, vane
   c. Gear, crescent, rotor
   d. Gear, pressure, rotor

2. Technician A says a positive-displacement pump delivers the same amount of fluid per revolution.
   Technician B says a positive-displacement pump does not require pressure regulation.
   Who is right?
   a. A only
   b. B only
   c. Both A and B
   d. Neither A nor B

3. The inner drive gear of a positive-displacement oil pump in a transmission is usually driven by the
   a. Input shaft
   b. Governor
   c. Torque converter hub
   d. Output shaft

4. Technician A says a variable-displacement vane pump may be driven by a pump driveshaft.
   Technician B says the displacement of a vane pump can be varied during transmission operation.
   Who is right?
   a. A only
   b. B only
   c. Both A and B
   d. Neither A nor B

5. Technician A says the transmission oil pump is driven by the engine to enable it to monitor engine operating demands.
   Technician B says the transmission oil pump supplies the transmission with a fluid flow when the engine is rotating.
   Who is right?
   a. A only
   b. B only
   c. Both A and B
   d. Neither A nor B

6. The pressure from which all other pressures are developed in an automatic transmission hydraulic system is
   a. Control
   b. Throttle
   c. Governor
   d. Mainline

7. Mainline pressure is developed and regulated by the
   a. Throttle valve
   b. Modulator valve
   c. Pressure regulator valve
   d. Detent valve

8. Which of the following operating conditions may require a higher mainline pressure?
   a. Operation under heavy load or reverse gear operation
   b. Closed-throttle downshift
   c. Part-throttle cruising
   d. All of the above

9. Technician A says throttle pressure decreases as engine load and torque increase.
   Technician B says throttle pressure increases as the accelerator pedal is depressed farther.
   Who is right?
   a. A only
   b. B only
   c. Both A and B
   d. Neither A nor B

10. Technician A says governor pressure remains constant as vehicle speed increases.
    Technician B says governor pressure decreases as vehicle speed increases.
    Who is right?
    a. A only
    b. B only
    c. Both A and B
    d. Neither A nor B

11. Technician A says throttle pressure is used to control upshifts and downshifts.
    Technician B says governor pressure is used to control upshifts and downshifts.
    Who is right?
    a. A only
    b. B only
    c. Both A and B
    d. Neither A nor B

12. Shift valves are sometimes referred to as
    a. Snap valves
    b. Detent valves
    c. Modulator valves
    d. Regulator valves

13. High throttle pressure may be produced by
    a. A wide-open throttle
    b. A heavily loaded engine
    c. Low intake manifold vacuum
    d. All of the above

14. Technician A says intake manifold vacuum assists spring pressure in a vacuum-operated throttle valve.
    Technician B says atmospheric pressure opposes spring pressure in a vacuum-operated throttle valve.
    Who is right?
    a. A only
    b. B only
    c. Both A and B
    d. Neither A nor B

15. Technician A says throttle pressure develops from govenor pressure.
    Technician B says vacuum-operated-throttle valves use a pushrod to connect the valve to a vacuum diaphragm.
    Who is right?
    a. A only
    b. B only
    c. Both A and B
    d. Neither A nor B

16. Maximum throttle pressure is never greater than
    a. Twice mainline pressure
    b. Half mainline pressure
    c. Mainline pressure
    d. None of the above

17. Technician A says a forced downshift may be controlled by a kickdown valve.
    Technician B says a forced downshift may be controlled by a detent valve.
    Who is right?
    a. A only
    b. B only
    c. Both A and B
    d. Neither A nor B

18. A transmission downshift valve may be controlled by
    a. Rods
    b. Cables
    c. Switches and solenoids
    d. All of the above

19. Technician A says the weights in a governor are moved by centrifugal force.
    Technician B says the weights in a governor are moved by throttle pressure.
    Who is right?
    a. A only
    b. B only
    c. Both A and B
    d. Neither A nor B

20. Technician A says that most of the valves in a transmission hydraulic system are housed in the valve body.
    Technician B says the valve body may be located in various positions depending on the type of transmission.
    Who is right?
    a. A only
    b. B only
    c. Both A and B
    d. Neither A nor B

5

Fluid Couplings and Torque Converters

In previous chapters, you learned how a transmission hydraulic system operates and how it controls a planetary gearset to select gear ratios. A transmission is not fully automatic unless it includes a device to couple and uncouple the engine and geartrain automatically. Either a fluid coupling or torque converter can accomplish this task. Although both transfer engine torque to the transmission, only a torque converter can increase the amount of torque being transferred.

This chapter explains the operation and construction of the torque converter, and examines how it was developed from the simpler fluid coupling. Although fluid couplings have not been used in automatic transmissions for many years, an understanding of fluid couplings will make the study of torque converters easier.

FLUID COUPLINGS

A fluid coupling consists of two elements, an impeller, also known as the pump, and a turbine. Each section resembles a doughnut that has been cut in half with a set of internal vanes that face each other when assembled (figure 5-1). Both components are enclosed in a sealed housing and act together as a single operating unit.

The **impeller** attaches to the engine through a flywheel or flexplate and turns as the engine rotates. The **turbine** connects to the transmission input shaft and provides the torque input to the planetary gearset. The impeller is the driving member, and the turbine is the driven member.

Fluid Flow and Resultant Force

The transmission oil pump keeps the fluid coupling full of pressurized automatic transmission fluid (ATF). As the impeller turns with the engine, its vanes scoop up fluid in the housing and throw it outward toward the turbine. As the fluid strikes the turbine

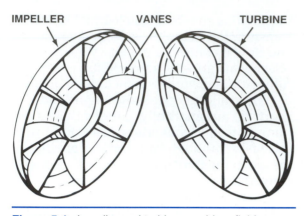

IMPELLER   VANES   TURBINE

Figure 5-1. Impeller and turbine provide a fluid coupling.

vanes, it rotates the turbine in the same direction as the impeller.

The moving fluid travels along two flow paths that are known as the rotary flow and the vortex flow. The **rotary flow** moves fluid in the same clockwise circular direction as the impeller rotation. This fluid flows around the axis of the engine crankshaft and the transmission input shaft (figure 5-2). As the fluid travels along the rotary flow path, centrifugal force moves it to the outer edge of the impeller. Because the impeller is curved, the fluid turns slightly as it strikes the outer edge of the impeller and flows into the turbine. This curvature moves the fluid in a second circular flow path at a right angle to the rotary flow path. This second flow path is the **vortex flow** (figure 5-2).

Fluid flows along both of the flow paths at the same time. The rotary flow, caused by impeller rotation, carries engine torque along with it. However, this engine torque cannot be transferred to the transmission without the vortex flow moving the fluid from the impeller to the turbine. Finally, the fluid leaving the impeller to enter the turbine exits as a combination of rotary and vortex flow (figure 5-3). The two flow paths combine to create a **resultant force** that directs the fluid from the impeller so that it strikes the turbine vanes at an angle. The angle and the resultant force may vary during different operating conditions.

Fluid Flow Turbulence

If the speed of one member of the fluid coupling is much faster than the speed of the other member, the result is fluid flow turbulence (figure 5-4). Turbulence swirls the fluid in all directions inside the coupling and greatly reduces the force available from the fluid flow. Turbulence is undesirable and engineers try to prevent and limit it. One way to limit turbulence is with a split guide ring. When added to the fluid coupling, the guide ring directs the fluid flow inside the coupling and steers it smoothly in the right direction (figure 5-5). This limits the force of any fluid flow that is counter to the rotary or vortex flow and improves the overall efficiency of the fluid coupling.

Speed Ratio

The efficiency of a fluid coupling is determined by how effectively the impeller can drive the turbine; **speed ratio** measures this coupling efficiency. To determine speed ratio, divide the speed of turbine rotation by the speed of impeller rotation; the result is expressed as a percentage. For example, if the impeller rotates at 1000 rpm, and the turbine rotates at 900 rpm, the speed ratio of the fluid coupling is 90 percent. If the impeller rotates but the turbine does not, the speed ratio is 0 percent, or zero speed ratio. Speed ratio will be zero with the vehicle stopped, engine at idle, and transmission in gear. The fluid coupling operates at maximum efficiency during a light-load steady-state cruise, and the speed ratio will be high.

Fluid Coupling Operation

When the engine turns at idle speed, the impeller does not generate enough force to drive the turbine and transmit torque to the transmission. As a result, the geartrain automatically uncouples from the engine. As the engine speeds up, so does the fluid flow and speed ratio produced by the impeller. At a low speed ratio the large vortex flow along the turbine vanes creates cross circulation between the impeller and turbine. Both the turbine vanes and the vortex flow work to oppose rotary flow, and at some

The Metallic Grapefruit

In 1938, Chrysler introduced the Fluid Drive, the first fluid coupling for a transmission. The company described the Fluid Drive as being "similar to two halves of a metallic grapefruit from which the fruit has been removed without damage to the sectional membrane." This two-element design uses an impeller and a turbine. The impeller attaches to the engine flywheel and the turbine attaches to a conventional single-disc clutch. The clutch drove the input shaft of a standard sliding-gear manual transmission.

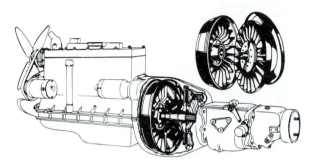

Although the Fluid Drive did not replace the mechanical clutch and transmission shift lever with an automatic shift system, it did allow the engine to idle in gear with the clutch engaged. It also reduced the number of times the driver had to shift by almost entirely eliminating forward gear shifts if the driver left the transmission in high gear. If the driver preferred, he could shift the transmission manually. In fact, as the 1940 Chrysler shop manual advised, "The transmission and clutch may be used in a conventional manner for shifting gears when flashing acceleration is desired."

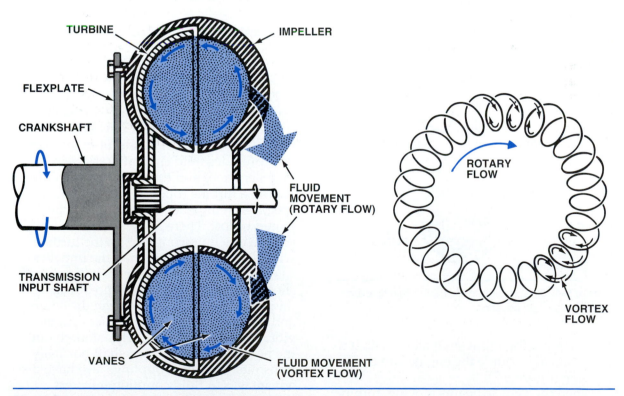

Figure 5-2. Fluid travels two paths—rotary and vortex flow.

point, vortex flow exceeds rotary flow. The resultant force direction is closer to the vortex flow direction when speed ratio is low (figure 5-6). When the resultant force of the fluid striking the turbine vanes becomes great enough, the turbine rotates, turning

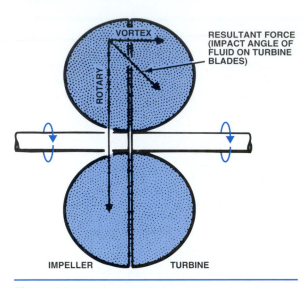

Figure 5-3. Fluid leaves the impeller at an angle.

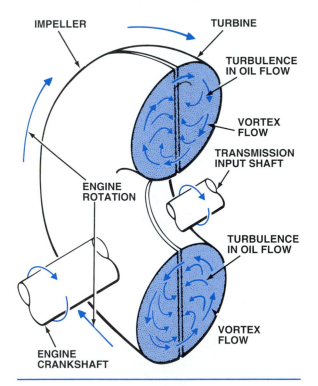

Figure 5-4. Speed difference creates fluid flow turbulence inside fluid coupling.

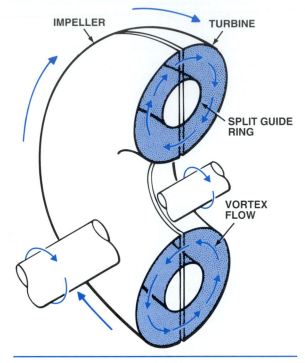

Figure 5-5. Split guide ring reduces fluid flow turbulence in a fluid coupling.

the transmission input shaft along with it to automatically couple the engine and transmission (figure 5-7).

When the vehicle begins moving, turbine speed approaches impeller speed and the speed ratio increases. At the same time, rotary flow increases while vortex flow decreases. The resultant force moves in the direction of the rotary flow to a point where the flow becomes almost completely rotary (figure 5-8). Under these conditions, the turbine is said to be coupled to the impeller.

Fluid flow is never completely rotary, because torque cannot transfer through the coupling without a vortex flow between the impeller and turbine. In addition, the vortex flow provides fluid circulation to keep the impeller vanes and turbine filled with fluid. Should a turbine rotate at exactly the same speed as an impeller, the coupling action would be lost. There is always some slippage in any fluid coupling, so the turbine will always turn slower than the impeller.

A fluid coupling also serves as a natural shock absorber since there is no direct mechanical connection between the engine and transmission. Also, it reduces engine vibration and noise and helps smooth out the power pulses the crankshaft normally transmits. But fluid couplings also have disadvantages. A fluid coupling transfers engine torque efficiently when the turbine moves nearly as fast as the impeller. Efficiency is high only when the speed ratio is high. When the speed ratio is low, the

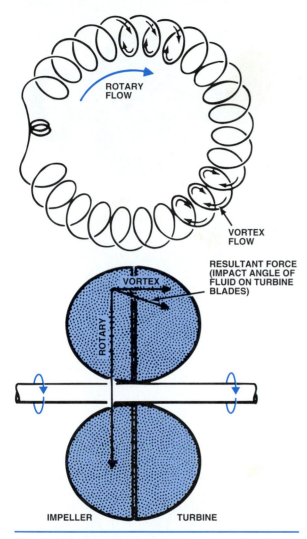

Figure 5-6. Low speed ratio—more vortex flow than rotary flow.

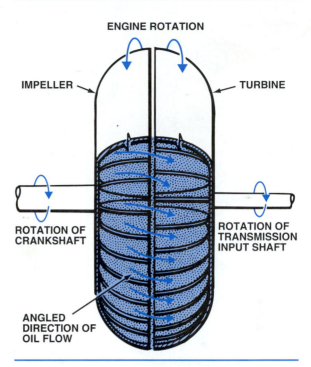

Figure 5-7. Turbine rotates when fluid resultant force overcomes vehicle inertia.

fluid coupling does not create enough fluid flow and torque transfer is less efficient. Additionally, a fluid coupling can only transfer torque; it cannot provide torque multiplication. The torque converter overcomes these problems and replaces the fluid coupling as the unit of choice for current automotive applications.

TORQUE CONVERTERS

In the early part of the 20th century, marine engineers seeking both gear and speed reduction using multiple turbines devel-

oped the torque converter. The first automotive use of a torque converter was on the 1948 Buick with a Dynaflow automatic transmission. Since that time a variety of multi-element torque converter designs have been used. Eventually, Ford developed a three-element torque converter design that became the industry standard among the domestic manufacturers.

Torque converters are more efficient than fluid couplings because they can increase, or multiply, the engine torque delivered to the transmission. Two advantages of a torque converter are quicker acceleration and better performance at low speeds. This is possible because a converter increases fluid flow and multiplies torque at low speed ratios. Torque converters have been used with all domestic automatic transmissions since 1964.

Torque Converter Construction

A typical torque converter consists of three basic elements contained in a sealed housing

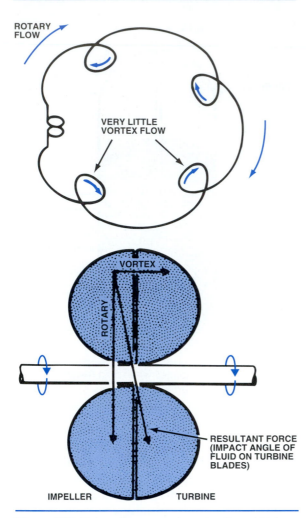

Figure 5-8. Rotary flow exceeds vortex flow at higher speed ratios.

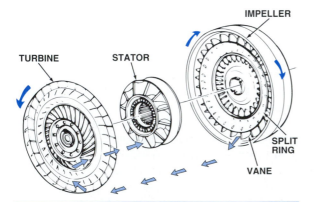

Figure 5-9. Typical torque converter—turbine, stator, impeller.

and is filled with pressurized transmission fluid (figure 5-9). The three elements of a standard torque converter are as follows:

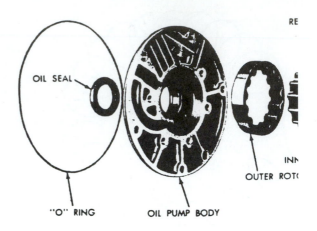

Figure 5-10. Curved vanes accelerate fluid flow and increase hydraulic advantage.

- Impeller
- Turbine
- Stator

The operation and construction of each member is similar to the fluid coupling. The impeller, also known as the pump, is the driving member and rotates with the engine. The impeller vanes pick up fluid in the converter housing and direct it toward the turbine. Fluid flow drives the turbine, and when the flow between the impeller and turbine is adequate, the turbine rotates and turns the transmission input shaft. A torque converter also contains the **stator**, or reactor, which is a reaction member mounted on a one-way clutch. Vanes on the stator multiply torque by redirecting fluid flow from the turbine back to the impeller. Like a fluid coupling, a torque converter can also utilize a split guide ring to reduce fluid flow turbulence. However, the guide ring is not considered a separate member.

The vanes used in each of the three elements of a torque converter are curved to increase the diversion angle of the fluid (figure 5-10). This also increases the force exerted by the fluid and improves the hydraulic advantage. The outlet side of the

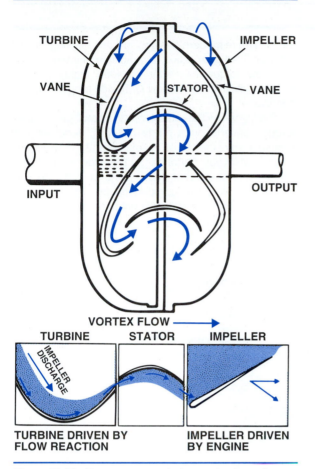

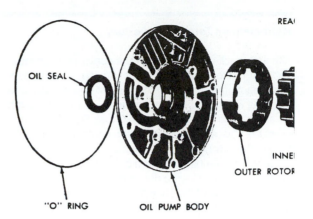

Figure 5-11. Vane curvature helps maintain optimum fluid flow.

impeller vanes accelerates the fluid as it leaves the impeller, in order to increase torque transfer to the turbine (figure 5-11). The inlet side of the turbine vanes absorb shock and limit power loss that occurs when flow between the impeller and turbine suddenly changes. The curve of the stator vanes is opposite to the curve of the impeller and turbine vanes (figure 5-11). Because the stator is located between the impeller and turbine, it adds to the original impeller flow and multiplies the force delivered to the turbine.

Early torque converters bolted together so they could be disassembled for service and repair (figure 5-12). Modern converters are single-piece, welded assemblies that cannot be disassembled or repaired easily. Although they can be rebuilt using specialized equipment, most shops simply replace welded converters as a unit if they fail. Some older torque converters also have

Figure 5-12. Nut-and-bolt construction used in early-model converters—modern converters are welded.

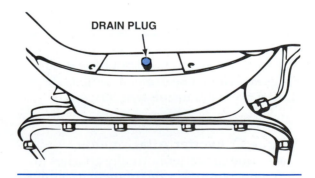

Figure 5-13. Torque converter drain plugs—once common, rarely seen today.

drain plugs to enable changing the fluid trapped in the converter when servicing the transmission (figure 5-13). Late-model

Multi-element Torque Converters

Although each element in a torque converter is an independent hydrodynamic member (driving, driven, reaction), each member may consist of more than one element. For example, the first automatic transmission on a domestic vehicle, the 1948 Buick Dynaflow transmission, had a torque converter containing five elements: the driving member consisted of two impellers, the reaction member consisted of two stators, and a single turbine served as the driven member.

The gearbox of the Dynaflow transmission had only a single forward speed instead of the two, three, or four found in more modern designs. In place of using several different fixed gear ratios, the multiple elements in the Dynaflow torque converter provided highly variable torque multiplication to allow for a wide range of driving conditions.

The Dynaflow transmission with its multiple-element torque converter was made possible, if not entirely practical, by the large-displacement, high-torque engines of its day. Although the Dynaflow worked well, it was very inefficient—both performance and fuel economy suffered in comparison to similar vehicles equipped with more conventional transmissions.

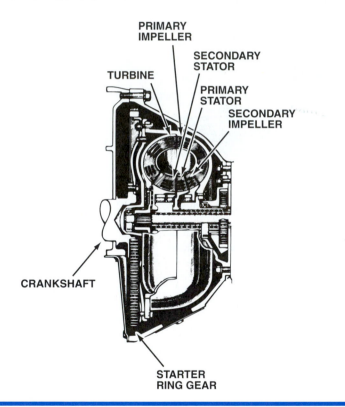

automotive converters do not have drain plugs and cannot be drained completely during normal transmission service.

Torque Converter Attachments

The torque converter normally attaches to the engine through a **flexplate** that mounts on the crankshaft flange of the engine (figure 5-14). The flexplate replaces the heavy flywheel used with a manual transmission. An important function of a flywheel is to smooth out engine pulsations and dampen vibrations. An automatic transmission does not require a conventional flywheel because the fluid in the torque converter provides enough mass to dampen engine vibrations. The flexplate compensates for any axial movement caused by wear or expansion of metal parts such as the transmission input and output shafts, and it allows for changes in endplay.

An external ring gear generally attaches to the outer rim of the flexplate. This ring gear engages the starter motor pinion gear to turn the engine during starting. On some older applications, such as the Ford C4 and Chrysler Torqueflite, the ring gear may be

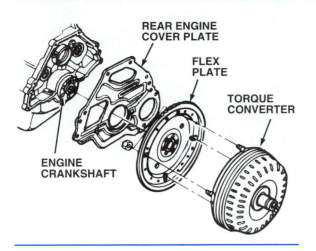

Figure 5-14. Flexplate mounting.

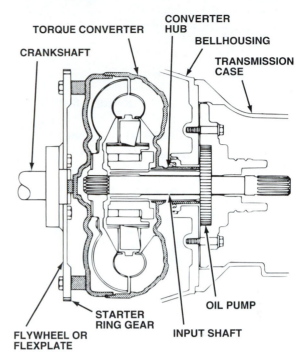

Figure 5-15. Torque converter hub directly drives oil pump on most rear-wheel drive transmissions.

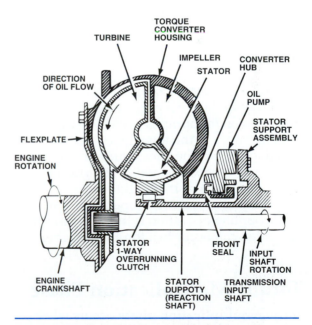

Figure 5-16. Transmission input shaft connects directly to the turbine through spines with an inline design.

welded to the outside of the torque converter cover.

There are several methods for driving the torque converter, but all arrangements mount the converter housing and impeller assembly to the flexplate so that it turns with engine rotation. Either an integral drive hub or a separate driveshaft connects the converter to the transmission oil pump. Both methods provide a link between the engine crankshaft and the transmission oil pump so that both rotate at the same speed and time. This ensures the pump will deliver fluid to the transmission whenever the engine turns. An integral hub is located on the converter housing and directly engages the pump (figure 5-15). Oil pump driveshafts generally pass through the converter inside a hollow input or transfer shaft and internally connect to the converter housing by splines.

Most rear-wheel drive (RWD) transmissions use an inline method to drive the converter and provide a direct mechanical connection between the turbine and the transmission input shaft. In a typical design, splines on the turbine connect it to the transmission input shaft and the stator hub mounts on a one-way overrunning clutch. The one-way clutch mounts on splines to a stationary extension of the oil pump called the stator support, or reaction shaft (figure 5-16). The converter drive hub at the rear of the torque converter housing passes over the stator support and through the front oil seal to drive the oil pump.

Many transaxles, and a few RWD transmissions, use an offset drive arrangement to conserve space. An offset drive design generally uses a drive chain to provide the

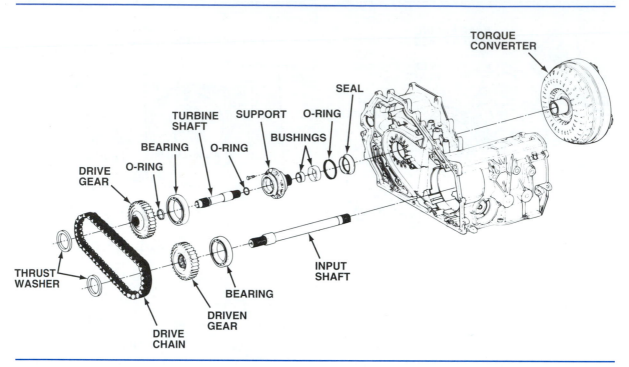

Figure 5-17. Turbine drives input shaft through a drive chain assembly on transaxles with an offset drive.

mechanical connection between the turbine and the input shaft (figure 5-17). The oil pump may be driven directly by the converter housing or by a separate driveshaft.

Torque Converter Operation

Fluid sent to the torque converter from the transmission oil pump is picked up by the rotating vanes of the impeller and transferred to the turbine vanes through the same rotary and vortex flow paths described for a fluid coupling. The major difference between torque converter operation and fluid coupling operation is that torque multiplication can occur in a torque converter.

Torque Multiplication Phase

Torque multiplication phase occurs when fluid leaving the turbine vanes strikes the concave, or front side, of the stator vanes. The stator vanes redirect this fluid so that it joins the fluid flow being delivered from the impeller to the next turbine vane (figure 5-18). The force of the fluid from the stator adds to the force of the fluid flowing from the impeller to increase the overall torque

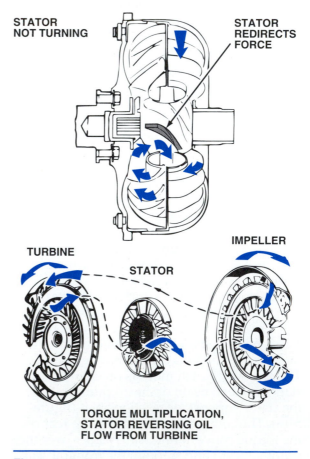

Figure 5-18. Torque multiplication.

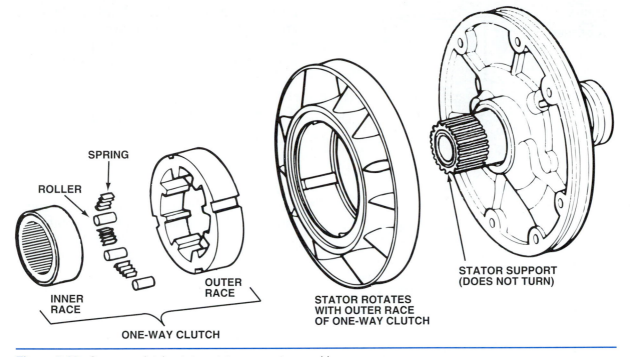

Figure 5-19. One-way clutch, stator, stator support assembly.

being transferred from the impeller to the turbine.

Torque multiplication occurs whenever the vortex flow makes a full cycle from impeller to turbine, then through the stator and back to the impeller. A torque converter multiplies torque in relation to the speed ratio. At low speed ratios the impeller is turning much faster than the turbine, so vortex flow is high and torque multiplication occurs. As turbine speed increases and approaches impeller speed, rotary flow increases, which reduces both vortex flow and torque multiplication. As the speed ratio approaches 90%, torque multiplication becomes minimal and a torque converter functions like a fluid coupling.

The stator redirects fluid flow because it remains stationary during the torque multiplication phase. The stator hub mounts on a one-way clutch, freewheeling in a clockwise direction, but locking when driven in a counterclockwise direction (figure 5-19). When fluid from the turbine strikes the concave face of the stator vanes, it tries to drive the stator counterclockwise. By locking the stator it can redirect the fluid back to the impeller.

Coupling Phase

When the speed ratio is 90% or more, fluid flow in the torque converter is mostly rotary flow and the angle of flow from turbine to stator increases. Fluid eventually strikes the convex, or back side, of the stator vanes rather than the concave (figure 5-20). As the force of fluid striking the back side becomes great enough to drive the stator clockwise, the one-way clutch overruns. With the clutch overrunning, the turbine, impeller, and stator all rotate in the same direction and at approximately the same speed. This is called the **coupling phase**. During this time, torque multiplication decreases and the torque converter operates like a fluid coupling.

The stator unlocks and freewheels once the angle of fluid flow changes enough to strike the opposite side of the stator vanes and rotate the stator clockwise. Should the stator remain locked, fluid can bounce off the vanes in a direction that opposes the fluid flow from impeller to turbine. Under these conditions, the torque converter would be working against itself, which would reduce efficiency.

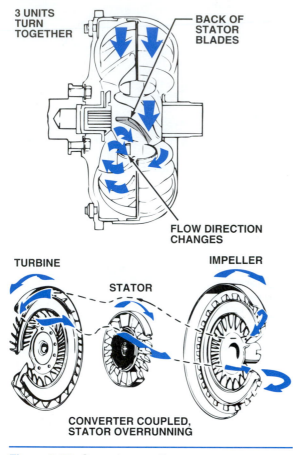

3 UNITS TURN TOGETHER

BACK OF STATOR BLADES

FLOW DIRECTION CHANGES

TURBINE

STATOR

IMPELLER

CONVERTER COUPLED, STATOR OVERRUNNING

Figure 5-20. Converter coupling.

Torque multiplication drops as the torque converter approaches the coupling phase because the stator no longer redirects fluid to increase the flow from impeller to turbine. When the torque converter reaches coupling speed, the turbine is traveling at nearly the same speed as the impeller, rotary flow is much greater than vortex flow, and the torque converter simply transmits torque like a fluid coupling.

Stall Speed

During converter stall, the impeller rotates but the turbine does not. This occurs just before the drive wheels of a vehicle begin to move. The greatest amount of stall occurs when the engine drives the impeller at the maximum speed possible without moving the turbine. The engine speed at which this occurs is called the torque converter **stall speed**. When the impeller rotates, but the turbine does not, the speed ratio is zero. This

is the lowest possible speed ratio and the greatest possible torque multiplication. Most modern torque converters multiply torque in the range of 2:1 to 2.5:1 at the stall speed.

Torque Converter Diameter

The outside diameter of a torque converter and the angle of its stator blades determine the stall speed of the converter. When both a small- and a large-diameter converter share the same stator blade angle and turn at the same speed, the smaller converter creates less centrifugal force to move the fluid inside. As a result, the small-diameter converter has a higher stall speed, multiplies torque at higher engine speeds, and will not couple until the engine reaches high speeds. In comparison, the large-diameter converter has a lower stall speed, multiplies torque at lower engine speeds, and couples at a lower engine speed.

Compare two converters of equal diameter with different stator blade angles turning at the same speed. One converter has a sharp or high-pitch stator blade angle while the other has a low stator blade angle. As the stator blade angle increases, the amount of fluid the blades can move decreases. As a result, torque converters with sharply angled stator blades have higher stall speeds, multiply torque at higher engine speeds, and do not couple until the engine reaches higher speeds. Torque converters with low-angled stator blades have lower stall speeds, multiply torque at lower engine speeds, and couple at somewhat lower engine speeds.

Vehicle manufacturers select torque converters to match the powertrain requirements and operating demands of each application. A vehicle with a large engine that produces a lot of torque at low rpm will often use a torque converter that couples at low speeds for greater fuel economy. Vehicles with smaller engines that produce less torque at low rpm will use a torque converter that allows the engine to operate higher in its torque curve, where more power is available. High-performance vehicles with automatic transmissions use small-diameter converters for the same reason.

Torque Converter Capacity

Another factor engineers consider when selecting a torque converter is the **torque converter capacity**. This aspect of the torque converter absorbs and transmits engine torque to the transmission without slipping. Any torque converter can only absorb a certain amount of engine torque. When that capacity is reached, the engine speed stabilizes at the stall speed and the torque converter slips. Because converter capacity affects engine speed, the engine and converter must be matched to obtain maximum efficiency.

Torque converter capacity limits engine speed as the load is placed on the impeller as it transmits torque to the turbine. The load is high when the vehicle first begins to move. As the vehicle gains momentum and turbine speed approaches impeller speed, the torque required to drive the impeller falls off and engine speed naturally rises. A high-capacity torque converter has a lower stall speed and can transmit engine torque with a minimum of slippage. High-capacity converters are efficient and provide good fuel economy at freeway speeds, but generally operate at higher speed ratios and provide less torque multiplication. A low-capacity torque converter has a higher stall speed and allows a greater amount of slip as it transmits engine torque. Low-capacity converters are generally less efficient at higher speeds, but operate well at low speed ratios and provide greater torque multiplication for better acceleration.

The engine and torque converter must be properly matched to get the best combination of acceleration and fuel economy. A converter whose capacity is too low for a given application will allow engine rpm to exceed the point of maximum torque output, reducing efficiency. A converter whose capacity is too high may prevent the engine from reaching a speed that produces maximum torque.

Variable-Pitch Stator

To gain the benefits of both high- and low-capacity torque converter designs, some manufacturers use torque converters with a variable-pitch stator. The variable-pitch sta-

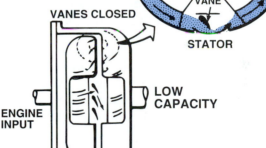

Figure 5-21. Variable-pitch stator operation.

tor has vanes that open or close to change the speed of the fluid flowing from the turbine to the impeller (figure 5-21). An electric solenoid activates a hydraulic piston built into the stator assembly to adjust the pitch of the blades.

Close the vanes of a variable-pitch stator and the fluid flow from the stator to the impeller increases. This high blade angle creates a low-capacity converter stage that allows engine rpm to increase for faster acceleration and extends the torque multiplication range to include higher speeds. Fluid speed drops when the vanes of a variable-pitch stator are at a low angle. This

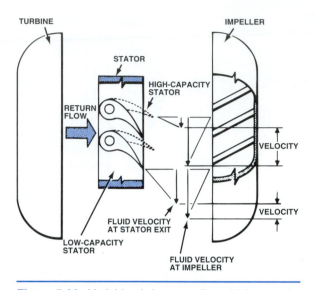

Figure 5-22. Variable-pitch stator allows high-capacity and low-capacity torque converter operation.

creates a high-capacity converter stage that allows the engine to couple more efficiently at lower speeds and provides better fuel economy (figure 5-22).

Buick was the first manufacturer to use a variable-pitch stator design, on the 1956 Dynaflow transmission. Over the next decade, several different variable-pitch stator designs appeared, but all were discontinued after a short production run. Eventually, variable-pitch designs were abandoned because they were both unreliable and fairly expensive to manufacture.

LOCKUP TORQUE CONVERTERS

Even the most efficient torque converters slip 3% to 6% during operation. This is because the fluid that transmits torque exhibits a type of slippage known as fluid shear. Fluid shear creates friction heat, but performs no work when the different layers of fluid slide past each other.

Eliminating torque converter slippage can improve fuel economy approximately 4% to 5% during freeway cruising. With the increased emphasis on fuel economy for late-model vehicles, this became an important goal for automotive engineers. An addi-

tional benefit to no slippage is a reduction of transmission operating temperature, which increases transmission life expectancy. Lockup torque converters reduce slippage by using a torque converter clutch (TCC) to lock the impeller to the turbine. Similar to a clutch for a manual transmission, a TCC uses a friction disc operated by a hydraulic piston to mechanically couple the turbine to the impeller. Engaging the clutch creates a mechanical connection between the engine and transmission, resulting in a direct drive ratio (1:1).

Some early automatic transmissions provided a direct mechanical lockup within the torque converter for high-gear operation. Both the 1949 Packard Ultramatic and 1950 Studebaker automatic transmissions had a TCC that locked the turbine to the impeller in high gear. However, early lockup converters were too expensive and unnecessary, considering the low fuel prices of the day. Consequently, both manufacturers discontinued them after a few years.

Chrysler revived the lockup torque converter in 1978 in response to demands for better fuel economy. Today, virtually all vehicles with automatic transmissions have a lockup torque converter. Early designs were strictly hydraulic or mechanical; most of today's vehicles regulate the operation of the TCC electronically.

Hydraulically Locking Torque Converters

Hydraulically locking torque converters use fluid pressure from the transmission hydraulic system to apply the TCC. Most modern torque converters are this type. When the clutch engages, the turbine and impeller lock and rotate together to function as a unit. A typical TCC consists of a large hydraulic piston located between the turbine and converter cover, which serves as a clutch plate. The clutch piston connects to the turbine, and the converter cover attaches to the impeller (figure 5-23A).

When the converter is unlocked, the fluid flowing from the impeller to the turbine, through the stator and back, provides the only connection between the engine

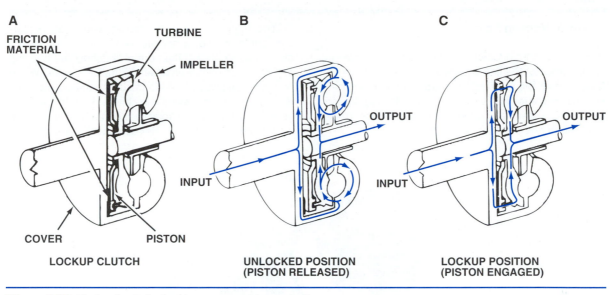

Figure 5-23. Hydraulically locked torque converter operation.

and transmission (figure 5-23B). During converter lockup, pressurized hydraulic fluid pushes the piston, along with the turbine, against the converter cover so there is no slippage between the turbine and impeller (figure 5-23C) Fluid flow plays no part in transmitting engine torque, as the converter cover, piston, and turbine mechanically connect the engine and transmission. Hydraulic pressure is maintained throughout lockup operation to keep the converter clutch components applied together tightly. Most transmissions redirect fluid pressure to the opposite side of the clutch piston to aid in converter clutch release.

Converter Clutch Control

The first hydraulic lockup converters were controlled entirely by hydraulic pressure and spool valves in the transmission valve body. Some later designs added simple electric switches and solenoids to control pressure to the converter clutch. Late-model hydraulic TCCs use an electronic control system to regulate the timing and application of the clutch.

Early hydraulic converter clutches will engage only in high gear because lockup in the lower gears reduces the torque multiplication needed for acceleration. Lockup may also be limited to specific vehicle speeds or operating conditions. For most vehicles,

lockup can occur at speeds over 25–30 mph (40–48 kph) after the transmission upshifts into high gear. Once lockup occurs, the clutch may disengage automatically during certain operating conditions, such as part- or full-throttle downshift. At these times, the increased acceleration requirements generally override the need for better fuel economy.

The more sophisticated electronic control systems of recent years regulate converter clutch application to meet the needs of a wide variety of speeds and operating conditions. These systems are capable of very precise control and can lock and unlock a converter clutch hundreds of times per minute to meet the vehicle demands of the moment. Some recent systems also allow partial lockup of the torque converter. Traditional lockup torque converters operate either locked or unlocked. Partial lockup converters allow a regulated amount of slippage at the clutch. This allows the converter to lockup smoothly, improving fuel economy and performance, without the drawback of shock to the driveline.

Lockup Converter Variations

Although all hydraulically locking torque converters operate similarly, there are minor variations in construction. Many of these design variations point out differences in the

Lockup Is Nothing New

When Chrysler introduced its lockup torque converter in 1978, it was not the first time this idea had been used. Back in 1949, the Packard Ultramatic transmission had a torque converter with a mechanical clutch that locked up for direct drive, and Studebaker automatics in the early 1950s had a similar lockup clutch.

The Packard Ultramatic transmission had a four-element torque converter with two turbines. The lockup clutch was located at the front of the converter housing and its driven plate was bolted to the first turbine. When hydraulic fluid was routed to the clutch housing, a movable driving plate locked the driven plate to the converter housing. This is exactly the same principle that was reintroduced by Chrysler almost 30 years later.

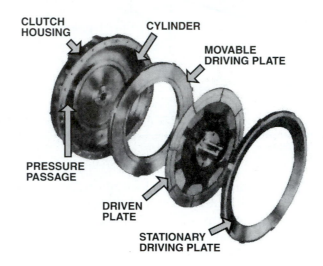

The Ultramatic clutch was controlled by applying governor and throttle pressure to opposite ends of a shift valve. Below 15 mph, the converter was always unlocked. Above 15 mph, governor pressure moved the shift valve to lock the clutch when throttle pressure dropped as the vehicle reached cruising speed. If the driver pressed hard on the accelerator for passing power, increased throttle pressure moved the shift valve against governor pressure to exhaust fluid from the clutch housing and unlock the converter.

way each manufacturer handles clutch damping and converter clutch apply.

Chrysler
Chrysler lines the inner surface of the converter cover with friction material on their lockup converters (figure 5-24). The clutch piston attaches to the outer edge of the turbine through a series of damping springs. The springs cushion initial clutch engagement and dampen the engine power pulses during lockup.

In low gear, hydraulic pressure on the front side of the piston pushes it away from the converter cover to keep the clutch unlocked (figure 5-25). Once the transmission shifts into high gear and the vehicle reaches minimum speed, pressure vents from the front chamber and mainline pressure applies to the back side of the piston, moving it for-

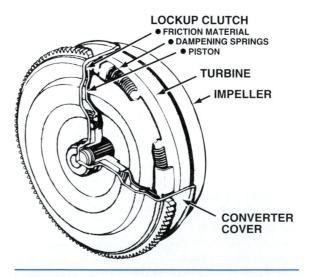

Figure 5-24. Chrysler lockup torque converter construction.

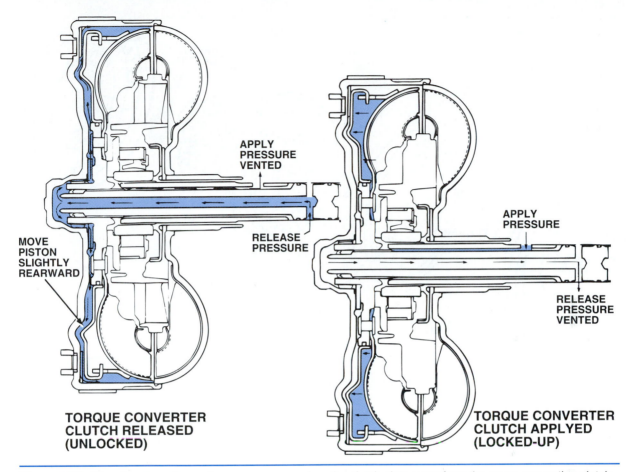

Figure 5-25. Chrysler converter—release pressure pushes the clutch plate away from the cover, preventing clutch engagement.

ward. This moves the piston into contact with the converter cover, and the friction material locks the turbine to the impeller. The clutch will disengage automatically during downshifts or when vehicle speed falls below the preset limit.

Early Chrysler lockup torque converters rely entirely on hydraulic pressures acting on spool valves in the transmission valve body to control lockup. In 1986, electric solenoid control was added to the basic hydraulic control system for some applications. Several years later, Chrysler introduced a transaxle with full electronic control. The most recent versions allow the TCC to operate under partial slip conditions. All current Chrysler systems feature full electronic control.

Ford
Ford hydraulic lockup torque converters operate similarly to the Chrysler design. The friction material is around the outer edge of the clutch piston, and splines connect the clutch piston to the turbine. To absorb shock and dampen engine power pulses, the Ford clutch piston uses a spring-type damper assembly built into the piston hub. Early Ford lockup converters were fully hydraulic. Some later clutches, such as that of the A4LD transmission, feature electronic solenoid control. These operate by hydraulic pressure and spool valves whose actions can be overridden by computer-controlled solenoids. In later applications, the clutch is controlled entirely by the electronic control system, with the most recent systems featuring a partial lockup.

General Motors
General Motors introduced its standard lockup torque converter on select 1980 models (figure 5-26). The clutch piston uses a band of friction material around the outer

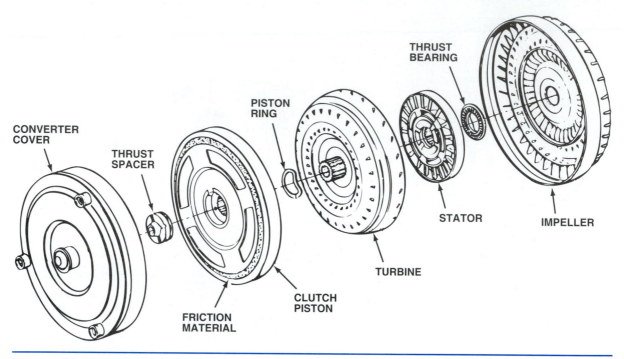

Figure 5-26. Typical GM hydraulic lockup converter.
General Motors Corporation, Service and Parts Operations

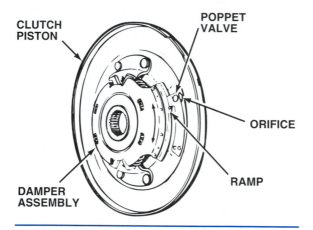

Figure 5-27. Built-in spring damper absorbs shock.
General Motors Corporation, Service and Parts
Operations

edge with several extra center blocks of friction material to support the piston evenly. There is no friction material inside the converter cover.

The clutch piston splines directly to the turbine and uses a spring-type torsional damper built into the back of the piston hub to dampen shock and vibration (figure 5-27). On certain models with diesel engines, the damper assembly includes a pair of poppet-

type pressure release valves. If engine braking becomes strong enough to rotate the damper assembly past a certain point, the valves open. This equalizes pressure on both sides of the piston, releasing the clutch and reducing the effect of engine braking.

A converter clutch solenoid controls lockup on early General Motors torque converters. On these models, the clutch operates only in high gear and simple electric switches control the solenoid. On later models, the electronic control system operates the solenoid and on some models the clutch applies in lower gears. Recent systems have full electronic control, and the latest of these feature a partial lockup torque converter.

Viscous Converter Clutch

In 1985, General Motors introduced a special type of hydraulic lockup converter on certain luxury vehicles: the **viscous converter clutch (VCC)**. The VCC is used on select Cadillac models with a 4T60E transaxle and offers maximum smoothness of power transmission.

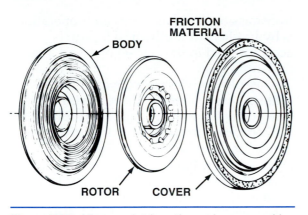

Figure 5-28. Viscous clutch — three-piece assembly. General Motors Corporation, Service and Parts Operations

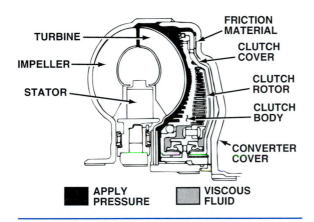

Figure 5-29. Silicone fluid allows small amount of slippage, in order to absorb shock. General Motors Corporation, Service and Parts Operations

The VCC piston assembly consists of a cover, body, and rotor. The cover and body seal together to contain the rotor (figure 5-28). The rotor is splined to the torque converter turbine. The rotor and body have a series of interlocking grooves, and the entire assembly is filled with a thick silicone fluid. The clutch friction material is on the face of the cover.

When the converter clutch engages, torque passes from the piston cover to the body, through the silicone fluid to the rotor, then to the turbine and transmission input shaft (figure 5-29). The silicone fluid itself allows a small amount of slippage between the body and rotor, in order to absorb the shock of engagement

and dampen engine vibration during lockup.

Technically, a VCC does not completely lock the converter, but the amount of slip that occurs is kept to a minimum by the silicone fluid. Typically, a VCC allows only about 40 rpm of slip at 60 mph (96 kph), which delivers excellent fuel economy and maximum smoothness.

Centrifugally Locking Torque Converters

Some torque converter designs do not rely on hydraulic pressure to lock the converter clutch. Instead, they actuate the TCC mechanically, or through a mixture of hydraulics and mechanics. Ford is the only domestic manufacturer to use mechanically locking torque converters. One popular design is the centrifugally locking unit used on the C5 transmission and the ATX transaxle.

Centrifugally locking torque converters connect the clutch disc to the turbine through a one-way clutch. A spring-type damper assembly built into the disc hub dampens engine pulses. The outer edge of the clutch disc supports a series of centrifugal clutch shoes that are held in place by return springs. Friction material lines the face of each clutch shoe.

As the vehicle accelerates and the turbine builds speed, centrifugal force pushes the clutch shoes outward toward the converter cover. When speed is great enough, the shoes contact the inside of the converter cover, locking the turbine to the impeller. When turbine speed drops below a certain level, the return springs retract the clutch shoes to unlock the converter.

When acceleration requires torque multiplication, or increased pulling power during lockup, the clutch shoes slip on the inside of the converter cover. This design also limits engine braking for maximum fuel economy, since the one-way clutch allows the turbine to overrun the impeller during coast or trailing throttle conditions. The centrifugally locking torque converter is simpler than hydraulically locking designs and will engage in any forward gear once the turbine speed rises above a preset limit. However, a centrifugally locking converter cannot be controlled as precisely as a hydraulically locking unit. In addition, both lockup speed and locking force can vary as the friction material on the clutch shoes wears. Finally, the greater amount of slippage that occurs with this type of lockup converter causes the release of more friction particles that can contaminate the transmission fluid.

Splitter-gear Torque Converter

Ford uses a splitter-gear torque converter on the ATX transaxle to increase fuel economy. A splitter-gear converter is similar to a hydraulic torque converter, with the exception that it contains a planetary gearset. This allows engine torque to be transmitted by a combination of hydraulic and mechanical means, depending on the gear selected. A simple planetary gearset replaces the piston and clutch assembly. The sun gear is splined to the turbine and planet carrier assembly, while the ring gear is splined to the converter cover. Two shafts split the power flow, the turbine shaft attaches to the sun gear, and the intermediate shaft connects to the carrier.

In first and reverse gears, engine torque transmission is 100% hydraulic, just as it is in a standard torque converter. In second gear, torque transmission is 38% hydraulic and 62% mechanical. In third gear, 7% of the torque transmits hydraulically, while 93% transfers by mechanical means. A spring-type damper assembly welded onto the converter cover absorbs engine vibration. The various torque splits available from a splitter-gear converter involve planetary gearset power flow, as well as the application of various clutches and bands in the transaxle that lock either the turbine shaft or intermediate shaft.

Split-Path Torque Converter

Ford uses the split-path torque converter, another mechanical variation, on the AOD

transmission. The basic converter operation is hydraulic, but mechanical lockup is accomplished in the gearset by using a second input shaft.

The split-path torque converter has two different input shafts to drive the transmission gears. A hollow turbine shaft splines to the converter turbine and to the forward clutch. Inside this shaft is a direct drive shaft, which splines to both the converter cover and the direct clutch hub. The turbine shaft is driven hydraulically at turbine speed, and the direct drive shaft is driven mechanically at engine speed. In first and second gears, torque input is entirely hydraulic. In third gear, torque is split between the two shafts so that 40% transmits hydraulically and 60% transmits mechanically. In fourth gear, torque transmission is completely mechanical, and the damper assembly in the converter cover absorbs shock and engine vibrations.

SUMMARY

Fluid couplings and torque converters transmit torque, as well as coupling and uncoupling the engine and transmission. A torque converter can multiply torque, whereas a fluid coupling cannot. Fluid couplings and torque converters use vane turbines and impellers to develop fluid flow and transfer engine torque. Fluid moves through a fluid coupling or converter in rotary and vortex flow paths. Rotary flow carries engine-rotating torque; vortex flow transfers that torque from the impeller to the turbine. The combined rotary and vortex flow creates a resultant force that drives the turbine.

Speed ratio is a comparison of impeller and turbine speeds expressed as a percentage and is a measure of coupling efficiency. At low speed ratios, vortex flow is high, rotary flow is low, and coupling efficiency is low. At higher speed ratios, vortex flow is low, rotary flow is high, and coupling efficiency is greater. Torque converters are more efficient than fluid couplings at lower speed ratios because they can multiply engine torque. Torque is multiplied by installing a stator, a third element with vanes installed between the turbine and impeller. Torque multiplication occurs at low speed ratios when vortex flow is high and fluid leaving the turbine strikes the front sides of the stator vanes. This action redirects the fluid so it joins the flow being delivered from the impeller to the turbine.

Both fluid couplings and torque converters are most efficient when fully coupled. Coupling occurs as the speed ratio approaches 90% and turbine speed is close to impeller speed. At this point, rotary flow is high and fluid leaving the turbine strikes the back sides of the stator vanes. This causes the stator one-way clutch to overrun, allowing the stator to rotate with the impeller and turbine. Torque multiplication then ceases.

The stall speed of a torque converter is the maximum speed at which the impeller can be driven without turning the turbine. The stall speed is also the speed at which maximum torque multiplication occurs. A small diameter torque converter has a higher stall speed than a large diameter converter. Torque converter capacity is the ability of a converter to transmit engine torque without slipping. High-capacity converters have low stall speeds and transmit torque with minimal slippage, but they operate at higher speed ratios and provide less torque multiplication. Low-capacity converters have high stall speeds and allow greater slippage, but they operate at lower speed ratios and provide greater torque multiplication. A variable-pitch stator allows a converter to provide some of the benefits of both high- and low-capacity designs.

Lockup torque converters connect the turbine to the impeller mechanically to eliminate slippage and improve fuel economy. Hydraulically locking torque converters use fluid pressure to apply a clutch piston splined to the turbine against the inside of the converter cover. Centrifugally locking converters use centrifugal force to move a set of clutch shoes attached to a clutch disc outward against the inside of the converter cover. For direct mechanical connections, a damper assembly or viscous coupling is required to smooth clutch engagement and absorb engine power pulses during lockup.

Most hydraulically locking torque converters operate only under certain vehicle speed and operating conditions. Early systems engage only in high gear, while later systems can engage in several gears. Clutch application can be controlled solely by mechanical or hydraulic means, or by a combination of hydraulic, electrical, and electronic components. Centrifugally locking torque converters are simple; they require no external controls and can apply in any forward gear whenever turbine speed reaches a preset point.

Splitter-gear torque converters contain a planetary gearset and damper assembly that allow engine torque to be transmitted by a combination of hydraulic and mechanical means, depending on the gear selected. Split-path torque converters use two input shafts to split the torque input hydraulically and mechanically.

Review Questions

Choose the single most correct answer. Compare your answers to the correct answers on page 213.

1. Technician A says the impeller is attached to the engine and turns as the engine rotates.
   Technician B says the turbine is attached to the engine and turns as the engine rotates.
   Who is right?
   a. A only
   b. B only
   c. Both A and B
   d. Neither A nor B

2. Technician A says the turbine provides torque input to the transmission gearset through the input shaft.
   Technician B says the impeller is the driving member and the turbine is the driven member.
   Who is right?
   a. A only
   b. B only
   c. Both A and B
   d. Neither A nor B

3. Technician A says the impeller vanes of a fluid coupling pick up fluid and force it inward toward the turbine.
   Technician B says the impeller fluid that strikes the turbine vanes causes the turbine to turn in the opposite direction of the impeller.
   Who is right?
   a. A only
   b. B only
   c. Both A and B
   d. Neither A nor B

4. Technician A says the fluid flow in a fluid coupling travels in two flow paths called the rotary and vortex flow.
   Technician B says the rotary and vortex flow in a fluid coupling occur at the same time.
   Who is right?
   a. A only
   b. B only
   c. Both A and B
   d. Neither A nor B

5. Technician A says rotary flow is in the same direction as impeller rotation and carries engine torque.
   Technician B says the vortex flow is at a right angle to the rotary flow and transfers engine torque to the turbine.
   Who is right?
   a. A only
   b. B only
   c. Both A and B
   d. Neither A nor B

6. The combination of rotary and vortex flow produces a
   a. Torpid force
   b. Multiplication force
   c. Coupling force
   d. Resultant force

7. Technician A says the split guide ring is used to limit fluid turbulence.
   Technician B says turbulence occurs when the impeller and turbine turn at the same speed.
   Who is right?
   a. A only
   b. B only
   c. Both A and B
   d. Neither A nor B

8. Technician A says that speed ratio is a measure of coupling efficiency.
   Technician B says speed ratio is calculated by dividing the speed of the turbine rotation by the speed of the impeller rotation.
   Who is right?
   a. A only
   b. B only
   c. Both A and B
   d. Neither A nor B

9. Technician A says the disadvantage of a fluid coupling is that it is most efficient at low speed ratios.
   Technician B says the disadvantage of a fluid coupling is that it cannot provide torque multiplication.
   Who is right?
   a. A only
   b. B only
   c. Both A and B
   d. Neither A nor B

10. Technician A says that at low speed ratios there is more vortex flow than rotary flow.
    Technician B says that at high speed ratios there is more vortex flow than rotary flow.
    Who is right?
    a. A only
    b. B only
    c. Both A and B
    d. Neither A nor B

11. Technician A says the vanes in a torque converter are straight rather than curved like those in a fluid coupling.
    Technician B says a torque converter has no split guide ring because there is no turbulence in a torque converter.
    Who is right?
    a. A only
    b. B only
    c. Both A and B
    d. Neither A nor B

12. Torque converters use a stator as a
    a. Drive member
    b. Reaction member
    c. Driven member
    d. Pump regulator

13. Technician A says the vanes in each element of a torque converter are curved to increase mechanical advantage.
    Technician B says the stator vanes curve in the same direction as the turbine and impeller vanes.
    Who is right?
    a. A only
    b. B only
    c. Both A and B
    d. Neither A nor B

14. Technician A says most torque converters no longer use drain plugs and are replaced as a unit if they fail.
    Technician B says automatic transmissions do not require a flywheel because the starter ring gear is attached to the outside of the torque converter.
    Who is right?
    a. A only
    b. B only
    c. Both A and B
    d. Neither A nor B

15. Which of the following is *not* a typical connection for a torque converter and automatic transmission?
    a. The turbine is splined to the input shaft.
    b. The torque converter hub drives the oil pump.
    c. The impeller is splined to the reaction shaft.
    d. The stator one-way clutch is mounted on an extension of the oil pump.

16. Technician A says the torque multiplication phase can occur when the stator one-way clutch begins to freewheel.
    Technician B says the torque multiplication phase can occur when the stator one-way clutch locks up.
    Who is right?
    a. A only
    b. B only
    c. Both A and B
    d. Neither A nor B

17. Technician A says the coupling phase can occur when the stator one-way clutch begins to freewheel.
    Technician B says the coupling phase can occur when the stator one-way clutch locks up.
    Who is right?
    a. A only
    b. B only
    c. Both A and B
    d. Neither A nor B

18. Technician A says converter stall occurs when the turbine rotates but the impeller does not.
    Technician B says maximum torque multiplication occurs at the converter stall speed.
    Who is right?
    a. A only
    b. B only
    c. Both A and B
    d. Neither A nor B

19. Technician A says that large-diameter torque converters have high stall speeds.
    Technician B says there is no torque multiplication during the converter coupling phase.
    Who is right?
    a. A only
    b. B only
    c. Both A and B
    d. Neither A nor B

20. Technician A says a low-capacity torque converter has a low stall speed.
    Technician B says a high-capacity torque converter has a high stall speed.
    Who is right?
    a. A only
    b. B only
    c. Both A and B
    d. Neither A nor B

6

Apply Devices

In previous chapters of this *Classroom Manual* it was explained how a planetary gearset produces an output drive when the transmission is holding one member of the gearset while driving a second member. The **apply devices** are the mechanical assemblies that provide these holding and driving forces. Automatic transmissions typically use transmission bands, multiple-disc clutches, and one-way clutches as apply devices.

Transmission bands, along with the servos that activate them, are holding devices. Although bands always provide a holding force, they cannot provide a driving force. A servo is a device that uses hydraulic pressure acting on a piston to tighten and apply a transmission band. The planetary gearset member held by the band is known as a reaction member.

A clutch piston hydraulically applies multiple-disc clutches. Multiple-disc clutches, or clutch packs, can either be holding or driving devices. Depending on transmission design, the clutch may either hold a reaction member or apply an input drive to the gearset.

Most automatic transmissions also use a one-way clutch, also referred to as an overrunning clutch. A one-way clutch is a mechanical device that locks up in one direction to prevent a gearset member from rotating so that it functions as a reaction member, but unlocks and overruns in the opposite direction to allow free rotation. A one-way clutch is considered an apply device, even though it is not hydraulically operated.

This chapter examines the general design and operation of transmission bands, servos, multiple-disc clutches, and one-way clutches. It also discusses the hydraulic system components associated with the operation of these devices.

TRANSMISSION BANDS

A **transmission band** stops and holds one planetary gearset member so that another

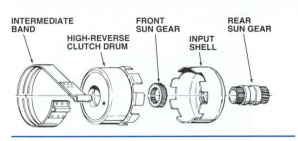

Figure 6-1. Gearset members held stationary when band applies.

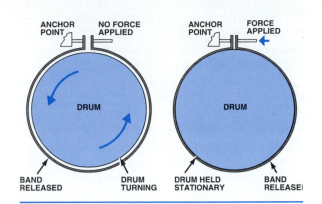

Figure 6-2. Band tightens around drum to prevent rotation.

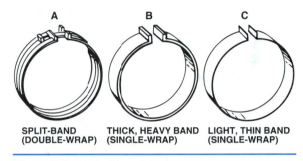

Figure 6-3. Typical band designs.

member can react against the held member and develop output motion. The reaction member has a control surface for the band to ride on known as a drum (figure 6-1). The band provides holding force around the outside of the drum, closing tightly to keep it from turning. A transmission band is a holding device and is not capable of driving any member of the planetary gearset.

The inner surface of the band that contacts the drum is lined with special friction material that adjusts the **coefficient of friction** between the band and drum to provide the proper amount of slip during application and release. Friction material composition depends on band usage and design. The most commonly used friction materials are paper, asbestos, and semi-metallic particles that bond to the band with a special heat-resistant adhesive. Often, the band lining is grooved for lubrication purposes and heat dissipation.

At its simplest, the band wraps around the drum, with one end anchored to the case and the other end connected to a hydraulic actuator called a servo. Force is applied to the band by hydraulic pressure working against the servo piston. As pressure applies, the band contracts tightly around the rotating drum and stops it through the frictional force that develops between the band and drum (figure 6-2). How much frictional force develops depends upon the length and width of the band, apply pressure of the servo, surface area of the drum, and amount of mechanical force applied to the end of the band.

Band Designs

Transmission bands vary in size and construction depending on the amount of torque they handle (figure 6-3). Transmission bands are made of cast iron or steel with friction material lining the inside surface. Transmission design and component size dictate the type of band used. Bands fall into one of the following two categories:

- Single-wrap
- Double-wrap

The single-wrap band is a simple one-piece design, while the double-wrap band is a split band with overlapping ends. Bands may also be classified as either flexible or fixed depending on how well they hold their shape when they are off of the drum.

A transmission band can be positioned to allow band apply force to work with or against the direction of drum rotation. If force applies in the direction of rotation, the band is self-energizing because drum rotation aids in tightening the band. Drum movement adds to the apply force so less hydraulic pressure is required at the servo.

The double-wrapped band is better suited for self-energizing action and conforms better to the circular shape of a drum than the single-wrap band (figure 6-3A). Also, the double-wrap band provides more holding force than the single-wrap band for a given apply pressure. As a result, the double-wrap band provides smoother shifts. However, the single-wrap transmission bands are less expensive to produce than double-wrap bands and work well in many applications. A large, heavy, and rigid single-wrap band may be used when a considerable amount of force is needed to hold a gearset member (figure 6-3B). However, a thinner, lighter version of the single-wrap band is more common (figure 6-3C).

Band design allows some slippage during application, which prevents the gearset members from stopping too abruptly. A sudden stop would cause a harsh shift and could possibly damage the transmission. On the other hand, too much slippage would cause a band to burn from the heat of apply friction, which would cause the band lining to become glazed and useless.

Transmission band slippage increases as the clearance between the band and drum increases due to normal wear of the friction lining. Too much band-to-drum clearance can also affect transmission shift timing, and some applications require periodic adjustments to maintain proper clearance. Many older automatic transmissions require a manual band adjustment as part of the normal service procedure. However, newer transmissions adjust band clearance automatically and do not require periodic service.

HYDRAULIC SERVOS

A hydraulically operated piston that travels inside a machined cylinder bore applies the transmission band. This piston-and-cylinder assembly is known as a servo (figure 6-4). A piston return spring normally holds the servo piston in its unapplied position. To apply the band, hydraulic fluid under pres-

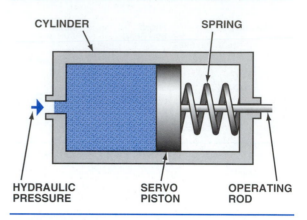

Figure 6-4. Servo—hydraulic piston-and-cylinder assembly.

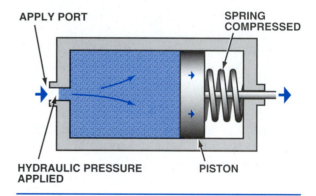

Figure 6-5. Hydraulic pressure moves piston to apply the band.

sure enters the servo cylinder and acts on the piston. The piston begins moving once hydraulic pressure overcomes spring force. A mechanical rod and linkage attaches to the piston and connects it to the band. As the piston moves, the linkage applies the band by tightening it around the drum.

Several different servo designs control the application and release of transmission bands. In the simplest design, the servo applies the band when hydraulic pressure against the piston forces the servo operating rod toward the band (figure 6-5). The band releases when hydraulic pressure to the apply port is cut off or exhausted. As hydraulic pressure drops, the return spring on the opposite side of the piston returns the piston to its unapplied position (figure 6-6). A disadvantage of this simple design is that spring force alone may not provide enough release clearance. Too little clearance can allow the friction material to contact the

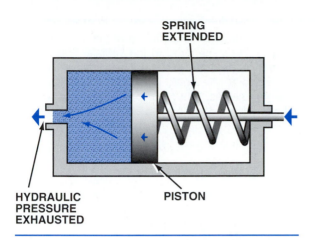

Figure 6-6. Spring force returns piston, releasing the band.

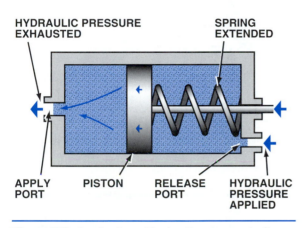

Figure 6-7. Application of hydraulic pressure to the spring side assists piston return and band release.

drum and drag when the band is not applied. This drag will generate friction heat, which can ruin the band and overheat the transmission fluid.

A combination of spring force and hydraulic pressure solves this release clearance problem (figure 6-7). Once hydraulic pressure on the servo apply side of the piston exhausts, pressure is routed to the release side of the piston. This release pressure works with spring force to retract the piston, linkage, and band. These designs quickly move the piston back to its unapplied position, ensuring the transmission band fully releases and has sufficient clearance. To eliminate any possibility of the band dragging, release pressure is maintained until the next band application.

Servo Force

The servo piston area is relatively large, which allows it to use mainline pressure to develop a large amount of apply force. This force is necessary to hold the band tightly enough around the drum to stop it quickly and keep it from slipping. Different operating conditions may require the band to stop a drum faster or slower to regulate shift timing, or hold the drum tighter against a greater torque load. Servos use varying hydraulic pressures to adjust the apply force as required.

Consider a servo piston with a surface area of 3 in^2 (1935 mm^2) operating in a hydraulic circuit where pressure ranges from 50 psi to 100 psi (345 kPa to 690 kPa). If the pressure is 50 psi (345 kPa), the force applied by the piston to the operating rod equals the hydraulic fluid pressure times the area of the piston, which equals 150 psi (1034 kPa). This amount of force could stop and hold a drum with a fairly light torque input, or with little resistance against the output unit. However, a transmission operating under a greater load would need a greater force. Servos can do so because the apply pressure increases along with an increase in engine load. If hydraulic apply pressure rises to 100 psi (690 kPa), the servo will develop 300 psi (2069 kPa) of apply force. This doubles the force with which the band tightens around the drum.

Servo Linkages

Servo **rods** and **struts** transfer the servo apply force to the transmission band. Rods are round metal bars and struts are flat metal plates. These may be used at either, or both, ends of the band. Linkages connect the band to the servo or an anchor (figure 6-8).

Rods and struts may be incorporated into three operating linkage configurations. The servo linkage types are as follows:

- Straight
- Lever
- Cantilever

Straight linkage uses a rod or strut to transfer force from the servo piston

Contracting-Band Brakes

The automatic transmission band that operates planetary gearset members was developed from an external contracting-band wheel brake design found on early vehicles. In that design, a flexible metal band lined with friction material wrapped around the outside of a brake drum attached to the wheel. The center of the band was anchored to the vehicle chassis and the free ends were joined by a cantilever linkage connected to the brake pedal through a series of rods and cables. When the pedal was applied, the linkage clamped the band around the drum to slow the vehicle.

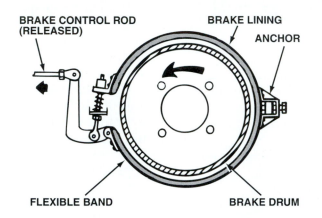

External contracting-band brakes were used for some years, but wore quickly because the lining was exposed to the elements. They could also drag or lockup if hard use caused the brake drum to overheat and expand. As vehicles got heavier and faster, internal expanding-shoe brakes, and later disc brakes, replaced external contracting-band brakes. However, even in recent times, contracting-band brakes have been used as parking brakes on the driveshafts of some Chrysler cars and many light trucks.

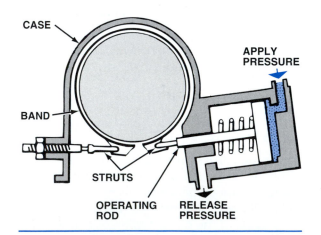

Figure 6-8. Rods and struts—vital parts of servo linkage.

directly to the free end of the band (figure 6-9). Bands may use straight linkage when the transmission design allows it to act directly on the band. A straight linkage design can be used only where the servo can be made large enough to hold a band when maximum torque is applied to the drum. Most older transmissions use this design.

A lever linkage is used when the servo location prevents it from acting directly on the band. This type of linkage redirects the inline force of the servo through a lever to the rod or strut that acts on the end of the band (figure 6-10). A lever linkage can also increase the hydraulic apply force if the lever arm is longer on the servo side of the pivot pin (fulcrum) than on the rod or strut side. This allows the lever to provide a mechanical advantage and multiply the force applied to the band.

A **cantilever** linkage uses a lever that acts on both ends of a band at once (figure 6-11). In this design, neither end of the band is anchored to the case. As the servo piston applies force, the piston-operating rod pivots the lever to apply force to one end of the band through a rod or strut. At the same time, the cantilever pulls the other end of

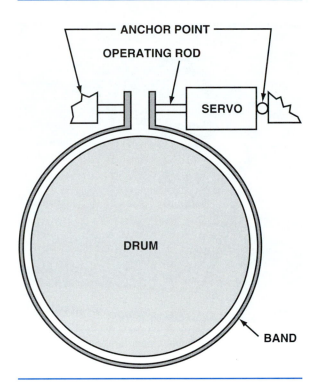

Figure 6-9. Straight linkage design.

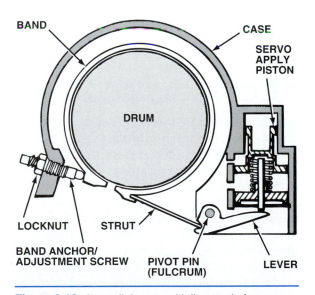

Figure 6-10. Lever linkage multiplies apply force.

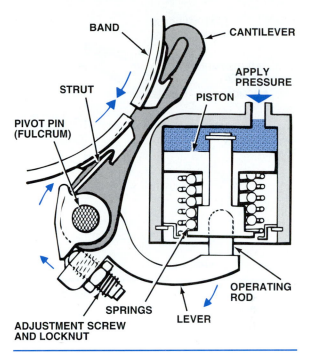

Figure 6-11. Cantilever linkage.

centering and contracts more evenly around the drum.

Servo Linkage Adjustment

Straight and lever linkage arrangements may require manual band adjustment to maintain clearance between the band and drum. Clearance is generally set using an adjustment screw that doubles as the fixed anchor for the band. On some applications, the adjustment screw passes through the transmission case where it is accessible from the outside (figure 6-12). On other applications the adjustment screw is internal and you remove the oil pan to access it. Adjustments are made by turning the screw and then securing the adjustment with a locknut. This straightforward design makes band adjustment a relatively simple job.

Some cantilever linkages also require a manual adjustment. With a cantilever design the screw and locknut are inside the transmission case on the linkage itself (figure 6-11). The oil pan must be removed to perform the band adjustment. Adjustment is usually scheduled to coincide with regular fluid service intervals.

the band toward the pivot pin. These two actions pull the band ends together to tighten the band around the drum and increase the band apply force through mechanical advantage. Cantilever designs also reduce band wear and smooth out band applications because apply action is self-

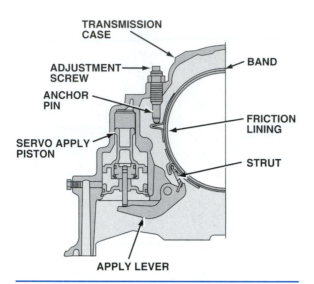

Figure 6-12. The fixed-band anchor is also an adjustment screw.

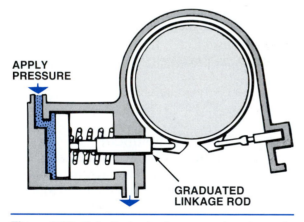

Figure 6-13. Selectively sized servo apply rods used to adjust band clearance.

Many late-model transmissions use a graduated servo rod rather than an adjustment screw to control band clearance (figure 6-13). Piston travel is measured using a depth gauge or special transmission tool (figure 6-14). Proper clearance is established by selecting the correct size servo rod. Servo rods are calibrated to allow the proper amount of piston travel and supply a specific amount of force. Selective servo rods usually do not require periodic maintenance. However, when overhauling the transmission or replacing the band measure piston travel, select the correct rod to obtain proper clearance.

Figure 6-14. Piston travel measurement.

Note: A description of tools and specific band adjustment procedures are outlined in Chapter 3 of the *Shop Manual* "Transmission Disassembly, Cleaning, and Inspection."

ACCUMULATORS

An automatic transmission uses one or more accumulators in the hydraulic system as a type of shock absorber. Accumulators cushion the hydraulic application of servos and clutches and are necessary because of pressure surges. Surges occur naturally as hydraulic fluid accelerates through the system, or when fluid flow rapidly changes direction. Rapid surges may cause an apply device to shudder, jerk, or engage harshly leading to rough shifts and eventual damage to the transmission.

An accumulator cushions, or dampens, hydraulic pressure surges by temporarily diverting part of the fluid flow in a hydraulic circuit into a parallel circuit or chamber. The diversion allows pressure in the main apply circuit to increase gradually and provides a smooth engagement of the band or clutch. Accumulators fit into two classifications: piston type or valve type.

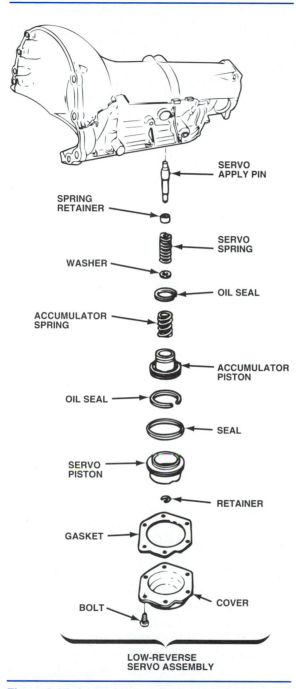

Figure 6-15. Integral accumulator combined with a servo in a single bore.

Piston-type accumulators look and function much like servo pistons. In fact, some piston-type accumulators share a bore with one of the transmission servos. This common bore design is known as an integral accumulator (figure 6-15). Additionally, piston accumulators that install in a dedicated bore in the transmission case are known as independent accumulators (figure 6-16).

Valve-type accumulators use a spring-loaded spool valve to absorb hydraulic surges. Similar in function to a piston accumulator, the valve-type accumulator temporarily diverts or delays a portion of the hydraulic flow that applies a servo or clutch. These accumulators are located in the transmission valve body.

Independent Piston-Type Accumulators

A simple hydraulic circuit for an apply device that uses an independent piston-type accumulator is shown in figure 6-17. When the shift valve opens to apply pressure to the intermediate servo, part of the fluid diverts to the accumulator. The fluid pressure acts at the same time on both the servo piston and accumulator piston. This causes pressure in the apply circuit to increase more gradually than it would if it were acting only on one piston. The accumulator looks and works like the servo it cushions, except there is no linkage connecting the piston to an apply device.

As hydraulic pressure enters both circuits, the accumulator piston offers much less resistance than the servo piston because it represents a much lighter load. As a result, the accumulator piston moves first and absorbs any surges as the fluid fills the accumulator cylinder. Once the accumulator piston reaches the end of its travel, cushioning is complete and pressure begins to build in the servo cylinder. This pressure acts on the servo piston to apply the intermediate band.

The cushioning action of the accumulator can be modified under certain driving conditions by applying an auxiliary pressure to the spring side of the accumulator piston. Auxiliary hydraulic pressure adds to the spring force acting on the piston, which allows the accumulator to adjust the cushioning to meet the demands of different operating conditions. This type of accumulator is found in Chrysler Torqueflite transmissions and some General Motors transmissions, such as the Hydramatic 4L80-E.

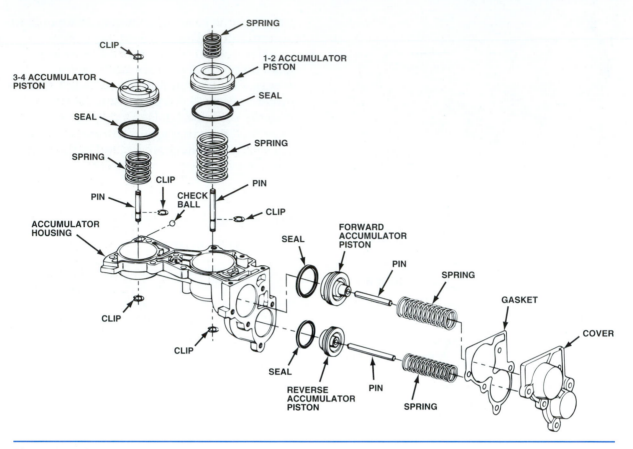

Figure 6-16. Independent accumulator installs in a dedicated bore.

Integral Piston-Type Accumulators

An integral piston-type accumulator installs in the same bore as a servo piston. In these applications, the accumulator piston is usually part of the apply circuit for a servo other than the one with which it is combined. In the hydraulic circuit shown in figure 6-18, the accumulator piston for the intermediate clutch shares the same bore as the servo piston for the low-reverse band.

When the low-reverse band and the intermediate clutch are both released, accumulator pressure applies to the top-side of the accumulator piston (figure 6-18A). This bottoms the accumulator piston inside the hollow servo piston while holding the servo in the released position.

As the intermediate clutch applies, part of the fluid from that circuit is routed into the accumulator through an internal passage in the accumulator piston (figure 6-18B). The fluid then enters the chamber between the accumulator piston and servo pistons, and forces the accumulator piston to the top of its bore against spring pressure and accumulator pressure. Just as with an independent accumulator, this cushions the pressure increase during intermediate clutch application.

While the accumulator is in operation, intermediate clutch pressure is applied to the top of the low-reverse servo piston. This pressure continues to hold the servo in the released position. Several Hydra-matic transmissions use integral piston-type accumulators.

Valve-Type Accumulators

A valve-type accumulator provides basically the same cushioning effect as a piston-type accumulator. These valves often work together with a restricting orifice to regulate

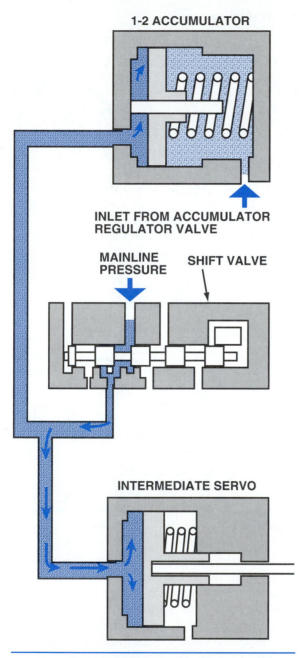

1-2 ACCUMULATOR

INLET FROM ACCUMULATOR REGULATOR VALVE

MAINLINE PRESSURE   **SHIFT VALVE**

INTERMEDIATE SERVO

Figure 6-17. Independent piston-type accumulator cushions intermediate servo application.

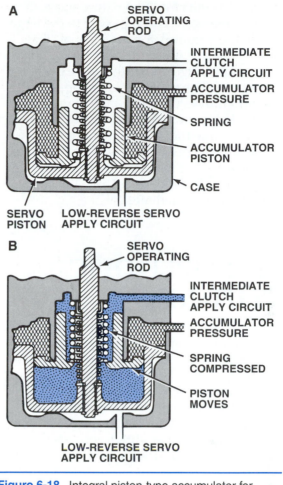

A

SERVO OPERATING ROD
INTERMEDIATE CLUTCH APPLY CIRCUIT
ACCUMULATOR PRESSURE
SPRING
ACCUMULATOR PISTON
CASE
SERVO PISTON
LOW-REVERSE SERVO APPLY CIRCUIT

B

SERVO OPERATING ROD
INTERMEDIATE CLUTCH APPLY CIRCUIT
ACCUMULATOR PRESSURE
SPRING COMPRESSED
PISTON MOVES
LOW-REVERSE SERVO APPLY CIRCUIT

Figure 6-18. Integral piston-type accumulator for intermediate clutch.

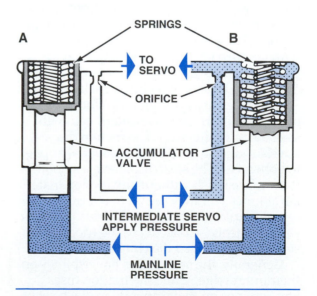

SPRINGS
A   **B**
TO SERVO
ORIFICE
ACCUMULATOR VALVE
INTERMEDIATE SERVO APPLY PRESSURE
MAINLINE PRESSURE

Figure 6-19. Valve-type accumulator.

pressure build-up. Before the servo apply circuit opens, there is no pressure in the circuit and the mainline pressure acting on the small end of the valve spool overcomes spring force to hold the valve bottomed in the bore (figure 6-19A).

As intermediate servo pressure enters the apply circuit, it passes through an orifice that delays pressure build-up. The fluid in the circuit splits into two paths: one path leads to the servo and the other to the large end of the accumulator valve spool. The combination of fluid pressure and spring force on the large end of the valve overcomes mainline pressure at the opposite end and moves the valve in its bore (figure 6-19B). Valve movement creates an additional volume that allows more fluid flow. The result is a pressure drop that combines with a delay in pressure build-up caused by the restricting orifice to cushion the application of the intermediate servo.

MULTIPLE-DISC CLUTCHES

Like a transmission band, a multiple-disc hydraulic clutch is a type of apply device. However, multiple-disc clutches have some advantages over bands. Clutches have more friction area so they can develop more force and handle more torque than a band. Also, a multiple-disc clutch is self-adjusting.

The **multiple-disc clutch** consists of plates, a piston, a drum, and a snapring (figure 6-20). The piston returns to an unapplied position via a return spring assembly. Some clutches use only a single return spring, while others may use several. Some transmissions use a special wave-type spring to return the piston and cushion clutch applications. These springs are kept in position with a return spring retainer and held in place by a snapring. The entire assembly is commonly known as a **clutch pack**.

The plates of a multiple-disc clutch assembly consist of friction discs alternated with steel discs (figure 6-21). The friction discs have a rough surface friction material applied to both faces. The steel discs have a smooth, flat surface finish without any friction material; at times you may see them referred to as separator plates, apply plates, drive plates, or simply "steels." Collectively, the friction and steel discs are called the **clutch plates**.

Generally, the steel plates have splines on their outer edge, while the friction discs have splines on their inner edge. Each set of splines engages matching splines on a shaft, drum, planetary gearset member, or the

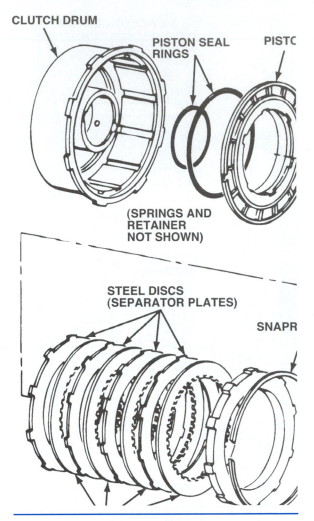

Figure 6-20. Multiple-disc clutch assembly.

transmission case. When the clutch applies, hydraulic pressure acting on the piston squeezes the two sets of plates together to mechanically connect the two components that engage the splines of the discs.

The piston compresses the clutch plates against a thicker reaction plate known as the **pressure plate**. Pressure plates may be used at one or both ends of the clutch pack and are available in selective sizes for adjusting clutch pack clearance. The pressure plate and clutch assembly components fit into either a **clutch drum** or machined bore in the transmission case. Snaprings retain all the clutch assembly components and are available in selective sizes for adjusting clearance (figure 6-22). Although a multiple-disc clutch is an apply device similar to a transmission band, it differs from a band because it can be used to drive members of

Figure 6-21. Friction and steel discs placed alternately in a multiple-disc clutch assembly.

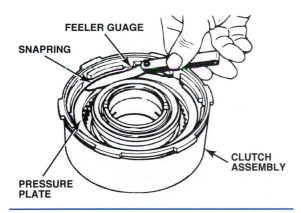

Figure 6-22. Selective pressure plate or selective snapring is used to adjust assembled clearance.

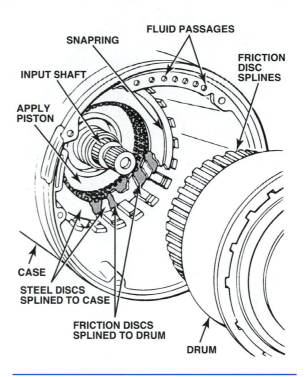

Figure 6-23. Holding clutch—one set of discs engages splines on the case, the other set engages splines on the drum.

planetary gearsets as well as hold them. There are two types of multiple-disc clutches, as follows:

- Holding
- Driving

Holding Clutches

An example of a holding clutch is shown in figure 6-23. In this arrangement, splines on the inner edge of the friction discs engage matching splines on the outside of the clutch drum. The steel discs, alternated with the friction discs, have splines on their outer edge that engage matching splines machined into the transmission case.

As long as there is running clearance between the friction and steel discs, the drum can rotate in either direction. However, applying the clutch eliminates any clearance as the two sets of discs are pressed together with great force. This locks the discs together to stop the rotation of the drum. The drum is held as long as hydraulic apply pressure to the clutch piston is maintained.

A holding clutch is an open design and usually fits into either a machined area of the case or in a special support that bolts to the case. Internal passages in the case route fluid to the apply piston.

Driving Clutches

There are two types of multiple-disc driving clutches and both types are commonly used in automotive transmissions. In one configuration, splines connect a set of friction discs to the transmission input shaft so that these

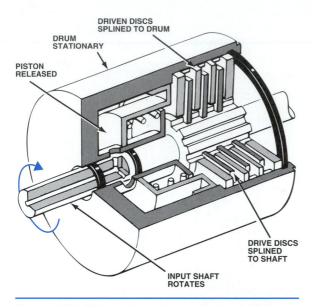

Figure 6-24. When piston releases, input shaft turns but does *not* drive the drum.

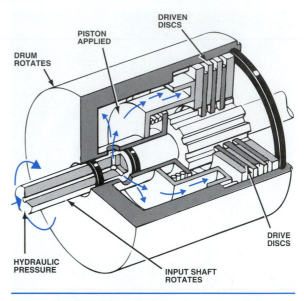

Figure 6-25. Piston applied—clutch discs lock together, input shaft drives the drum.

discs function as the driving member (figure 6-24). The alternating set of steel discs splines to the inside of the clutch drum and serves as the driven member. When the clutch is released, the drive discs rotate with the input shaft, but they do not drive the driven discs that spline to the drum.

When the clutch applies, the piston takes up clearance and forces both sets of discs firmly together. Now, the input shaft and drum rotate together at the same speed and torque transfers from one gearset member to another (figure 6-25). A passage inside the input shaft carries fluid to the clutch apply piston.

With the second driving clutch configuration, the drum connects directly to the input shaft so the drum always rotates with the shaft (figure 6-26). Splines connect the steel discs to the inside of the drum and the friction discs to the outside of a clutch hub. When the clutch applies, hydraulic pressure compresses the clutch pack to lock the drum and clutch hub together. The input shaft then drives the output shaft and both turn at the same speed.

CLUTCH OPERATION

To explain how a hydraulic clutch operates, refer to the typical multiple-disc driving

clutch shown in figure 6-26. In this design, the apply piston in the rear of the drum is held in place by return springs and a spring retainer secured by a snapring. Unless the clutch is applied, spring force retracts the piston to create clearance between the discs.

To apply the clutch, pressurized fluid enters the drum through an internal passage in the input shaft. The fluid acts on the piston and moves it against return spring force to clamp the clutch plates together and hold them against the pressure plate (figure 6-26A). The friction between the discs then locks the clutch drum to the hub, causing them to turn as one unit.

To release the clutch, hydraulic fluid to the apply side of the piston is cut off and exhausted. The piston return springs, which were compressed when the clutch was applied, are now free to expand and move the piston back, allowing the clutch discs to disengage (figure 6-26B).

Clutch Vent Port and Check Ball

Even when a multiple-disc clutch is not applied, residual fluid may remain behind the apply piston. Centrifugal force can throw this fluid toward the outside of the drum. As the fluid reaches the outer edges

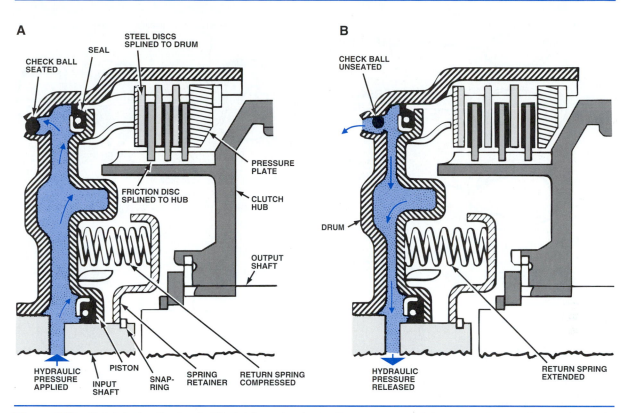

Figure 6-26. Clutch hydraulic circuit: (A) clutch apply—hydraulic pressure on piston compresses return spring and clamps discs together; (B) clutch release—hydraulic pressure exhausts, return springs retract the piston to free discs.

of the clutch drum, it can spread out, develop a considerable amount of pressure, and actually apply force against the piston. This can cause partial engagement of the clutch pack, which could ruin the shift quality and burn, glaze, or warp the clutch discs.

To relieve any residual fluid pressure, a vent port with a check ball is built into the clutch. During clutch application, full hydraulic pressure behind the clutch piston forces the check ball against its seat to contain the pressure within the drum (figure 6-26A). When the clutch releases, centrifugal force exceeds the residual hydraulic pressure. This moves the check ball away from its seat to allow excess fluid to escape through the open vent port (figure 6-26B).

The vent port and check ball do not necessarily have to be in the drum. In some clutches, they are located in the piston. Other transmissions have a metered orifice in either the clutch drum or the clutch piston. Regardless of where the devices are located, they perform the same task (figure 6-27).

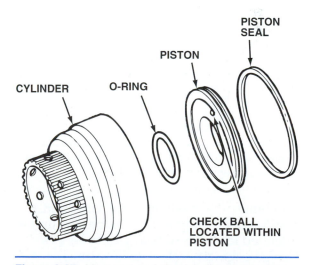

Figure 6-27. Vent port and check ball in clutch piston.

Clutch Piston Return Springs

The two most common types of return piston springs are coil and Belleville. The type of spring that is used depends on clutch piston size, shift programming, and transmission load rating. Some manufacturers use

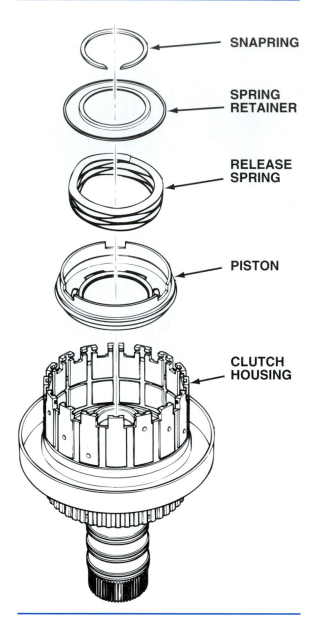

Figure 6-28. Multiple-disc clutch—using single large compression spring to return clutch piston.

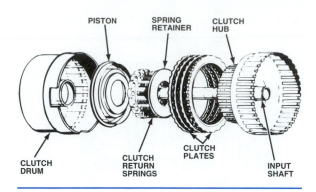

Figure 6-29. Spring retainer with several small compression springs.

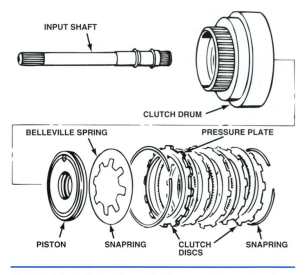

Figure 6-30. Belleville or diaphragm spring acts as a return spring.

different spring designs in the same transmission depending upon whether the unit is intended for light- or heavy-duty service. Design engineers calculate how much spring force is needed to release the piston quickly enough to keep the clutch from dragging while offering the least possible resistance when the piston applies.

Coil return springs may use either a single, large spring to return the clutch piston (figure 6-28) or several smaller springs held in place by a spring retainer and snapring (figure 6-29). A group of small springs will generally develop more force than a large single spring and are used where there are higher torque loads. Another type of multiple-disc clutch return spring is the **Belleville spring** (figure 6-30). Also called a diaphragm spring or over-center spring, a Belleville spring acts as both a piston return spring and clutch apply assist device.

The outer circumference of a Belleville spring is held in place by a snapring that fits into a machined groove inside the drum. As the clutch piston applies, it contacts the inner ends of the fingers of the spring and bends them into contact with the pressure plate to apply the clutch. Because the spring fingers contact the pressure plate near their outer edge, they act as levers to increase the clutch apply force. A Belleville spring can increase mechanical advantage by approximately 25 percent. When apply pressure to the clutch piston is cut off, the Belleville spring returns to its original shape. This pushes the piston back to its original position and releases the clutch.

CLUTCH APPLICATION AND CONTROL

The amount of pressure exerted on the piston along with the rate at which the fluid is allowed to enter the clutch assembly determines shift quality with a multiple-disc clutch. Some clutch circuits include an accumulator, like those described earlier, to achieve a smooth application and yet maintain good holding power once the clutch is fully applied. However, accumulators are not the only way to control shift quality.

Some apply circuits control the rate of fluid entering the clutch assembly with a restrictive orifice in the feed circuit (figure 6-31). The orifice reduces the initial apply pressure by delaying full fluid flow, but allows full pressure to act on the piston once pressure equalizes on both sides of the orifice. The orifice in this example is coupled with a check ball and unrestricted exhaust port. During clutch application, the check ball seats and the orifice restricts pressure to provide smooth engagement (figure 6-31A). When the clutch releases, the check ball unseats to open the unrestricted port allowing fluid to exhaust quickly and release the clutch (figure 6-31B).

In addition to the orifices and accumulators, many late-model electronic transmissions use electronic controls to regulate shifting. Several electronic strategies are available for precisely controlling clutch application and improving shift quality. One common strategy is shift overlap. Shift overlap occurs when one apply device engages just as another releases. Overlap prevents flare-up and harsh shifts to ensure a smooth transition between gears.

Many electronic transmissions also regulate the buildup of hydraulic pressure elec-

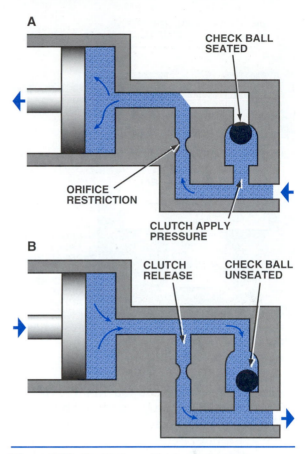

Figure 6-31. Restricting orifice in apply circuit smooths clutch application.

tronically with solenoids. This control strategy allows the onboard computer to adjust apply pressures to the shift circuits in response to engine load and vehicle operating conditions. To improve shift quality, the control system provides a carefully controlled pressure increase to the apply devices as the shift occurs.

Variable Clutch Holding Force

Many multiple-disc hydraulic clutches require less holding force under light operating conditions. For example, operating in high gear demands less engine torque than operating in reverse gear. With less torque transmitted through the gearset, the bands and clutches require less holding force to

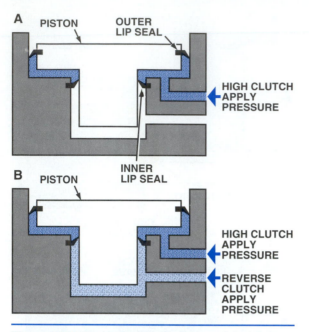

Figure 6-32. Torque demand met by applying pressure to different areas of piston.

control the gearset members. In these cases, piston apply force can be modified by applying the clutch piston through two separate hydraulic circuits (figure 6-32). In this design, the backside of the piston is acted on by fluid pressure in two chambers that are separated by an inner lip seal. As in all clutches, an outer lip seal contains fluid behind the piston.

In high gear, pressurized fluid from the high clutch apply circuit flows into the high clutch chamber (figure 6-32A). This chamber allows hydraulic pressure to act on only a portion of the total piston surface area, thus limiting application force to less than maximum. The one-way sealing action of the inner lip seal prevents hydraulic pressure from entering the reverse clutch apply chamber.

Additional application force is needed in reverse gear, so pressurized fluid is also fed into the reverse clutch apply chamber (figure 6-32B). When both apply circuits are pressurized, the pressure acts on the entire surface area of the piston to apply maximum force. The inner lip seal is generally ineffective at this time because pressure is equal in both chambers. However, if pressure in the reverse clutch chamber should exceed that in the high clutch chamber, the

inner lip seal allows pressure to bypass into the high clutch chamber, ensuring maximum clutch application force.

ONE-WAY CLUTCHES

Another type of automatic transmission device in common use is the **one-way clutch**, or overrunning clutch. Like a transmission band, a one-way clutch is always a holding device. However, they can work together with a drive clutch to provide input. One-way clutches are either roller or sprag clutches. However, the roller clutch is more common.

One-Way Roller Clutch

A one-way roller clutch consists of a hub, rollers, and springs that fit inside a drum (figure 6-33). The inner circumference of the drum has a series of machined ramps, or cam cuts, to accommodate the rollers and springs. Each ramp is narrower at one end than it is at the other.

If you hold the drum while rotating the hub clockwise, the rollers will compress their springs and move toward the larger end of the ramps. This unlocks the clutch because there is enough clearance between the rollers and the drum for the hub to freewheel.

Rotate the hub counterclockwise while holding the drum. The rollers move toward the narrow end of the ramp wedging themselves between the hub and drum to lock the clutch. With the rollers at the narrow end of the ramp there is no roller-to-drum clearance. Therefore, the hub cannot turn counterclockwise because the drum is being held.

One-Way Sprag Clutch

A **one-way sprag clutch** consists of a hub and a drum separated by a number of figure-eight-shaped metal pieces called **sprags** (figure 6-34). Sprags lock and unlock the clutch in a manner similar to the rollers in a one-way roller clutch. The shape of a

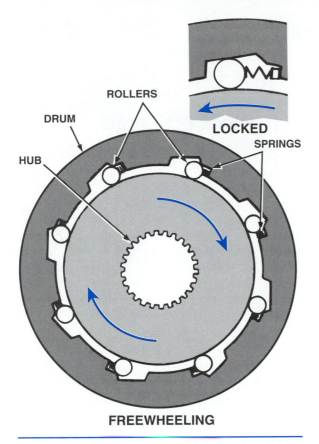

Figure 6-33. One-way roller clutch locks when hub rotates counterclockwise, freewheels when it rotates clockwise; lockup occurs when rollers wedge between drum and hub.

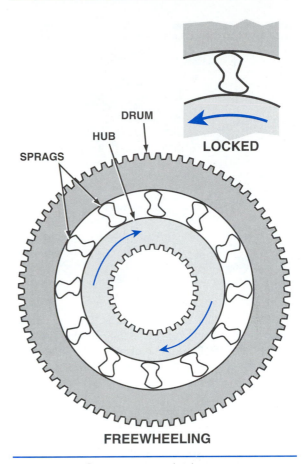

Figure 6-34. One-way sprag clutch.

sprag provides two effective working lengths. The direction the sprag tilts determines if working length is short or long.

When the clutch hub in the illustration rotates clockwise, the sprags tilt and open a space between themselves, the hub, and the drum. This unlocks the clutch and allows the hub to freewheel. The one-way clutch assembly allows clockwise hub rotation at all times. Hold the drum while rotating the hub counterclockwise and the sprags tilt to wedge themselves between the drum and hub, locking the two parts together.

One-Way Clutch Applications

One-way clutches have some advantages over other types of apply devices. First, they

are mechanical devices and do not require hydraulic pressure to operate. Second, they apply and release almost instantly, unlike bands and multiple-disc clutches. Finally, a one-way clutch that holds the reaction member of a planetary gearset can release that member automatically as soon as the reaction member turns faster than, or overruns, its respective drive member. The same holds true should the device try to rotate in the opposite direction.

INTERACTION OF APPLY DEVICES

Automatic transmissions use planetary gearsets controlled by various combinations of bands, multiple-disc clutches, and one-way clutches to provide forward and

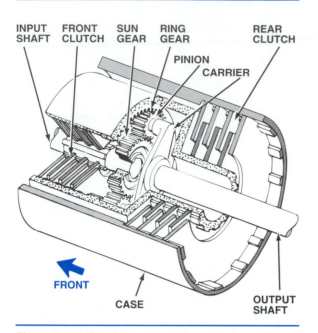

INPUT SHAFT | FRONT CLUTCH | SUN GEAR | RING GEAR | REAR CLUTCH
PINION
CARRIER
FRONT
CASE
OUTPUT SHAFT

Figure 6-35. Simple two-speed transmission with both clutches released (gearset in neutral)—one planetary gearset and two multiple-disc clutches.

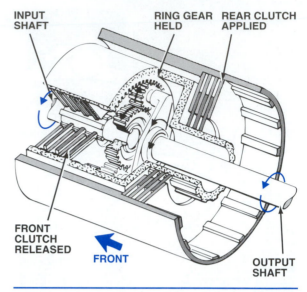

INPUT SHAFT | RING GEAR HELD | REAR CLUTCH APPLIED
FRONT CLUTCH RELEASED
FRONT
OUTPUT SHAFT

Figure 6-36. Low gear—front clutch releases and rear clutch applies.

reverse gear ranges. Precisely how this is done varies by transmission. The following sections explain some basic ways in which apply devices interact within a transmission to control planetary gearset operation.

Basic Two-Speed Transmission

If you combine two multiple-disc clutches with a single planetary gearset, it is possible to build a simple two-speed automatic transmission (figure 6-35). The two forward gear ranges are obtained by holding the ring gear and locking it to the transmission case and by turning the ring gear with the input shaft. To do this, a front clutch is installed between the input shaft and the inside of the ring gear. Also, a rear clutch is installed between the outside of the ring gear and inside the transmission case.

In neutral, both clutches are released (figure 6-35). The sun gear splines to the input shaft and both rotate clockwise as viewed from the front. Resistance from the rear wheels holds the output shaft and the carrier that attaches to it. Therefore, the planet pinions, which are driven by the sun

gear, rotate counterclockwise, driving the ring gear counterclockwise. However, because the ring gear is not connected to the output shaft, the wheels are not being driven.

To obtain low gear, the front clutch releases and the rear clutch applies (figure 6-36). The rear clutch holds the ring gear and locks it to the transmission case. The planet pinions are still driven counterclockwise by the sun gear. However, because the ring gear is held, the pinions walk around the inside of the ring gear, driving the carrier clockwise. The carrier then drives the output shaft in gear reduction, or low gear.

The front clutch applies and the rear clutch releases when the transmission shifts into high gear (figure 6-37). The front clutch locks the sun and ring gears together. Now, the entire gearset turns clockwise as a unit because two members of the planetary gearset are locked together. The pinions then turn the carrier, which drives the output shaft in direct, or high gear.

This simple transmission provides only two forward speeds and no reverse. However, it does provide a good basic example of how multiple-disc clutches are used as driving and holding devices for a planetary gearset.

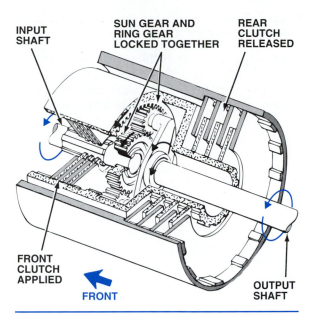

INPUT SHAFT

SUN GEAR AND RING GEAR LOCKED TOGETHER

REAR CLUTCH RELEASED

FRONT CLUTCH APPLIED

FRONT

OUTPUT SHAFT

Figure 6-37. High gear—front clutch applies and rear clutch releases.

Engine Braking

In normal low-gear operation, the one-way clutch holds the ring gear when engine torque drives the sun gear and the ring gear attempts to turn counterclockwise. However, when the vehicle is coasting, the situation is reversed, and the drive wheels are providing torque to the transmission gears. This makes the carrier the input member of the planetary gearset, and causes the pinions to walk around the sun gear and drive the ring gear clockwise. The one-way clutch then overruns, and there is no longer a direct connection between the engine and the drive wheels. As a result, engine compression *cannot* be used for braking.

The band around the ring gear in our second type of transmission is used to shift into manual low gear. In manual low gear, the band applies to hold the ring gear and keep it from rotating in *either* direction. This maintains a direct connection between the engine and rear wheels, enabling the driver to use engine compression for braking.

SUMMARY

The mechanisms that hold and drive planetary gearset members are called apply devices. The apply devices used in an automatic transmission include bands, multiple-disc clutches, and one-way clutches. Bands and one-way clutches are holding devices only; multiple-disc clutches can be holding or driving devices.

Bands may be either a double- or single-wrap design, and they come in several thicknesses depending on the torque load they carry. A hydraulic servo that acts through a linkage applies the band. A straight linkage transmits the servo force directly to the band; lever and cantilever linkages transmit servo force indirectly and can increase the amount of force applied.

Some servo hydraulic circuits contain an accumulator to smooth the buildup of pressure and dampen pressure surges by temporarily diverting part of the fluid into a parallel circuit or chamber. Accumulators may be either piston type or valve type. Piston-type accumulators are further classified as independent designs that have their own bore or integral designs that share a bore with a servo piston.

Multiple-disc hydraulic clutches consist of a set of friction discs alternated with a set of steel discs. One set of discs attaches to a component by inner splines; the other set of discs attaches to a second component by outer splines. When hydraulic pressure acting on the piston forces the disc sets together, the clutch locks to connect the two components that spline to the discs.

Multiple-disc clutch application may be controlled and smoothed with accumulators, restricting orifices, and dual hydraulic apply circuits. Multiple-disc clutches use clutch piston return springs to ensure the clutch piston fully releases when there is no apply pressure. Spring force is often assisted with hydraulic release pressure. A fluid vent port and check ball also aid in a quick release and prevent partial clutch application due to centrifugal force.

One-way clutches are either roller or sprag type. Both designs freewheel in one direction and lock up in the other. One-way clutches are purely mechanical devices that do not require hydraulic pressure apply.

Review Questions

Choose the single most correct answer. Compare your answers to the correct answers on page 213.

1. Transmission apply devices consist of
   a. Multiple-disc clutches
   b. Hydraulic servos
   c. One-way clutches
   d. All of the above

2. Technician A says a transmission band is used as a drive device only.
   Technician B says a transmission band is used as a holding device only.
   Who is right?
   a. A only
   b. B only
   c. Both A and B
   d. Neither A nor B

3. Technician A says the amount of force that a band develops against a drum is determined by the length and width of the band.
   Technician B says the amount of force that a band develops against a drum is determined by the servo apply pressure and the servo linkage type.
   Who is right?
   a. A only
   b. B only
   c. Both A and B
   d. Neither A nor B

4. Technician A says a double-wrap band provides greater holding force than a single-wrap band.
   Technician B says a single-wrap band is able to match the circumference of a drum more closely than a double-wrap band.
   Who is right?
   a. A only
   b. B only
   c. Both A and B
   d. Neither A nor B

5. The hydraulic apply force of a servo equals the system pressure times the surface area of the servo piston. Therefore, a pressure of 125 psi applied to a 4-in^2 piston would exert _____ pounds of force.
   a. 300
   b. 350
   c. 500
   d. 550

6. Technician A says that a band that is positioned to apply force in the direction of drum rotation is a self-energizing band.
   Technician B says the drum rotation of a self-energizing band aids in band application and requires more servo apply pressure.
   Who is right?
   a. A only
   b. B only
   c. Both A and B
   d. Neither A nor B

7. Technician A says a servo piston is normally held in its unapplied position by a piston return spring.
   Technician B says a transmission band is normally held in its unapplied position by the servo linkage.
   Who is right?
   a. A only
   b. B only
   c. Both A and B
   d. Neither A nor B

8. Technician A says a cantilever servo linkage is used with a band that is anchored to the case at one end.
   Technician B says a cantilever servo linkage is convenient because it can be adjusted from outside the transmission.
   Who is right?
   a. A only
   b. B only
   c. Both A and B
   d. Neither A nor B

9. Technician A says a straight servo linkage design is usually best because it can apply force directly to the band.
   Technician B says some servo linkage designs are capable of increasing the apply force through mechanical advantage.
   Who is right?
   a. A only
   b. B only
   c. Both A and B
   d. Neither A nor B

10. Periodic transmission band adjustments are not required when the servo linkage is a _____ type.
    a. Cantilever
    b. Lever
    c. Strut
    d. Graduated rod

11. Accumulators are used in the transmission hydraulic system to
    a. Delay the pressure buildup on an apply device
    b. Cushion the shock of a sudden pressure change
    c. Provide smoother shifts
    d. All of the above

12. Technician A says an accumulator may be either a spool valve in the valve body, or a piston in a servo bore.
    Technician B says some accumulators may be installed in a separate bore in the transmission case.
    Who is right?
    a. A only
    b. B only
    c. Both A and B
    d. Neither A nor B

13. Technician A says that when an accumulator reaches the end of its stroke, the pressure on the apply device increases to full value.
    Technician B says that when an accumulator reaches the end of its stroke, the pressure on the apply device increases to twice the pressure at the shift valve.
    Who is right?
    a. A only
    b. B only
    c. Both A and B
    d. Neither A nor B

14. Technician A says a multiple-disc holding clutch is used to lock the input and output shafts together.
    Technician B says a multiple-disc driving clutch is used to lock the planetary ring gear to the transmission case.
    Who is right?
    a. A only
    b. B only
    c. Both A and B
    d. Neither A nor B

15. The diaphragm-type return spring used in some multiple-disc clutches is also called a
    a. Coil spring
    b. Belleville spring
    c. Ackerman spring
    d. Roller spring

16. Technician A says a multiple-disc clutch can act as a driving clutch.
    Technician B says a multiple-disc driving clutch is an apply device.
    Who is right?
    a. A only
    b. B only
    c. Both A and B
    d. Neither A nor B

17. Technician A says a check ball is used in some clutch drums to provide an escape for any fluid remaining in the drum when the clutch is released.
    Technician B says a check ball is used in some clutch drums to prevent the clutch from releasing when the fluid is exhausted.
    Who is right?
    a. A only
    b. B only
    c. Both A and B
    d. Neither A nor B

18. Technician A says that transmission gearshift quality often depends on how a multiple-disc clutch is timed and applied.
    Technician B says that many transmissions control the rate of fluid flow into a multiple-disc clutch apply circuit with a restrictive orifice.
    Who is right?
    a. A only
    b. B only
    c. Both A and B
    d. Neither A nor B

19. The most common type of one-way clutch used in an automatic transmission is the _____ type.
    a. Sprag
    b. Roller
    c. Belleville
    d. Bendix

20. Technician A says a one-way clutch locks up whenever it overruns.
    Technician B says one advantage of a one-way clutch is that it requires less hydraulic pressure to apply.
    Who is right?
    a. A only
    b. B only
    c. Both A and B
    d. Neither A nor B

7

Transmission Fluids, Filters, and Coolers

Automatic transmission hydraulic systems require special fluids to operate properly and have long service lives. Filters keep these fluids clean and prevent wear or damage to the transmission components. Vehicles with automatic transmissions also have coolers that lower transmission operating temperatures by removing excess heat from the fluid.

AUTOMATIC TRANSMISSION FLUIDS

Automatic transmission fluid (ATF) is the vital operating fluid of every automatic transmission. Automatic transmission fluid performs the following jobs in the transmission:

- Torque transfer
- Cooling
- Cleaning
- Lubrication
- Shift control
- Apply device operation

Torque Transfer

The planetary gearsets in an automatic transmission are in constant mesh and do not require a driver-operated clutch for shifting. Because an automatic transmission does *not* mechanically connect to the crankshaft, there is no need of a clutch to prevent the engine from stalling when the vehicle brakes to a stop. With an automatic transmission, ATF circulates through a torque converter, transferring engine power to the transmission hydraulically (figure 7-1). Unless the torque converter is operating in lockup mode, the ATF provides the *only* connection between the engine crankshaft and the transmission input shaft.

Cooling, Cleaning, and Lubrication

The torque converter, transmission gears, bands, and clutches create a great deal of

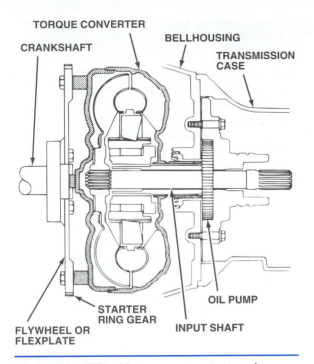

Figure 7-1. ATF inside torque converter transfers engine torque to transmission.

heat during operation. The ATF circulates through and over these parts and cools them by absorbing some of the heat. The hot fluid then circulates through an oil cooler to lower its temperature before returning to the transmission.

Automatic transmission fluid also lubricates as it circulates in the hydraulic system. In most transmissions, the fluid returning from the oil cooler goes directly into the lubrication circuit that feeds **bushings**, bearings, and gears. In other designs, fluid from the cooler flows into the sump where the pump draws it up, directs it to the pressure regulator valve, and then sends it through the transmission.

As it cools and lubricates the transmission, ATF also works to clean internal parts. Special additives in the fluid prevent rust, oxidation, and varnish buildup. Additives also help keep fluid contaminants in suspension so they can be trapped in the filters. The combination of all the additives in a particular ATF is referred to as the performance additive package (figure 7-2).

Shift Control and Apply Device Operation

The ATF circulates under pressure through the transmission valve body to move the valves that control transmission shifting (figure 7-3). As described previously, hydraulic pressure that develops in the oil pump is controlled by regulating valves that sense engine torque and road speed. Pressure and flow from the regulating valves operate the switching valves that time and control the gear changes.

Finally, ATF operates the apply devices in the transmission. The clutches and bands apply and release by fluid pressure. This happens when the switching valves direct fluid through the hydraulic circuits to these apply devices.

GENERAL ATF PROPERTIES

Automatic transmission fluid can be a petroleum-based oil, a synthetic lubricant, or a combination of the two. Most vehicle manufacturers install a petroleum-based fluid on the assembly line and recommend using the same ATF when servicing the transmission. However, some manufacturers fill their transmissions with a semi-synthetic fluid during assembly. Both synthetic and semi-synthetic fluids are available from aftermarket suppliers (figure 7-4).

In general, an ATF blend consists of about 85% to 90% base oil, or base stock. The performance additive package makes up the remaining 10% to 15%. Because the base oil is the largest component of an ATF, it has the largest impact on how the fluid performs. Base oil affects viscosity, oxidation, foaming, and flash point. Additives might modify these qualities somewhat, but the base stock determines the starting point.

Miscibility Test

Although fluids from several manufacturers might meet the same set of specifications, this does not mean they are exactly the

ADDITIVE TYPE	PURPOSE
Anti-foam agents	Prevent air bubble formation
Anti-oxidant agents	Prevent sludge, varnish, and acid formation
Anti-swell agents	Prevent seals from swelling or hardening
Anti-wear agents	Combat friction to prevent wear
Corrosion inhibitor	Prevent corrosion
Dispersant	Hold contaminants in suspension
Friction modifiers	Establish friction characteristics
Pour point depressant	Improve low temperature flow
Red dye	Identify fluid type

Figure 7-2. List of typical additive package ingredients.

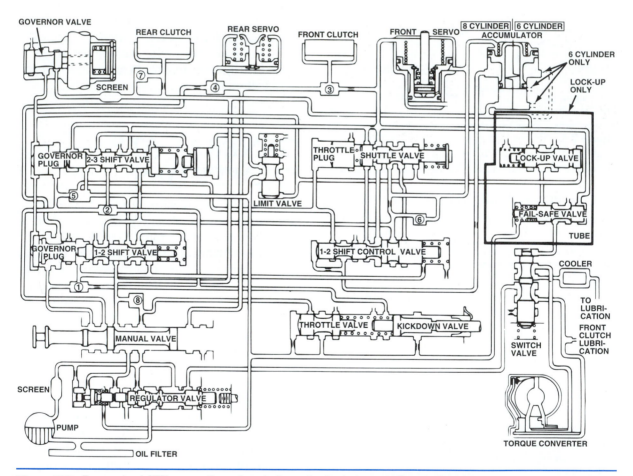

Figure 7-3. Pressurized ATF moves the valves in the valve body to control gear changes.

same in their chemical composition. To ensure compatibility between different brands of fluid, every fluid must pass a **miscibility** test. In a miscibility test, ATF samples are mixed with several reference fluids. These mixtures are subjected to extreme high and low temperatures that are above and below normal operating range. To pass the test, the ATF must remain completely mixed at all times and there cannot be any color change.

Viscosity Tests

The **viscosity** test measures the internal friction, or resistance to flow, of a liquid. The viscosity, composition, and wax content of

Figure 7-4. Aftermarket synthetic ATF.

the base stock are the key factors in determining the flow characteristics of an ATF. Wax has the greatest affect of these factors. In order to achieve the required low-temperature performance, an ATF must have a base oil with low wax content. The additive package contains chemicals that modify the fluidity of the base oil.

Temperature affects the viscosity of a fluid. Viscosity increases at low temperatures and decreases at high temperatures. In comparison to other automotive lubricants, ATF has a low viscosity and remains fluid even in sub-zero temperatures. The higher the viscosity of a fluid, the greater is its resistance to flow. If fluid viscosity is too high on a cold start-up, there is a lapse between the time the engine starts and when fluid actually reaches the control valves, apply devices, and heavily loaded transmission parts. This delays shift action, increases band and clutch slippage, accelerates wear, and can lead to transmission failure. Additives called pour-point depressants improve the low temperature flow characteristics of ATF.

As ATF warms up, viscosity lowers and the fluid thins out and flows easily. However, if the viscosity is too low the lubricating film between critical parts may break down and allow the parts to make contact. This loss of lubrication causes rapid wear that quickly leads to severe damage. In addition, lowered viscosity at higher temperatures increases the chances of internal and external fluid leakage. Additives called "viscosity index improvers" enable ATF to maintain a higher viscosity at extremely high temperatures.

Flash Point and Flame Point Tests

Automatic transmission fluid blends must meet minimum specifications for flash and flame point. The **flash point** is the temperature at which the vapors from heated ATF ignite when exposed to an open flame. The **flame point** is the temperature at which ATF actually begins to burn when exposed to an open flame. Generally, both temperatures are above 300°F (149°C) for petroleum-based ATF and above 400°F (204°C) for synthetic ATF. Flame point is always higher than flash point.

Foaming Test

The rapidly spinning components inside an operating automatic transmission can agitate ATF and churn it into foam. When this happens, air bubbles in the fluid reduce lubrication and the transmission hydraulic system is unable to function properly because the air in the fluid compresses. Minor foaming can delay shift action and cause erratic gear changes. Heavy foaming increases clutch and band slippage that can generate extreme heat, accelerate wear, and result in fluid breakdown that leads to transmission damage. This can also cause the fluid to exit the vent or filler tube and start a fire as the fluid contacts the hot exhaust system of a vehicle.

To avoid these problems, ATF contains anti-foaming agents that help prevent air bubble formation and limit the life span of bubbles that do form. The effectiveness of these additives is checked in a series of laboratory tests. During these tests a constant fluid temperature is maintained while the sample is agitated in a controlled manner for a specified time. Depending on the exact test being performed, there must be either no sign of foam on the surface of the fluid, or the amount of foam and the time it takes to subside must fall within certain limits.

Oxidation Resistance Test

The extreme high temperature of an ATF operating under heavy loads subjects the fluid to **oxidation** of the oil molecules. Resistance to oxidation is critical to any lubricant because oxidation greatly shortens the functional life of ATF. Oxidation causes the formation of varnish, sludge, and acids that can result in transmission damage. Varnish can inhibit valve movement; sludge can plug screens and fluid passages; acids can corrode metal components, friction elements, and seals. Automatic transmission fluids blended with the same additive package at the same treat rate, but with different base stocks, have been shown to have different oxidation rates in controlled tests.

Automatic transmission fluid base oils oxidize during a chain reaction process initiated by the attack of oxygen brought on by high temperatures. The threat of oxidation is significant in an automatic transmission, as the rate at which these chemical reactions occur can double for every 18°F (10°C) rise in temperature. To combat such heat-related fluid breakdown, the additive package contains chemicals known as oxidation inhibitors. Oxidation inhibitors are designed to disrupt such a chain reaction, but how effective they are depends upon the quality of the base stock.

How effective an ATF is in resisting oxidation is measured by installing the fluid into a test transmission, then operating the transmission through a strictly controlled test cycle. Afterwards, the fluid is drained and chemically analyzed for breakdown, while the transmission is disassembled and its parts inspected for physical damage and deposits.

Rust, Corrosion, and Compatibility Tests

Automatic transmission fluid also contains additives called corrosion inhibitors that prevent the rusting or etching of metal components. Copper alloys such as brass or bronze are particularly sensitive to corrosion. These materials are typically used in the construction of the transmission oil cooler.

Corrosion resistance properties are tested by immersing small pieces of the various metals used in a transmission into heated ATF. After a preset period of time, the metal samples are removed from the fluid for evaluation. Metal samples are weighed to check for metal loss and visually inspected for signs of staining or physical damage.

Automatic transmission fluid must be compatible with rubber, nylon, and Teflon®, as well as other synthetic materials used for seals, check balls, speedometer gears, and other transmission parts. Compatibility with these materials is also checked by immersing samples of them in temperature-controlled ATF. After a specified time, samples are measured to check for excessive swelling or softening of the material and visually inspected for signs of physical deterioration.

Friction and Wear Tests

A number of additives are blended into ATF to help prevent the fluid from breaking down due to friction and wear. Anti-wear additives such as zinc, sulfur, and phosphorus combat friction. Detergent additives help keep the transmission clean. Dispersant additives hold contaminants suspended in the fluid so the filter can trap them. In addition, additives called **friction modifiers** determine the frictional properties of an ATF.

Friction and wear tests determine how well an ATF protects the transmission over its projected operating life and how well the fluid maintains its frictional properties under simulated operating conditions. During the friction and wear tests, the ATF is installed into a freshly rebuilt test transmission. The transmission is then subjected

FLUID TYPE	FRICTION MODIFIED	NON-MODIFIED	OBSOLETE
TYPE A	X		X
TYPE A, SUFFIX A	X		
DEXRON®-B	X		
DEXRON®-IIC	X		X
DEXRON®-IID	X		X
DEXRON®-IIE	X		X
DEXRON®-III	X		
TYPE F			
1P		X	X
2P		X	
TYPE G		X	
TYPE CJ	X		X
TYPE H	X		X
MERCON®	X		
MOPAR ATF PLUS	X		

Figure 7-5. Fluid type application chart.

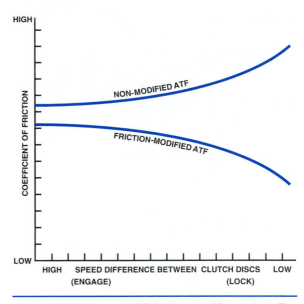

Figure 7-6. Effects of ATF friction modifiers on coefficients of friction.

to several hundred hours of controlled cycle operation. For the duration of the test, shift times must remain within specified limits. Afterwards, the fluid is analyzed to ensure there is no deterioration of its frictional properties, while the transmission is torn down and inspected for cleanliness and physical condition.

ATF FRICTION PROPERTIES

Automatic transmission fluid blends fall into two basic groups, friction-modified fluids and non-modified fluids (figure 7-5). Friction-modified fluids include Type A fluid, DEXRON®, MERCON®, and MOPAR® ATF-Plus, while Type F and Type G fluids are examples of non-modified fluids. The two types act in opposite ways within the transmission, but to explain how they differ, we must first define two terms: **static friction** and **dynamic friction**.

Static friction is the **coefficient of friction** between two surfaces that are in fixed, or nearly fixed, contact with each other. Dynamic, or kinetic, friction is the coefficient of friction between two surfaces that have relative motion between them—such as when they are sliding against each other. Under normal conditions, the coefficient of static friction is higher than that of dynamic friction. This is why it is harder to *start* an object moving than it is to *keep* it moving.

With a non-modified ATF, the coefficient of friction *increases* as the band or clutch

applies and the relative motion decreases. A non-modified ATF provides an *increasing* coefficient of static friction that is ultimately *greater* than the dynamic friction present before lockup (figure 7-6). These fluids promote positive engagement by preventing excessive slippage during clutch or band application. With a friction-modified fluid, the coefficient of friction *decreases* as the bands and clutches apply. Therefore, the coefficient of static friction with a friction-modified fluid is *less* than the coefficient of dynamic friction. Modifying the friction properties allows a transmission manufacturer to control shift quality and feel by adjusting the amount of slippage that occurs during a clutch or band application.

Fluid Type and Transmission Design

Engineers must consider ATF friction properties when they design a transmission and calibrate its shift action. Due to the increasing coefficient of static friction with a non-modified fluid, transmissions using these blends can achieve positive engagement and good shift action using smaller bands and clutch packs (figure 7-7). Also, each clutch pack can operate with fewer discs. The drawback to a non-modified fluid is that the

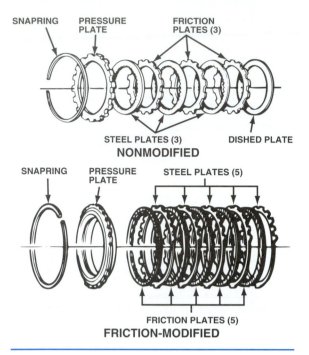

Figure 7-7. Clutch pack designs for non-modified and friction-modified fluids.

low coefficient of dynamic friction requires bands and clutches to be applied quickly and with high hydraulic pressure in order to avoid excessive slippage. Transmissions that operate with non-modified fluid generally have a firm shift feel with distinct rpm changes between gears.

Friction-modified fluids require a different approach to transmission design, construction, and shift programming. The main advantage of a friction-modified ATF is a relatively high coefficient of dynamic friction. When combined with lower clutch and band application pressures, these fluids provide a very smooth shift feel. However, low apply pressure can lead to excessive slippage, which can result in heat damage. Transmissions operating with friction-modified ATF generally use larger bands and clutch packs with more plates. Typically, these transmissions will exhibit a smooth, seamless flow of power with almost undetectable shifts under light loads.

Improper Fluid Use

The consequences of using the wrong ATF in a transmission vary depending on the

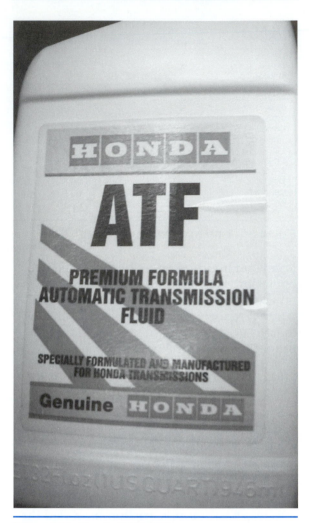

Figure 7-8. Honda OEM ATF.

type of fluid originally specified by the vehicle manufacturer. Honda, Toyota, and Chrysler products, for example, are very particular about ATF use. Only OEM fluids should be used in these applications (figure 7-8). When a friction-modified ATF is used in a transmission designed for a non-modified blend, the result is excessive band and clutch slippage. The slippage can be especially prevalent under high-torque conditions such as trailer towing or hill climbing. Pronounced slippage accelerates friction material wear and greatly reduces transmission service life.

When a non-modified ATF is used in place of a friction-modified fluid, harsh or abrupt shifts usually occur. The change in shift characteristics is usually noticeable to the driver and may increase the load on certain components. However, it is less likely to create a serious long-term problem and has little affect on the service life of the transmission.

Installing the correct friction-modified ATF in a late-model electronic transmission is also a concern. Not all friction-modified fluids are the same, and different brands are blended for specific applications. Torque converter clutch shudder is a common problem that often results from either using the wrong ATF or from breakdown of the fluid due to wear or overheating.

Universal Transmission Fluids and Additives

Some oil companies have developed protectant additives (figure 7-9) and full-synthetic ATF blends with good performance for a wide variety of automatic transmissions. These additives and synthetic fluids are sometimes known as universal fluids, and their makers claim they can be used in any automatic transmission.

Contrary to these claims, it remains a fact that no single ATF can be both friction-modified and non-modified. As explained earlier, these two types of fluids operate fundamentally in opposite ways. A synthetic fluid formulation may meet *some* of the requirements for both types of fluid, and may even work well under certain driving conditions. However, it would have to defy the laws of chemistry in order to meet *all* of the requirements for both types of fluid.

Avoid using any product that has not been approved by the transmission manufacturer. Installing the wrong fluid can result in poor performance and possibly void any warranties that are in effect.

SPECIFIC ATF TYPES

The first ATF was straight mineral engine oil dyed red to identify transmission leaks. Limited additives were introduced to improve low-temperature performance,

reduce sludge and varnish formation, and resolve any compatibility problems with different metals, rubbers, and friction materials used in the transmission. Over time, more advanced ATF blends met the increasing needs of more modern transmission designs. The most popular blends are briefly described in the following sections.

GM—DEXRON® Fluids

General Motors introduced DEXRON® ATF in 1967 to meet the increased operating temperatures of newer automatic transmissions. DEXRON® ATF is a friction-modified fluid that improves high- and low-temperature performance and provides better oxidation resistance than previously used fluids. There have been four generations of DEXRON® fluid since its original introduction back in 1967. The latest formulation in the DEXRON® family offers further performance improvements and material compatibility.

Saturn Transaxle Fluid

Saturn uses a highly friction-modified transaxle fluid for all of its transmission applications—manual as well as automatic (figure 7-10).

Ford—MERCON® Fluid

Ford introduced MERCON®, a multipurpose friction-modified fluid, in 1987 (figure 7-11). With the release of MERCON®, Ford was able to reduce the number of fluids needed to service their family of automatic transmissions. MERCON® is the ATF of choice for all Ford transmissions that require friction-modified fluid.

MOPAR® ATF-Plus Fluid

In 1987 Chrysler developed MOPAR® ATF-Plus. This fluid is recommended for all DaimlerChrysler automatic transmissions

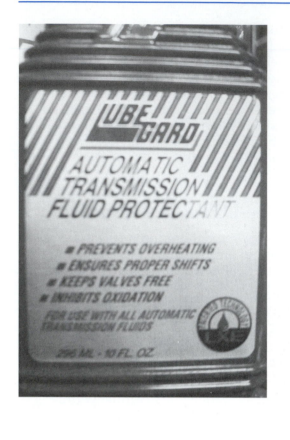

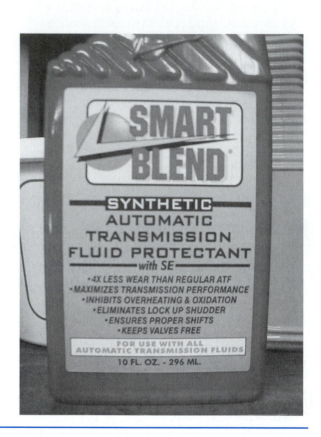

Figure 7-9. Aftermarket fluid protectant.

that use a lockup torque converter. MOPAR® ATF-Plus is a friction-modified fluid specifically designed to eliminate the possibility of shudder when the TCC is operating in a partial lockup mode. While DEXRON® and MERCON® fluids perform satisfactorily in many older Chrysler transmissions, MOPAR® ATF-Plus is the only fluid recommended for new DaimlerChrysler applications. Chrysler ATF+3 is used in all rear wheel drive applications and is highly friction modified (figure 7-12).

Proprietary ATF Types

The previous sections describe the most common types of ATF, but these are not the only fluids available. In some cases, a vehicle manufacturer may require a special fluid

that meets some additional requirement unique to a particular application. Several import manufacturers such as Mercedes-Benz, Toyota, and Volkswagen recommend their own proprietary brand of ATF for use in their automatic transmissions.

TRANSMISSION FILTERS

Transmission fluid filters remove particles or contaminants present in the fluid so that these contaminants do not circulate through the transmission where they can increase wear and cause valves or solenoids to stick. Transmission filters are located inside the transmission case between the pickup for the oil pump and the bottom of the sump

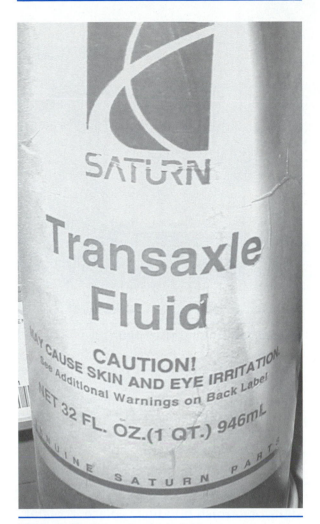

Figure 7-10. Saturn transaxle fluid.

Figure 7-11. Ford MERCON® fluid.

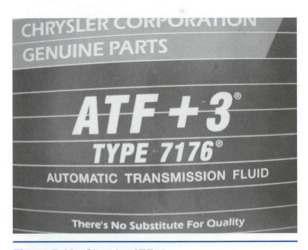

Figure 7-12. Chrysler ATF+3.

(figure 7-13). The filter must be positioned so that it is always submerged in fluid, but high enough above the bottom of the pan to prevent any debris that accumulates from clogging the filter. Three common types of automatic transmission filters are as follows:

- Screen
- Paper
- Felt

Some automatic transmissions are available with optional deep pans that replace the standard parts to provide greater oil capacity for increased cooling. Transmissions with such pans require special filters that are longer and extend down to the bottom of the pan to pick up the ATF.

Screen Filters

The oldest type of transmission filter is the metal screen filter, which is nothing more than a fine wire mesh designed to trap contaminants (figure 7-14). A screen filter should be cleaned every time the transmission is serviced and should be replaced if it is torn, broken, or clogged. A screen

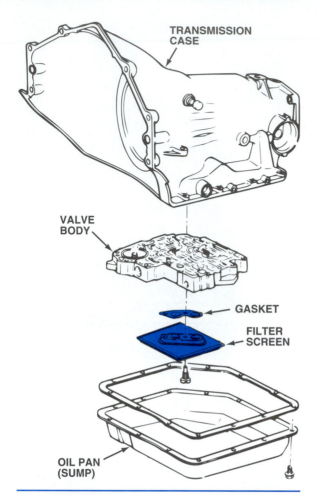

Figure 7-13. Typical automatic transmission primary filter installation.

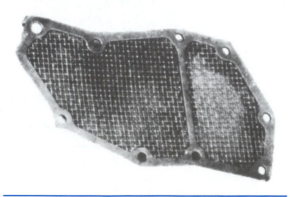

Figure 7-14. Metal screen filter.

with varnish buildup on its mesh surface can be soaked in carburetor cleaner, flushed in solvent, and reused. If the varnish cannot be removed in this manner, replace the filter.

Newer synthetic screen filters are similar to the metal screen design, but the

Figure 7-15. Synthetic screen filter.

mesh is made of nylon or polyester (figure 7-15). These have a finer mesh than a metal screen, which makes them able to filter out smaller particles. A synthetic filter screen can be washed with solvent to remove trapped particles; however, it cannot be soaked in carburetor cleaner to remove varnish. If a synthetic screen filter is broken, torn, or clogged, or shows any signs of varnish buildup, replace it. Metal and synthetic screen filters are **surface filters**. A surface filter traps contaminants on its surface, and as the particles collect, fluid flow is reduced. Because of this, the mesh openings in screen filters must be large enough to allow small particles to pass through or the filter will become clogged. Most metal screen filters have mesh openings of about 130 microns (0.005 inch or 0.13 mm); typical synthetic screen filter openings are roughly 100 microns (0.004 inch or 0.10 mm) in size. Even larger particles with irregular shapes, such as slivers, can pass through these relatively large mesh openings.

Paper Filters

Paper transmission filters are made of an oil-resistant fabric that is often enclosed in a metal housing (figure 7-16). The fabric may be made of a natural material such as

Figure 7-16. Paper filter elements—typically encased in a metal housing.

Figure 7-17. Felt filter—trap contaminants within the filter matrix rather than on the surface.

trap particles as small as 59 microns (0.0025 inch or 0.06 mm). Most late-model transmissions use this type of filter.

cellulose, but many newer designs use a synthetic fiber such as Dacron®. Paper filters cannot be cleaned and should be replaced whenever the transmission is serviced.

Paper filters are also surface filters with the same limitations as screen filters, but they are more efficient and can trap a greater number of smaller-sized particles. Some transmissions with paper filters have an oil bypass that redirects fluid flow around the filter to prevent pressure loss should it become clogged. However, such a bypass directs contaminated fluid into the transmission, where it may cause further problems.

Felt Filters

Felt filters are made from specially treated polyester fibers that are randomly spaced and not woven. Like paper filters, felt filters cannot be cleaned and should be replaced whenever the transmission is serviced.

Unlike screen and paper filters, felt filters are **depth filters**. A depth filter traps contaminant particles within the matrix of the filter material rather than on its surface (figure 7-17). As a result, they are able to trap finer particles and hold larger quantities of contaminants with little or no restriction in fluid flow. A quality felt filter can

Secondary Filters

Although every automatic transmission uses a primary oil filter to filter the fluid taken from the sump, many transmissions also use additional filters. These secondary filters are usually small screen filters used to keep foreign materials out of critical components such as pumps, valve bodies, governors, and solenoids. Some secondary filters are located in the valve body while others may be located in various passages throughout the transmission (figure 7-18). These are screen-type filters that must be serviced during an overhaul. Although they can sometimes be cleaned and reinstalled, it is always preferable to replace them.

Inline filters, another type of secondary filter, install into the transmission cooler lines (figure 7-19). These filters are an aftermarket item and are not provided as original equipment. Generally, technicians install an inline filter as a precautionary measure after rebuilding a transmission. An inline filter collects any contaminants that remain in the oil cooler after flushing, or particles that slip by the primary filter. Once an inline filter is installed, it should be replaced whenever the transmission is serviced. These are disposable filters and cannot be cleaned.

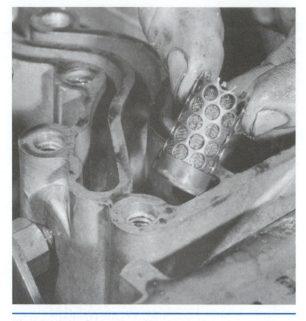

Figure 7-18. Secondary filters provide extra measure of protection.

ATF OPERATING TEMPERATURE		PROJECTED ATF SERVICE LIFE	
°F	°C	MILES	KM
175	80	100,000	160,000
195	90	50,000	80,000
215	100	25,000	40,000
235	115	12,500	20,000
255	125	6,250	10,000
275	135	3,000	5,000
295	145	1,500	2,500
315	155	750	1,200
335	170	325	500
355	180	160	250
375	190	80	125
390	200	40	65
410	210	20	32

Figure 7-20. ATF service life with respect to operating temperature.

Figure 7-19. Typical in-line filter.

TRANSMISSION OIL COOLERS

During transmission operation, ATF undergoes a great deal of stress and strain that can shorten its service life. Under normal operating conditions, ATF must efficiently dissipate the heat naturally generated by clutch and band slippage, friction between moving parts, and fluid shear in the torque con-

verter. Heat is the number one cause of transmission fluid failure. Excessive heat chemically breaks down transmission fluid, rendering it useless. Overheated ATF lubricates poorly and has low oxidation resistance. Continued use of overheated fluid allows varnish to form and may result in sticking valves, erratic shifting, glazed or burned friction materials, and the need for a transmission overhaul.

The performance specifications for petroleum-based ATF are established using an operating temperature of about 175°F (80°C). At this temperature, the service life of a typical ATF is roughly 100,000 miles (160,000 km). Above that temperature, the useful service life of a transmission fluid declines rapidly. Raising the operating temperature to 195°F (90°C) cuts fluid life in half to 50,000 miles (80,000 km). Raising the temperature to 215°F (100°C) reduces ATF life to 25,000 miles (40,000 km). At 410°F (210°C), the transmission fluid would only survive for 20 miles (32 km) (figure 7-20).

An automatic transmission uses an oil cooler to maintain fluid temperatures within safe operating limits. Oil coolers are mounted outside the transmission and act as a heat exchanger to draw heat off the fluid before it returns to the transmission. The following types of oil coolers are commonly used on automatic transmissions:

- Oil-to-water
- Oil-to-air

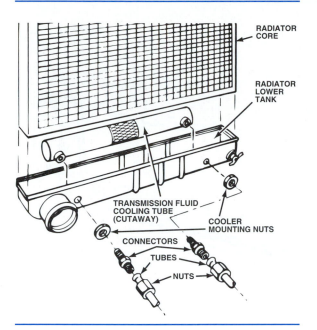

Figure 7-21. Typical oil-to-water cooler installation.

A single cooler of either type may be used to cool an automatic transmission. In heavy-duty applications, one of each cooler type may be plumbed in series for added cooling capacity.

Oil-to-Water Coolers

Most passenger vehicles use an oil-to-water cooler as original equipment. These units are built into the engine radiator and use the engine cooling system to dissipate heat (figure 7-21). The heat exchanger, or cooler tube, is located in the bottom tank of a downflow radiator or the outlet tank of a crossflow radiator (figure 7-22).

Hot ATF travels from the transmission to the cooler, which is surrounded by engine coolant. Under normal conditions, the temperature of the ATF will be higher than that of the engine coolant in the radiator. Therefore, the ATF transfers heat to the coolant, which in turn transfers heat to the air passing through the radiator. Once cooled, ATF returns to the transmission.

Two steel lines connect the transmission hydraulic system to the oil cooler (figure 7-23). The lines end in fittings that thread into matching fittings on the transmission case and cooler assembly. Some vehicles use a

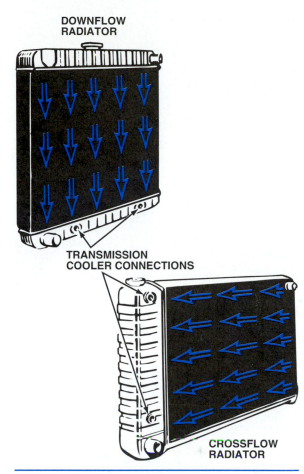

Figure 7-22. Transmission oil cooler—mounted in lower tank of a downflow radiator, outlet tank of a crossflow radiator.

short length of reinforced high-pressure hose to allow a more flexible connection between the steel lines and cooler (figure 7-24). These hoses allow for the small amount of movement between the transmission and radiator as the powertrain flexes due to torque loading.

Fluid flows to the cooler under pressure from the torque converter circuit, because that is where most of the heat is generated (figure 7-25). Therefore, the fitting for the delivery line to the oil cooler is usually close to the torque converter at the front of the case (figure 7-26). The cooler return line may route fluid into the lubrication circuit or back to the sump, so return fitting locations will vary by transmission.

The advantages of oil-to-water coolers are their compact size and relatively low cost. This type of cooler also assists transmission warm-up on cold starts because the engine

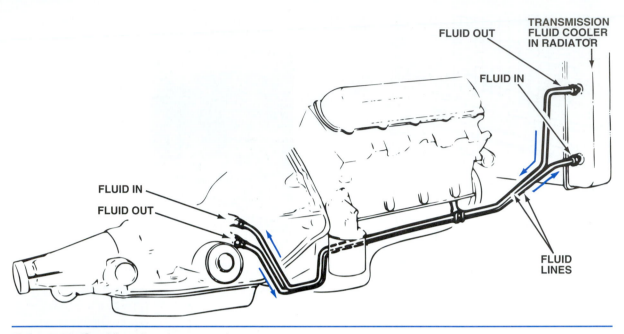

Figure 7-23. Steel line oil cooler connections.

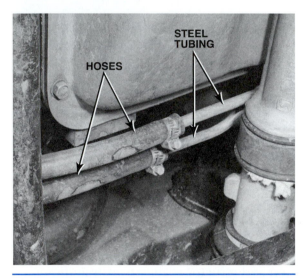

Figure 7-24. Cooler connections with rubber hoses that allow movement.

coolant warms to operating temperature faster than ATF. Coolant heat transfers to the ATF under these conditions. A disadvantage of an oil-to-water design is that an overheating engine will also overheat the transmission if coolant temperature exceeds ATF temperature. Also, a leaking cooler can contaminate both the engine cooling system and transmission hydraulic system. In addition, this design is generally less efficient at reducing fluid temperatures than an oil-to-air cooler.

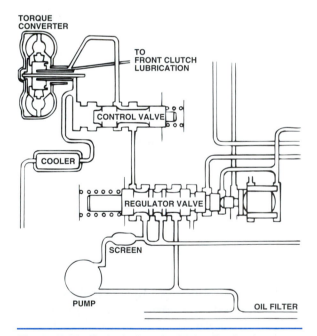

Figure 7-25. Typical oil cooler hydraulic circuit.

Oil-to-Air Coolers

Vehicles with a heavy-duty cooling system or trailer-tow package often use an auxiliary oil-to-air cooler, which is available as a dealer-installed or aftermarket option (figure 7-27). Auxiliary oil-to-air coolers mount in front of the radiator, air condition-

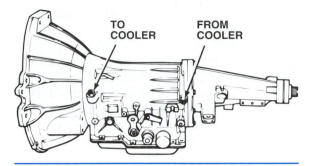

Figure 7-26. Typical cooler line connection locations for a RWD transmission.

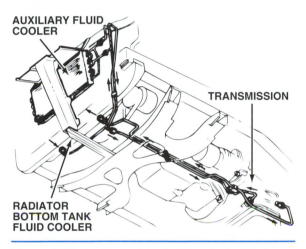

Figure 7-27. Auxiliary oil-to-air oil cooler installation.

ing condenser, or elsewhere in an unobstructed air stream. An air-to-oil transmission cooler acts like a small radiator; heat from the ATF transfers directly into the cooler fins, where it is dissipated by the passing airflow.

Although oil-to-air coolers are more expensive than oil-to-water coolers, they are also able to provide greater reductions in fluid temperature. This is because the temperature difference between the hot ATF and the outside air is much greater than the difference between hot ATF and heated engine coolant.

Most oil-to-air coolers are auxiliary units that install in series with a standard oil-to-water cooler. Fluid flows from the transmission to one cooler, then through the other cooler before it returns to the transmission. A few applications use oil-to-air coolers as the sole oil cooler, though this practice is relatively rare. Oil-to-air coolers eliminate the possibility of a fluid leak between the engine

cooling system and transmission hydraulic system, but they also prevent using coolant heat to aid transmission warm-up.

ATF CHANGE INTERVALS

Even with two transmission coolers, ATF operating temperatures often exceed the 175°F (80°C) ideal operating temperature. This can occur at points inside the transmission where friction creates momentary hot spots, but it is most likely to result from severe service such as trailer towing, operation in extreme high or low temperatures, and constant driving in stop-and-go traffic. These situations make fluid temperatures climb rapidly, which result in fluid breakdown that eventually leads to burned bands and clutches causing slippage during shifts.

Because of fluid breakdown, vehicle manufacturers recommend the transmission fluid be changed periodically. Fluid change intervals were frequent in the early years of automatic transmissions. However, improvements in fluid and transmission technologies gradually led to less frequent change intervals. Today, some manufacturers claim that in normal use the ATF is good for the life of the vehicle and need never be changed. However, these same manufacturers recommend ATF change intervals as short as 15,000 miles (24,000 km) when the vehicle is used in severe service. A large percentage of the vehicles on the road are operating under what the manufacturer considers severe service conditions.

Field experience shows that the normal fluid operating temperature in most vehicles is actually about 190° to 195°F (88° to 90°C). This means that ATF breaks down continuously whenever the vehicle is being driven; this is a severe service situation.

SUMMARY

The ATF transmits all of the power from the engine to the transmission when the torque converter clutch (TCC) is disengaged.

Automatic transmission fluids (ATF) perform a number of different functions, including lubricating, cleaning, cooling, shift control, and apply device operation. ATF can be a petroleum-base, a synthetic, or a combination of the two.

Automatic transmission fluids can be either non-modified or friction-modified. With a non-modified ATF, the coefficient of friction increases as a band or clutch applies; in a friction-modified ATF, the coefficient of friction decreases during clutch and band application. Transmissions are designed to operate with a specific type of ATF, and using the wrong fluid can result in internal damage.

Filters remove debris and contaminants from the fluid to protect transmission components. Screen filters use a wire or nylon mesh to trap particles. Paper and felt filters use a fabric made of cellulose or a synthetic fiber. All automatic transmissions use a primary filter at the oil pump inlet, and many use one or more secondary filters to keep

foreign materials out of critical circuits and components.

Transmission oil coolers help keep fluid operating temperature within design limits to prevent chemical breakdown. Most original equipment transmission coolers are oil-to-water designs that are built into the engine radiator. Oil-to-air coolers often supplement the cooling capacity of the radiator-mounted cooler. These coolers mount in an unobstructed airstream and transfer heat from the fluid into the air passing over the cooler. Oil coolers usually connect to the hydraulic system with steel lines and reinforced rubber hoses.

Many transmissions operate above the general design temperature, and partial fluid breakdown occurs whenever the vehicle is driven. To protect a transmission from damage caused by deterioration of the fluid, it is good practice to change the ATF at regular intervals.

Review Questions

Choose the single most correct answer. Compare your answers with the correct answers on page 213.

1. Technician A says ATF is used to cool, clean, and lubricate an automatic transmission.

   Technician B says ATF is used to operate the shift valves and transmit engine torque.

   Who is right?
   a. A only
   b. B only
   c. Both A and B
   d. Neither A nor B

2. Technician A says ATF uses additives to enhance or provide special fluid properties.

   Technician B says ATF is actually a blend of several kinds of fluids and ingredients.

   Who is right?
   a. A only
   b. B only
   c. Both A and B
   d. Neither A nor B

3. Technician A says a torque converter uses ATF to provide the hydraulic coupling between the engine and transmission.

   Technician B says ATF may be blended to assist fluid shear in the torque converter and reduce torque multiplication.

   Who is right?
   a. A only
   b. B only
   c. Both A and B
   d. Neither A nor B

4. Technician A says ATF always flows through the cooler, and then it returns to the oil sump.
   Technician B says ATF always flows from the cooler directly into the lubrication circuit.
   Who is right?
   a. A only
   b. B only
   c. Both A and B
   d. Neither A nor B

5. Which of the following are not used as additives in an automatic transmission fluid?
   a. Miscibility and viscosity additives
   b. Anti-wear and anti-foaming agents
   c. Oxidation enhancers
   d. Dispersants and detergents

6. Technician A says the quality and feel of a transmission shift depends on the amount of slippage that occurs when a band or clutch is applied.
   Technician B says ATF uses friction modifiers to control the amount of slippage that occurs when a band or clutch is applied.
   Who is right?
   a. A only
   b. B only
   c. Both A and B
   d. Neither A nor B

7. Technician A says ATF friction modifiers work by modifying the coefficient of friction between surfaces.
   Technician B says ATF blends fall into two groups called friction-increased fluids and friction-decreased fluids.
   Who is right?
   a. A only
   b. B only
   c. Both A and B
   d. Neither A nor B

8. Technician A says a friction-modified ATF provides a more positive grab as the band or clutch applies and prevents excessive slippage.
   Technician B says a non-modified ATF provides a more positive grab as the band or clutch applies and prevents excessive slippage.
   Who is right?
   a. A only
   b. B only
   c. Both A and B
   d. Neither A nor B

9. Technician A says the type of ATF you use in a late-model transmission is relatively unimportant, because any modern ATF lubricates well.
   Technician B says ATF type has no bearing on transmission design.
   Who is right?
   a. A only
   b. B only
   c. Both A and B
   d. Neither A nor B

10. Technician A says transmissions that use a friction-modified ATF are usually known for their firm shifts.
    Technician B says transmissions that use a non-modified ATF usually have larger bands and clutches.
    Who is right?
    a. A only
    b. B only
    c. Both A and B
    d. Neither A nor B

11. Technician A says transmission filter types can be generally classified as surface filters or depth filters.
    Technician B says transmission filters can be generally classified as primary filters or secondary filters.
    Who is right?
    a. A only
    b. B only
    c. Both A and B
    d. Neither A nor B

12. Transmission filters can be made of
    a. Synthetic fibers
    b. Paper or felt
    c. Metal or nylon screens
    d. All of the above

13. Technician A says many transmissions use secondary filters to provide further protection to important circuits.
    Technician B says the secondary filters should be changed whenever a transmission is serviced.
    Who is right?
    a. A only
    b. B only
    c. Both A and B
    d. Neither A nor B

14. Technician A says transmission operating temperature does not affect the service life of ATF.
    Technician B says age is the main factor that causes ATF to oxidize.
    Who is right?
    a. A only
    b. B only
    c. Both A and B
    d. Neither A nor B

15. The most common type of original equipment transmission oil cooler is the _____ design.
    a. Crossflow
    b. Oil-to-air
    c. Downflow
    d. Oil-to-water

16. Technician A says ATF operating temperature is a major factor in determining fluid service intervals.
    Technician B says poor shift quality could indicate a need to change the transmission fluid.
    Who is right?
    a. A only
    b. B only
    c. Both A and B
    d. Neither A nor B

17. Technician A says after-market oil-to-air coolers are normally mounted in place of the original oil-to-water cooler.
    Technician B says oil-to-air coolers are more efficient in heavy traffic and low-speed applications.
    Who is right?
    a. A only
    b. B only
    c. Both A and B
    d. Neither A nor B

Chapter

8

Gaskets, Seals, Bushings, Bearings, Washers, and Snaprings

Every automatic transmission contains secondary parts that play an important role in normal transmission operation. Gaskets and seals contain fluid within the transmission case and prevent pressurized fluid from leaking out of the various hydraulic circuits. Bushings, bearings, and thrust washers support and align the shafts, reduce friction between moving parts, and control the movement of component assemblies within the transmission. Snaprings hold various assemblies together and locate components inside the transmission case.

GASKETS

A gasket seals the space between two parts with irregular surfaces. In an automatic transmission, some gaskets seal parts together in order to contain ATF; other gaskets help channel fluid from one part of the transmission to another. The gaskets used in automatic transmissions are made of paper, cork, rubber, plastic, or synthetic materials. A gasket that combines two or more of these materials is called a composition gasket.

Gasket Compressibility

Depending on the specific application, transmission gaskets require varying amounts of **compressibility**. Compressibility is the ability of a gasket to conform to irregularities in the sealing surfaces. Gaskets with less than 20 percent compressibility are known as "hard" gaskets; those that can be compressed more than 20 percent are "soft" gaskets. A plain paper gasket is a common type of hard gasket; a cork and rubber composition gasket is a common type of soft gasket (figure 8-1).

Hard gaskets seal well when both mating surfaces are smooth, flat, and rigid. A good example is a valve body that fastens to a transmission case. Both are castings that have machine-finished mating surfaces. Also, hard gaskets allow good torque retention; they do not "relax" over time, allowing

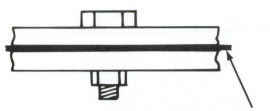

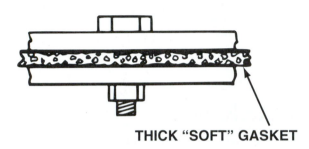

Figure 8-1. Hard and soft gaskets—differing degrees of compressibility.

the fasteners holding the assembly together to loosen.

Soft gaskets do an excellent job of sealing where one or both mating surfaces are irregular or subject to distortion when tightened. A good example is a stamped steel oil pan that bolts to a cast transmission case. The case surface has a machine finish, but the surface of the stamped oil pan will easily distort. A soft gasket here will compress to fill slight gaps and surface irregularities as the pan bolts are drawn up. The tradeoff for high compressibility is a weakness in the area of torque retention. Soft gaskets tend to relax over time, reducing the amount of joining force provided by the fasteners that hold the assembly together. The following two types of gaskets are used in modern automatic transmissions:

- Pan
- Mating assembly

Pan Gaskets

The oil pan gasket on most automatic transmissions is a soft gasket that is 1/16 to 1/8 inch (1.5 to 3.0 mm) thick (figure 8-2). Early pan gaskets were made entirely of cork, which was a good sealing material but was

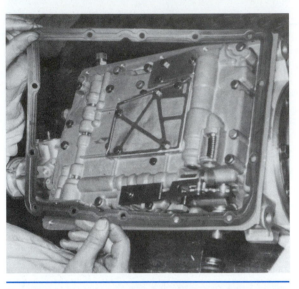

Figure 8-2. Pan gasket—soft gasket example.

unstable when used alone because it shrank and cracked with age. Cork also acted as a wick and would pull transmission fluid through the gasket, which gave the appearance of a leak. Now, the typical oil pan gasket is a composition of cork and rubber. The rubber provides added stability and improves fastener torque retention.

Some pan gaskets use a "sandwich" construction with a stiff reinforcing layer in the center. Others have metal inserts surrounding the pan bolt openings to prevent overtightening. Yet others are made of synthetic rubber compounds that offer added sealing benefits. A few transmissions do not use a pan gasket; instead, a bead of room temperature vulcanizing (RTV) silicone sealant is placed between the pan and transmission case to create an oil-tight seal (figure 8-3). Aftermarket gaskets are available for applications that originally used RTV to seal the pan.

A recent trend in original equipment oil pan gasket technology is the reusable gasket. These gaskets are made of a pliable rubber compound that does not weather or crack with age. Reusable gaskets are easy to recognize because they are thicker and softer than a standard gasket.

Mating Assembly Gaskets

Gaskets that seal smooth and rigid mating surfaces, such as those that seal the extension housing, valve body, and pump are made of

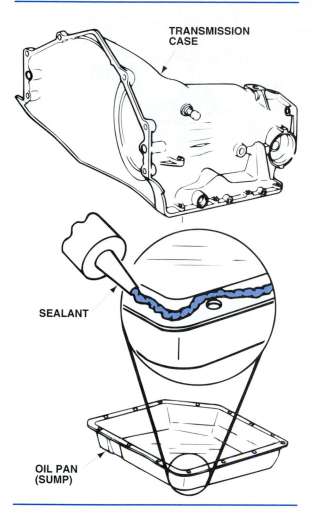

TRANSMISSION
CASE

SEALANT

OIL PAN
(SUMP)

Figure 8-3. RTV silicone—used in place of a gasket in some applications.

"hard" thin cellulose paper (figure 8-4). Some servo and governor covers also use paper gaskets. Thin paper gaskets are desirable in these applications because they are unlikely to compress and allow the retaining fasteners to loosen over time.

In addition to providing a seal, paper gaskets between the separator plate and valve body can help direct fluid flow from one half of the valve body, through the separator plate, to a different circuit in the other half of the valve body (figure 8-5). Manufacturers frequently use these gaskets to make running design changes in the transmission, or to use the same transmission case and valve body in several vehicle applications. A valve body gasket that blocks certain circuits between valve body halves in one application might open or enlarge the same circuits in another application.

Gasket Sealants

Gasket sealants are not recommended except for specific applications when servicing, repairing, or overhauling automatic transmissions. In most situations, quality gaskets and flat, clean surfaces are all that is needed to establish a proper seal.

Sealants should never be used on pump and valve body gaskets because excess sealant may get into the hydraulic system and block passages or cause valves and check balls to stick. Also, avoid applying gasket sealant to a highly compressible gasket because the sealant may act as a lubricant and cause the gasket to slip out of the joint.

Using RTV sealant in place of a pan gasket is acceptable in some applications, as is a light application of non-hardening sealant on thin paper gaskets used for cast transmission pans and extension housings. Non-hardening sealants may also be used on the outer surface of a metal-clad lip seal. However, if a metal-clad seal has a rubber coating on its outer circumference, a sealant is not necessary.

TRANSMISSION SEALS

Rubber, metal, and Teflon® seals used in automatic transmissions each come in three types: Rubber seals are O-ring, square-cut (lathe-cut), and lip seals; metal and Teflon® seals are the open-, butt-, and locking-end seals.

Static and Dynamic Seals

The seals listed previously fall into one or both of two categories: static and dynamic. A **static seal** blocks the passage of fluid between parts that are in fixed positions relative to each other. There can be no or little movement of either part if a static seal is used. Movement can cause a leak and damage the seal.

A **dynamic seal** blocks the passage of fluid between parts that have relative motion between them. Dynamic seals are

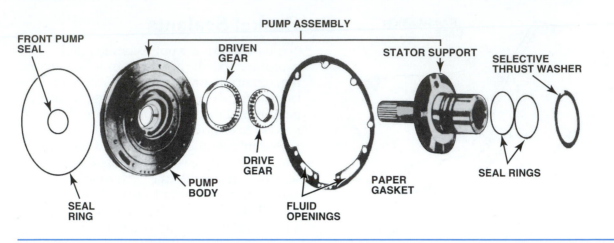

Figure 8-4. Hard paper gaskets—commonly used between oil pump body and transmission case.

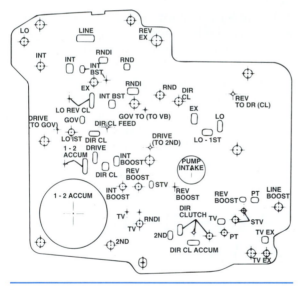

Figure 8-5. Valve body gasket holes direct fluid flow.

required where there is axial or rotational motion between the parts. **Axial motion** is movement back and forth along the length of a shaft, or parallel to the centerline (axis) of the shaft. **Rotational motion** is present when one of the parts being sealed turns (rotates) in relation to the other.

RUBBER SEALS

Early automatic transmissions required only a handful of rubber seals, but a typical modern transmission uses considerably more (figure 8-6). Rubber seal materials must have three main characteristics: abra-

sion resistance, compatibility with ATF, and sealing ability across a wide range of operating temperatures. A seal without good abrasion resistance wears quickly—especially during occasional periods of dry running when full lubrication is temporarily unavailable. If a rubber seal is incompatible with ATF it can soften, swell, and fail quickly. When a seal operates at temperatures below its design range, it may become brittle and crack; when it operates above its design range, it may soften and leak. All of these circumstances result in seal deterioration that can lead to fluid leaks, loss of pressure, poor shift quality, or even transmission failure.

Rubber Compounds

Natural rubber alone will not meet the operating demands of a modern transmission seal, so manufacturers use a blend of synthetic materials to improve seal characteristics. Seal design and materials are improving to the point where the service life of the typical seal exceeds that of most other transmission parts. These advances in seal life are primarily the result of research into synthetic rubber compounds.

Early seals were made of a synthetic rubber **polymer** called neoprene. Compared to natural rubber, neoprene was less brittle and more resistant to oil, heat, and oxidation. But compared to the more advanced synthetic rubber **copolymers** now available,

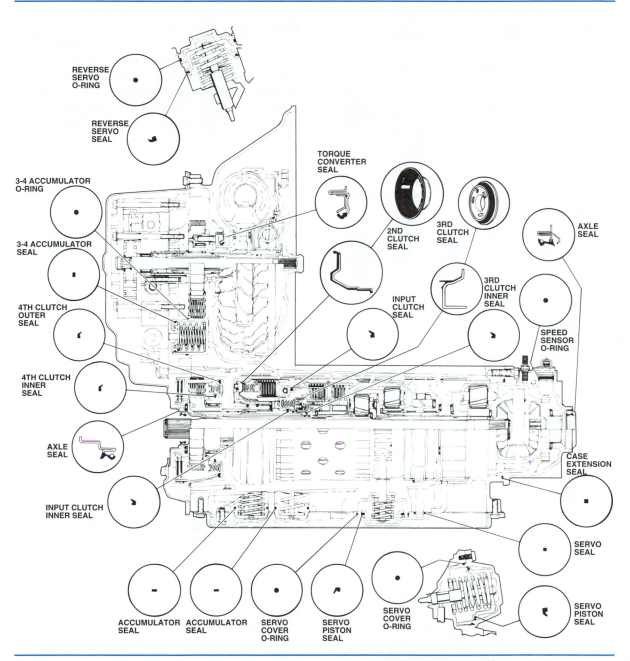

Figure 8-6. Seal locator chart shows location and seal types (4T60-E transmission). General Motors Corporation, Service and Parts Operations

neoprene is only a fair seal material and is seldom used today. The synthetic rubbers used for modern transmission seals break down into the following four groups:

1. Nitrile
2. Polyacrylic
3. Silicone
4. Fluoroelastomer

Nitrile Rubbers

Nitrile rubbers such as Buna N have excellent abrasion resistance and very good ATF compatibility. Nitrile rubber can also be formulated to work well in temperatures ranging from −40°F to 280°F (−40°C to 138°C), as shown in figure 8-7. However, when a nitrile-rubber seal is designed to be durable at high temperatures, its low-

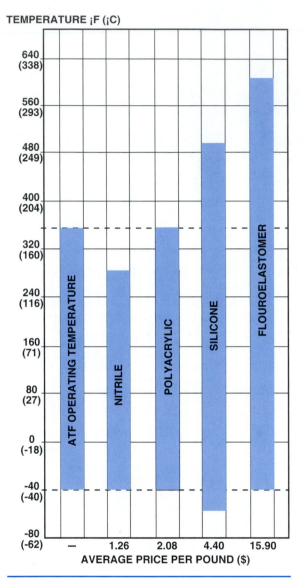

Figure 8-7. Operating temperature/materials cost chart.

Polyacrylic Rubbers

Polyacrylic rubbers such as polyacrylate or Vamac® have only fair abrasion resistance, but very good ATF compatibility. The advantage of polyacrylic over nitrile-rubber seals is that they work better at higher temperatures and hold up well in temperatures as high as 350°F (177°C). Like nitrile rubber, polyacrylic seal materials are usually black or grayish-black in color.

The disadvantages of polyacrylic seals are their high cost, poor dry-running ability, and, with certain formulations, limited low-temperature performance. Despite these drawbacks, polyacrylic compounds are suitable for some transmission seals and are frequently used for pump and piston seals, as well as in other temperature-critical applications.

Silicone Rubbers

Silicone rubbers are soft **elastomers** that have relatively poor resistance to abrasion and offer only fair ATF compatibility. An advantage of silicone is that it works extremely well over a wide temperature range of −80° to 350°F (−62° to 177°C). Although some silicone rubbers may be gray or blue in color, most are red or orange.

The disadvantages of silicone rubber include high cost, low tolerance of certain oxidized oils, and relative softness. The softness of silicone seals contributes to their poor abrasion resistance and makes them prone to handling and installation damage. In transmission applications, the use of silicone is primarily limited to oil pump seals.

temperature performance suffers. Similarly, designing a nitrile-rubber seal to remain flexible at low temperatures reduces its high-temperature durability. Nitrile-rubber seals are usually either black or grayish-black in color.

Nitrile rubber is among the least expensive seal materials, but it is inadequate for many transmission applications due to its limited operating temperature range. Nitrile-rubber transmission seals were common a few years ago but recently have given way to newer synthetic compounds that offer better high-temperature performance.

Fluoroelastomer Rubbers

Fluoroelastomer rubbers such as Viton® offer good ATF compatibility and excellent abrasion resistance. These compounds also have the best high-temperature performance and remain flexible from −40°F (−40°C) to 600°F (316°C). Fluoroelastomer rubbers are usually brown or black in color, but they may also be blue or green.

The main disadvantage of fluoroelastomer compounds is their extreme cost in comparison to all other seal materials. Due

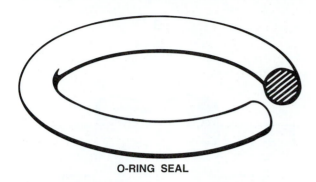

Figure 8-8. O-ring seal: limited range of axial motion—cannot be used where rotary motion occurs.

to their high price, use of fluoroelastomer seals is limited to rare instances in which the demands of the application cannot be met by any other seal material. Typical automatic transmission applications include check balls and speedometer drive seals.

RUBBER SEAL TYPES

The following three types of synthetic rubber seals are used in automatic transmissions:

- O-ring
- Square-cut
- Lip

O-Ring Seals

O-ring seals are round and have a circular cross section (figure 8-8). An O-ring works because it distorts slightly as the two parts it seals are fitted together. The O-ring fits loosely into and extends slightly past the edge of a machined groove on one of the parts (figure 8-9A). As the other part slips through the inside diameter of the O-ring, the O-ring compresses between the groove and the inner metal part (figure 8-9B). This pressure distorts the ring and forms a tight seal between the two parts.

O-ring seals are commonly used as static seals and have limited use as dynamic seals. Once the O-ring compresses, it remains in position and does not move. An O-ring on a clutch piston that moves inside

a cylinder or drum is an example of a dynamic seal. An O-ring will maintain a seal under these conditions providing the amount of axial motion is not too great. If the piston moves too far, the O-ring will roll in its groove, become damaged, and will not seal properly.

O-ring seals are never used where rotational motion occurs. As with excessive axial motion, rotation will cause an O-ring seal to shift and stretch unevenly so that it cannot maintain a seal.

Square-Cut Seals

Square, or lathe-cut, seals are circular seals that have a square or slightly rectangular cross section (figure 8-10). Like O-ring seals, square-cut seals are used in both static and dynamic seal applications. However, a square-cut seal can maintain an effective seal over a larger range of axial motion than an O-ring seal. This is because the shape of a square-cut seal prevents it from rolling over in its groove and becoming damaged. In a static application, a square-cut seal works much like an O-ring as it compresses during assembly to ensure a tight, close fit.

Square-cut seals operate well in dynamic applications under hydraulic pressure and are frequently used as clutch piston seals. When the piston moves, the outer edge of the seal slides along the cylinder wall but does not move as far as the inner edge of the seal that fits on the piston (figure 8-11). When hydraulic pressure releases, the flexed edge of a square-cut seal moves back to its original position and helps draw the piston back into the cylinder.

Square-cut seals are not used where rotational motion can occur. Rotation will cause a square-cut seal to bunch up in its groove and become damaged, much the same way as an O-ring seal.

Lip Seals

Lip seals are circular and made of rubber like O-ring and square-cut seals. However, the actual sealing is done by a thin, flexible lip that is molded as part of the seal. Two

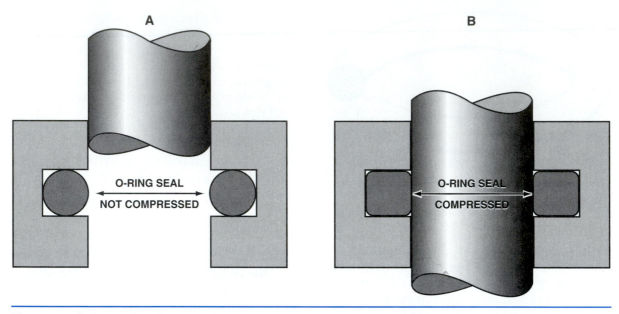

Figure 8-9. O-ring sealing characteristics.

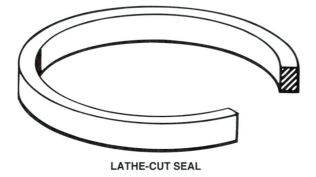

LATHE-CUT SEAL

Figure 8-10. Square-cut seal: effective where there is axial movement—cannot withstand rotary motion.

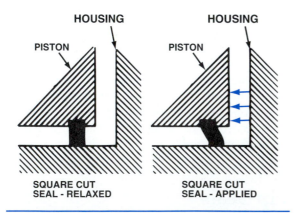

Figure 8-11. A square-cut seal compressed between a piston and its cylinder flexes in direction of moving piston.

types of lip seals are common in automatic transmissions, as follows:

- Shaft
- Piston

Shaft Seals

Shaft seals (figure 8-12) are a type of dynamic lip seal used where high rotational motion is present. A shaft seal has a metal outer shell that press fits into a bore machined in the transmission case. The rubber seal is bonded to the inside of the shell with a garter spring holding the seal lip firmly against the rotating part. This type of seal is commonly known as a radial lip seal because the garter spring loads the lip radially against the rotating part. Because the seal lip firmly attaches to the rigid metal shell and the area that receives the rotational motion is very small, the shaft seal will not distort the way an O-ring or lathe-cut seal would.

Shaft seals are found at the front and rear transmission; one rides on the torque converter hub and the other on the transmission output shaft. The job of these seals is to keep ATF within the transmission. To do this, a shaft seal is always installed with its lip fac-

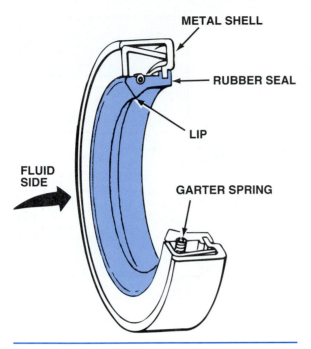

Figure 8-12. Shaft seal: used for rotary sealing—seal lip installed facing the fluid to be contained.

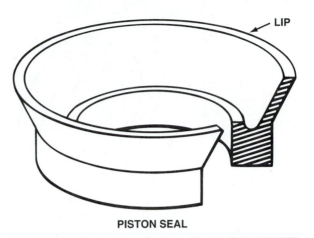

PISTON SEAL

Figure 8-13. Piston seals—type of lip seal that permits axial movement while containing high hydraulic pressure.

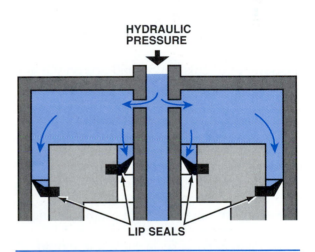

LIP SEALS

Figure 8-14. Hydraulic pressure forces seal lip against wall.

ing the fluid to be contained. Shaft seals are not designed to contain highly pressurized fluids and can rarely hold back more than about 15 psi (103 kPa) without leakage.

Piston Seals

Piston seals are a type of dynamic lip seal used where large axial movements are present (figure 8-13). A piston seal is made entirely of rubber and is similar to a square-cut seal with a lip molded on. This design is used for the internal and external seals on servo and clutch pistons.

Unlike shaft seals, piston seals are designed to contain high hydraulic pressures. To do this, piston seals are always installed with the lip facing the source of hydraulic pressure. As pressure applies, the lip seal flares and presses harder against the cylinder wall forming a tighter seal (figure 8-14). When pressure relieves, the seal relaxes and can slide easily against the cylinder in either direction.

It is important to realize that lip seals, as used on pistons, are effective in only one direction. If fluid pressure applies to the

back side of the sealing lip, the lip collapses, allowing fluid to flow past the seal.

METAL SEALS

The metal sealing rings in automatic transmissions contain pressurized ATF and direct fluid flow to hydraulic circuits (figure 8-15). Three types of metal seals are in use: open-, butt-, and locking-end. Open-end seals have a small space between the ends of the seal when installed. The square-cut ends of butt-end seals touch, or butt against, each other.

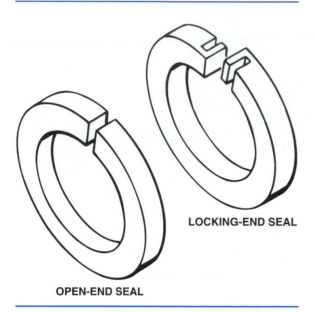

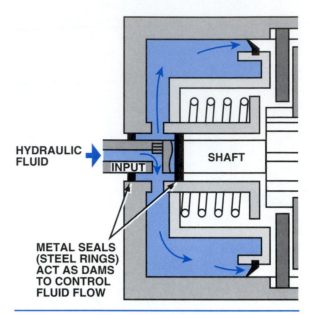

LOCKING-END SEAL

OPEN-END SEAL

Figure 8-15. Metal seal rings containing fluid to direct flow—locking and butt-end types shown.

Locking-end seals have small lips on the seal ends that interlock for better sealing.

Metal-seal rings are also known as oil rings, metal seals, or steel rings. All types of metal seals are commonly called steel rings; however, in addition to steel they might be made of cast iron, bronze, or aluminum. These sealing rings must be soft enough to seal well, yet strong and rigid enough to withstand the strain of high rotational and axial movement.

By design, these seals allow some fluid seepage past the ends of the ring. Therefore, they are used where an absolute fluid-tight seal is not required. Of the three types of seals, a locking-end seal permits the least amount of fluid seepage while an open-end seal permits the most.

Metal seals are often used as shaft seals, where they act as a dam to direct pressurized fluid from passages in a shaft or pump to a clutch drum (figure 8-16). Steel rings are also used on some accumulator and servo pistons.

TEFLON® SEALS

Teflon® seals are similar in construction to metal seals. They also perform the same tasks as steel rings and can be found in the

HYDRAULIC FLUID

INPUT

SHAFT

METAL SEALS (STEEL RINGS) ACT AS DAMS TO CONTROL FLUID FLOW

Figure 8-16. The seal rings in this clutch installation direct fluid flow from a passage in the input shaft into the clutch drum.

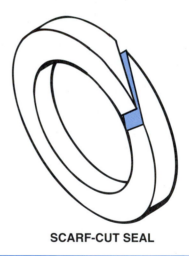

SCARF-CUT SEAL

Figure 8-17. Scarf-cut ends form a positive seal, keeping seepage to a minimum.

same locations inside the transmission. Teflon® seals are popular with transmission manufacturers because they are less expensive than metal seals and provide excellent sealing when new.

The ends of Teflon® locking-end seals vary slightly from the hooked ends of their metal counterparts, as they are cut at an angle (figure 8-17). This type of locking-end seal is generally called a "scarf-cut ring." Some original equipment Teflon® seals are a solid design and must be cut off for removal.

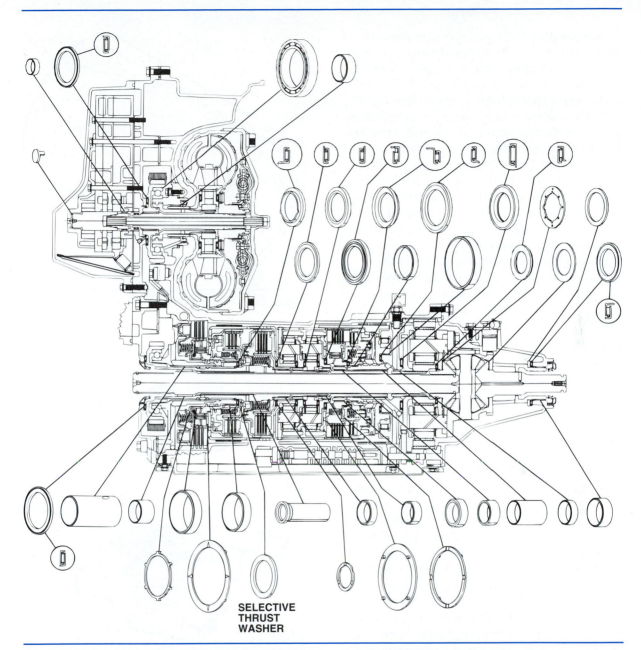

SELECTIVE THRUST WASHER

Figure 8-18. Bushing, thrust washer, and thrust bearing location chart (4T80-E transmission). General Motors Corporation, Service and Parts Operations

A disadvantage of a Teflon® seals is their relative softness, which makes them susceptible to scratches from contaminants circulating in the ATF. These scratches decrease sealing ability. In addition, metal particles can become impregnated in the soft face of a Teflon® seal, causing increased wear of the surface on which the seal rides. For these reasons, some manufacturers recommend that Teflon® seals be replaced with steel seals when the transmission is overhauled.

BUSHINGS, BEARINGS, AND THRUST WASHERS

Bushings, bearings, and thrust washers control axial and radial play within the transmission (figure 8-18). This movement must be minimized to limit transmission wear and ensure proper component location.

Radial play is the side-to-side movement, or side thrust, of the gears, drums, and hubs on a transmission shaft. Because automatic transmissions use planetary gears that are in continuous mesh, there is much less radial play than there is in a manual transmission that uses sliding gears. As a result, very few ball or roller bearings are used in automatic transmissions; bushings are used instead.

Axial play is the back-and-forth movement of a gear, gearset, hub, or drum along the axis of a shaft. A small amount of axial play is necessary in an automatic transmission for several reasons. First, it allows metal parts to expand without binding as the transmission reaches operating temperature. Second, it allows clutch drums and other parts to expand under hydraulic pressure. Finally, it allows fluid to escape between the parts when a clutch releases. However, excess axial play can cause clutch pack slippage, component wear, and damage. Thrust washers and bearings control axial play.

Bushings

A bushing is a cylindrical sleeve made of a soft metal that acts as a bearing. An assortment of bushings are used in an automatic transmission to support and align drums, shafts, gears, and other rotating parts. Bushings can be placed on a transmission shaft, pressed into a gearset component, or fit into a bore on the transmission case.

The bushings in an automatic transmission do not have to absorb much radial play, so they tend to wear very slowly. Some bushings function as a seal to restrict fluid between two components while others are designed to help direct fluid flow to a certain area. When a bushing does not function as a seal, it may have helical or diagonal oil grooves cut into its inner surface for better lubricant distribution (figure 8-19).

Thrust Washers

A thrust washer absorbs axial play to prevent automatic transmission parts from rubbing together and wearing out (figure 8-20). Because thrust washers are made of softer

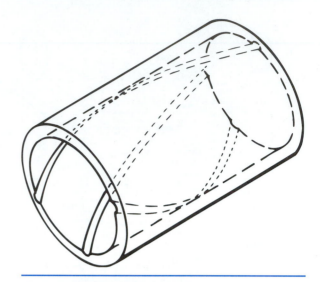

Figure 8-19. Bushings often have oil grooves.

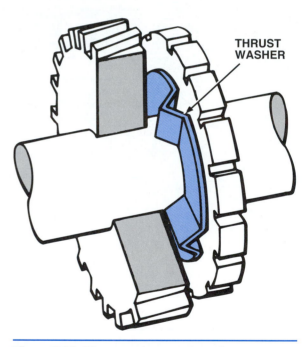

Figure 8-20. Thrust washers used to take up excess clearance.

materials than the components they separate, the thrust washers suffer the wear themselves. Typically, thrust washers are made of nylon, plastic, bronze, or soft steel with copper facings that are kept well lubricated to reduce friction.

Thrust washers often install on a transmission shaft between drums and gears or between drums and planetary gearset carriers. Several thrust bearings are used in a typical automatic transmission, and many

THICKNESS	COLOR	NUMERAL
.060 TO .064 IN (1.53 TO 1.63 mm)	YELLOW	1
.071 TO .075 IN (1.80 TO 1.91 mm)	BLUE	2
.082 TO .086 IN (2.08 TO 2.18 mm)	RED	3
.093 TO .097 IN (2.36 TO 2.46 mm)	BROWN	4
.104 TO .108 IN (2.64 TO 2.74 mm)	GREEN	5
.115 TO .119 IN (2.92 TO 3.02 mm)	BLACK	6
.126 TO .130 IN (3.20 TO 3.30 mm)	PURPLE	7

Figure 8-21. Thrust washer selection chart.

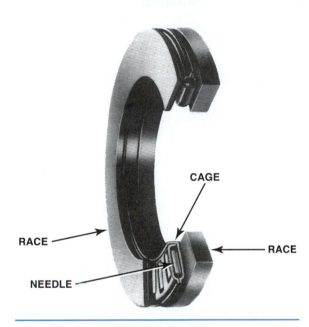

Figure 8-22. Roller-thrust bearings.

transmissions use selective-fit thrust washers to adjust transmission endplay (figure 8-21). Because they are designed to wear, replacement of thrust washers is necessary during a transmission overhaul.

Roller Thrust Bearings

Roller thrust bearings (sometimes known as Torrington® bearings, a brand name of roller thrust bearing) are rollers inside a cage that provide a low-friction connection between two races (figure 8-22). In some designs, the bearings and races are a complete unit; in other designs, the cage with the needles, or rollers, is one piece and each race is a separate unit.

Like thrust washers, roller thrust bearings reduce friction and prevent wear between drums and gears and between drums and planetary gearset carriers. Together with the

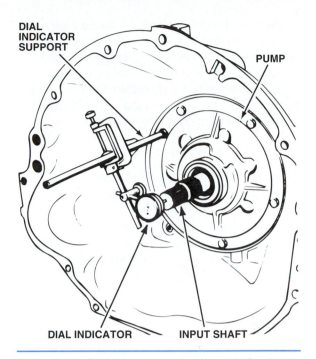

Figure 8-23. Endplay measured at input shaft using a dial indicator.

thrust washers, roller thrust bearings help control axial play in an automatic transmission. A thrust bearing is more expensive than a thrust washer, but it provides maximum protection.

Transmission Endplay

The free axial movement in an assembled transmission is called transmission **endplay**. A small amount of endplay is necessary to allow for expansion of the transmission components during operation and to allow room for lubrication. Manufacturers provide endplay specifications for each of their transmissions. As long as the endplay exceeds the minimum value, the transmission will not seize up when the metals expand as they warm up to operating temperature. In addition, if the endplay does not exceed the maximum value, the transmission can maintain sufficient hydraulic pressure even when cold.

Endplay is usually measured at the input shaft using a dial indicator (figure 8-23). The measurement is taken before a transmission is disassembled for overhaul so that the technician will be able to adjust the endplay during reassembly if needed. Endplay is also measured after the transmission is assembled to ensure that it is within the specified limits. These procedures are covered in detail in the accompanying *Shop Manual*.

Selective-Fit Thrust Washers

Transmission endplay is usually adjusted with selective-fit thrust washers that install at certain locations on the shafts. However, some transmissions use steel shims at the pump body or extension housing to set total endplay. The exact locations of the washers vary with each model of transmission. Selective-fit thrust washers are available in many thickness variations so that the proper sizes can be selected to establish the endplay within the specified limits. When overhauling a transmission, endplay should be set near the minimum measurement because it will increase as the thrust washers and other internal components wear.

SNAPRINGS

Internal and external snaprings are used as retaining devices in many places in automatic transmissions (figure 8-24). External snaprings hold clutch and gear assemblies in place on the transmission shafts, while internal snaprings hold servo piston retainers in their bores and hold clutch assemblies together.

The snaprings for some clutch assemblies come in different thickness variations and are used to adjust the amount of clearance within a clutch pack (figure 8-25). Some clutches also use a wave-type snapring to smooth clutch application (figure 8-26). Snaprings with holes in their ends, like those in figure 8-24, are called Truaro® snaprings, which require special pliers to remove and install. However, many snaprings in automatic transmissions have simple square or tapered ends, which can be removed with a small screwdriver.

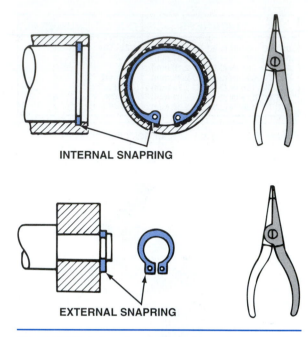

INTERNAL SNAPRING

EXTERNAL SNAPRING

Figure 8-24. Internal and external snaprings come in a variety of sizes and are used in a variety of locations.

Snaprings are stamped from sheet steel stock, and as a result, the edges on one side of the snapring may be sharp. Because of this, install a snapring so the side with the sharper edge faces away from any force that may be exerted on the ring.

SUMMARY

Transmissions require secondary parts that serve a vital role in transmission operations. These include gaskets, seals (that contain and channel ATF within the transmission), bushings, bearings, and thrust washers to support and align the shafts and reduce friction. Snaprings are also important transmission components, as they hold various parts together.

Two types of gaskets seal the space between parts with irregular surfaces. A plain paper gasket is an example of a "hard" gasket, which is less than 20 percent compressible and is best used when both mating surfaces are hard, flat, or smooth. "Soft" gaskets, such as cork or rubber compound gaskets, offer more than

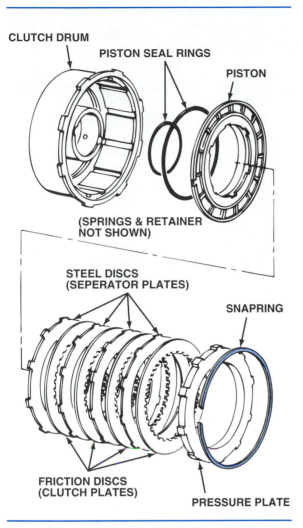

Figure 8-25. Internal snaprings holding a clutch assembly together—selectively sized to control clearance.

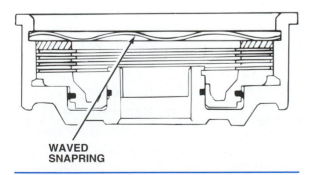

Figure 8-26. Wave-type snaprings sometimes used in clutch packs.

20 percent compressibility and are better suited to mating irregular surfaces that can be easily distorted. In order to meet the demands of the transmission, gaskets are constructed of paper, cork, plastic, rubber, and synthetics.

Sealing transmission parts can also be accomplished with rubber, metal, and Teflon® seals. Seals like these come in two forms: static and dynamic. Like gaskets, static seals block the passage of fluid between parts with no motion between them. Dynamic seals block fluid flow between parts that have relative motion between them. This motion can either be axial (movement back and forth) or rotational (when one part being sealed rotates in relation to the other). Modern transmission seals must offer high abrasion resistance, compatibility with ATF, and good sealing ability across a wide temperature range.

Bushings, bearings, and thrust washers control the previously mentioned axial play, as well as radial play (side-to-side movement of the gears, shafts, drums, and hubs). Bushings are metal sleeves, or cylinders, installed on a shaft or transmission case and act as bearings and seals for various transmission parts. Bushings do not have to absorb much radial play, so they wear very slowly.

Thrust washers, on the other hand, control only axial play in the transmission. By doing so they can adjust endplay within specified limits so the gearbox will not lose hydraulic pressure. Thrust washers, often composed of softer materials such as nylon, plastic, or bronze, are typically installed between the drums and the planetary gearset members.

Bearings also serve as axial control components. Bearings are rollers inside cages that reduce friction and prevent wear between drums and gears and between drums and planetary gearset members.

Internal and external snaprings are retaining devices that hold clutch and gear assemblies in place on transmission shafts, servo piston retainers in their bores, and clutch assemblies together. Some snaprings are designed to adjust clutch pack clearance and smooth clutch applications. All snaprings are installed with their sharp-edged side facing away from any force that may be exerted on the ring.

Review Questions

Choose the single most correct answer. Compare your answers to the correct answers on page 213.

1. Technician A says a hard gasket is used to seal surfaces that are irregular or subject to distortion.
   Technician B says a soft gasket is mostly used to seal machined surfaces.
   Who is right?
   a. A only
   b. B only
   c. Both A and B
   d. Neither A nor B

2. A gasket with good compressibility
   a. Sometimes has poor torque retention
   b. Is preferred for sealing smooth, rigid surfaces
   c. Can be replaced by a paper gasket if desired
   d. All of the above

3. Technician A says some transmissions use composition gaskets made of cork and rubber.
   Technician B says some valve body gaskets may be marked to indicate position and orientation.
   Who is right?
   a. A only
   b. B only
   c. Both A and B
   d. Neither A nor B

4. Technician A says some transmission manufacturers recommend RTV sealant in place of an oil pan gasket.
   Technician B says RTV sealant is frequently recommended in place of valve-body gaskets.
   Who is right?
   a. A only
   b. B only
   c. Both A and B
   d. Neither A nor B

5. Technician A says a non-hardening sealant can be used on the outer surface of a metal-clad lip seal.
   Technician B says you should not use sealant on a metal-clad lip seal if the outer surface is coated with rubber.
   Who is right?
   a. A only
   b. B only
   c. Both A and B
   d. Neither A nor B

6. Technician A says static seals are designed to be used with parts that move.
   Technician B says dynamic seals are designed to be used with parts that move.
   Who is right?
   a. A only
   b. B only
   c. Both A and B
   d. Neither A nor B

7. Which of the following is not a necessary characteristic of rubber seal materials?
   a. Compatibility with ATF
   b. Resistantance to abrasion
   c. Unlimited dry-running ability
   d. Wide temperature operating range

8. Technician A says most modern transmission seals are made of synthetic rubber.
   Technician B says most modern transmission seals are made of natural rubber.
   Who is right?
   a. A only
   b. B only
   c. Both A and B
   d. Neither A nor B

9. Technician A says O-ring seals are commonly used as static seals and have limited use as dynamic seals.
   Technician B says O-ring seals are frequently used in applications where rotary motion occurs.
   Who is right?
   a. A only
   b. B only
   c. Both A and B
   d. Neither A nor B

10. Technician A says square-cut seals can be used as static or dynamic seals.
    Technician B says square-cut seals work because they distort slightly under pressure.
    Who is right?
    a. A only
    b. B only
    c. Both A and B
    d. Neither A nor B

11. Technician A says lip seals are frequently used as shaft and piston seals.
    Technician B says lip seals are frequently used in applications where rotary motion occurs.
    Who is right?
    a. A only
    b. B only
    c. Both A and B
    d. Neither A nor B

12. Which of the following is not true of shaft seals?
   a. They are used where rotary motion is present.
   b. They are designed to contain high fluid pressures.
   c. They are dynamic seals.
   d. They often have a seal lip attached to a metal shell.

13. A lip-type piston seal
   a. Is installed with the lip facing the pressure source
   b. Is able to seal in only one direction
   c. Forms a tight seal as hydraulic pressure is applied
   d. All of the above

14. Technician A says Teflon® seal rings are used because they are much harder than the metal rings.
   Technician B says metal seal rings and Teflon® seal rings are basically the same except for the materials from which they are made.
   Who is right?
   a. A only
   b. B only
   c. Both A and B
   d. Neither A nor B

15. Technician A says transmission seal rings are designed to provide a highly fluid-tight seal.
   Technician B says a butt-end seal ring allows more fluid leakage than a locking-end seal ring.
   Who is right?
   a. A only
   b. B only
   c. Both A and B
   d. Neither A nor B

16. Technician A says radial play is the side-to-side movement of a part along its center axis.
   Technician B says axial play can be adjusted with selective-fit thrust washers or thrust bearings.
   Who is right?
   a. A only
   b. B only
   c. Both A and B
   d. Neither A nor B

17. Technician A says bushings can serve as a type of internal transmission seal by restricting or directing fluid flow.
   Technician B says bushings are used to support and align transmission components.
   Who is right?
   a. A only
   b. B only
   c. Both A and B
   d. Neither A nor B

18. Technician A says thrust washers wear out before the components they separate.
   Technician B says thrust washers are made of the hardest materials possible, such as tungsten and tool steel.
   Who is right?
   a. A only
   b. B only
   c. Both A and B
   d. Neither A nor B

19. Transmission endplay is
   a. The total axial play of the assembled transmission
   b. The total radial play of the assembled transmission
   c. Usually adjusted with steel shims
   d. Measured only after the transmission is overhauled

20. Technician A says external snaprings are often used to hold servo covers in place.
   Technician B says a selective-fit snapring may be used to adjust the clearance of a clutch pack.
   Who is right?
   a. A only
   b. B only
   c. Both A and B
   d. Neither A nor B

PART TWO

Transmission and Transaxle Electronics

Chapter Nine
Basic Computer and
Electronic Controls

Chapter Ten
Electronic Control Systems

Basic Computer and Electronic Controls

Today's automotive management systems use electronic components to keep the powertrain operating at peak efficiency with minimal emissions output and optimum performance. Included is the electronic control of shifting and torque converter clutch operation in automatic transmissions.

Early electronic systems controlled only torque converter clutch (TCC) operation. Over the years, technology has evolved and become more powerful, resulting in fully electronic automatic transmission (EAT) designs that control not only TCC and shifting functions, but hydraulic pressure development as well.

This chapter covers the basic principles associated with electronic operations, including computer control principles, sensors, actuators, and **On-Board Diagnostic** (OBD) systems.

COMPUTER CONTROL

Computer modules consisting of **integrated circuits** work with a network of sensors and actuators to regulate the automatic transmission, as well as other automotive functions. Computer technology enables engineers to simplify transmission designs, resulting in improved performance as well as reduced manufacturing costs.

The computer module (figure 9-1) is the heart of the electronic control system. It receives and processes information in the form of voltage signals from input devices, or **sensors**, and transmits voltage signals that regulate the outputs, or actuators, that control mechanical operations.

Some vehicles have many computer control modules that regulate a number of electronic systems such as climate control systems, antilock braking systems, automatic ride control systems, and of course powertrain control systems such as the engine and transmission. Earlier systems used engine control modules (ECMs) to regulate engine functions and a separate transmission control module (TCM) to regulate transmission functions. Most vehicles today

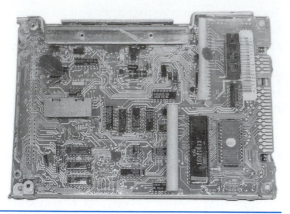

Figure 9-1. Integrated circuits inside a typical computer module.

use a powertrain control module (PCM) to regulate engine and transmission functions.

Computer Operating Principles

The operation of any computer system can be divided into the following four basic functions:

- Input
- Processing
- Storage
- Output

Inputs

A computer module receives voltage signals from sensor devices. In the case of a PCM, these voltage signals provide information about vehicle operating conditions such as engine temperature, engine speed, vehicle speed, transmission fluid temperature, and engine load, to name but a few (figure 9-2).

Processing

A computer module translates, or processes, input voltage signals into **binary** numbers (1s and 0s) that it compares with its programming instructions and other stored data. The module then makes logical decisions and sends the appropriate commands to various output devices in the system.

Storage

A computer module has an electronic memory to store its operating instructions and programs. Some modules have the ability to store input signals for later reference and updating internal files associated with operating conditions. Some modules, most PCMs in fact, can "remember" previous operating conditions and can adapt their output commands to current operating characteristics. In other words, the module has "learning" or "adaptive" capabilities commonly referred to as **adaptive learning memory**.

Outputs

After receiving and processing input data, the module transmits output commands to the appropriate actuators. The actuators are devices such as solenoids and relays that convert electrical signals into mechanical action.

Signal Conditioning

Computer modules can only process **digital** voltage signals. Some input signals must therefore be converted from **analog** to digital signals before the **microcomputer** or **central processing unit (CPU)** portion of the module can interpret the information.

Once input signals are properly converted, the information is directed to the microcomputer's memory where it is evaluated with respect to the module's programming.

The evaluation process (figure 9-3) allows the microcomputer to select the best possible choices for system control. Keep in mind that the process of filtering, storing, and analyzing signals, as well as making decisions, happens in a fraction of a second—as quickly as 1/1000 of a second (one millisecond).

Computer Memory

A control module makes decisions by comparing actual operating conditions to program data stored in memory. This programmed data tells the module how to process input signals and in what order; it also determines what output signals are

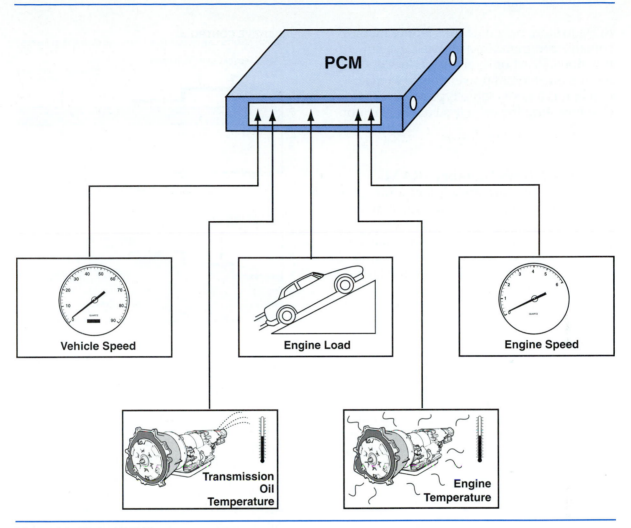

Figure 9-2. Typical PCM inputs.

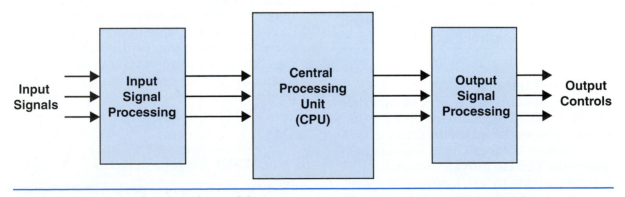

Figure 9-3. Information flow through a module.

required, when they are needed, and the proper order. Following are the different types of storage memory used in computer modules.

Read-Only Memory (ROM)

Read-only memory is permanently stored data that is programmed by the manufacturer and is always available. The module can only read the contents; it cannot use the

ROM to store new data. Read-only memory contains programming for basic system functions. Read-only memory does not require an external power source to maintain it; it is a nonvolatile type of memory, so disconnecting the vehicle's battery will not erase it.

Random-Access Memory (RAM)

Random-access memory is temporary storage space that the module uses as it makes calculations during vehicle operation. Random-access memory requires an external power source, which makes it volatile. In other words, it erases whenever the ignition is switched off or the battery is disconnected. Because RAM is where general data and ongoing calculations are stored, it does not matter that it is lost when the vehicle is shut off.

Nonvolatile RAM

Nonvolatile RAM is a special type of long-term random-access storage contained on a separate memory chip that is connected to battery voltage. This prevents stored data from being erased when the ignition is turned off or when the battery is disconnected.

Nonvolatile RAM is where the module stores information that is subject to change or update but must be retained when the ignition is off. This includes adaptive memory and diagnostic trouble codes.

Adaptive Memory

Adaptive memory is a type of storage that allows the PCM to modify its decision-making process based on the actual operating experience of the vehicle. This feature allows the PCM to provide superior shift control and quality by "learning" the specific operating conditions and characteristics of an individual vehicle (figure 9-4).

Adaptive strategies permit the PCM to compensate for changes in engine performance and normal friction material wear. The end result is a consistent shift quality throughout the life of the transmission. This learning capability is called adaptive learn-

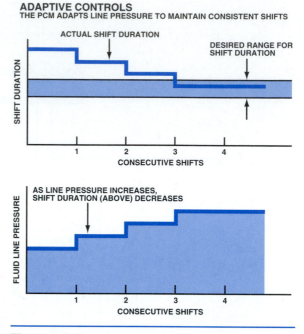

Figure 9-4. Adaptive memory.

ing, and the data is stored in a special section of the RAM.

Adaptive learning can be done on both a short- and long-term basis. On a short-term basis, the system corrects itself for momentary differences. The PCM stores short-term correction information in volatile RAM, so the adaptive strategy is lost when the ignition is switched off. If the same momentary conditions recur frequently enough, the adaptive strategy is moved into nonvolatile RAM to make the correction more permanent. Adaptive learning allows the control system to adapt to long-term wear or gradual changes in vehicle operation.

Program Instructions

Every module requires control instructions to operate correctly. These instructions, or programs, consist of several elements. Using a PCM as an example, the first element consists of the mathematical and logic instructions that tell the module how to process the data it receives. Second is the data pertaining to permanent or fixed vehicle traits, such

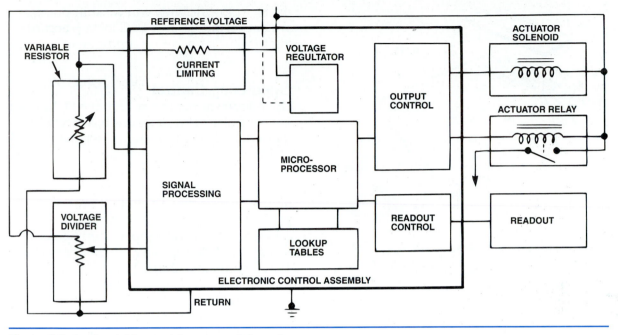

Figure 9-5. Lookup tables contain program information.

as the number of cylinders, engine displacement, and compression ratio. The last element includes the variable operating data and performance characteristics of the particular engine, transmission, and chassis that the PCM services.

The mathematical formulas and fixed traits are constant values that do not change over the operating life of the vehicle. Design engineers permanently store this information in the ROM as **lookup tables**. The PCM reads lookup tables to access information it uses to make calculations and generate the proper output (figure 9-5).

Design engineers determine how the PCM responds to variable conditions using a process called mapping. To establish a map, the powertrain is operated on a dynamometer and variable inputs are manually adjusted to obtain optimum settings for driveability, economy, and performance. This information is recorded in a dedicated section of the ROM known as **programmable read-only memory (PROM)**.

Real-world operating conditions are often quite different than what engineers can create on a dynamometer in a laboratory. As a result, PROM information does not always provide acceptable driveability; PROM programs are often updated and revised to rem-

edy situations encountered in field-testing or described in customer complaints.

On early computers, the PROM was often a separate chip that installed in the PCM (figure 9-6). With programming variables located on a replaceable chip, a technician could upgrade the control system without replacing the entire PCM. It also allowed a single base PCM to be used for a number of different vehicles by simply installing different PROM chips.

Late-model control systems use a flash electronically erasable programmable read-only memory (FEEPROM). These processors allow a technician to electronically program, or flash, a new set of instructions into the PROM using a scan tool. Flash programming offers a quick way to update the control system without having to remove the PCM or replace any hard parts.

PCM System Operating Strategies

Powertrain control modules have several operating modes or strategies that determine how they respond to input signals. The three most common operating modes

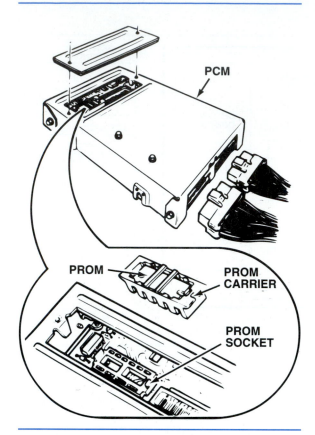

Figure 9-6. PROM chip contains operating instructions.

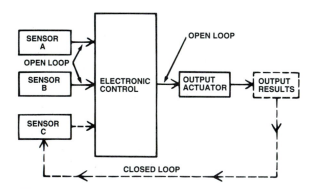

Figure 9-7. Closed-loop operation.

are closed-loop, open-loop, and default mode.

Closed-Loop Control

In closed-loop operation the PCM is in complete control of system operations. The PCM issues output commands based on input and **feedback** signals from system sensors (figure 9-7). Closed-loop operation allows

the PCM to efficiently control shift points, system pressures, and TCC lockup according to vehicle operating conditions.

Open-Loop Control

Open-loop simply means that the PCM does not control system functions based solely on input data. One circumstance when the PCM is in open-loop mode includes initial startup. Powertrain control modules operate in open-loop until the engine has been running for a prescribed period of time and a prescribed operating temperature is achieved. When in the open-loop operating mode, the PCM typically will not provide TCC lockup, and shift scheduling is typically modified according to established program parameters. Although the PCM does not respond to input data, it does continuously monitor input data such as engine coolant temperature (ECT) transmission oil temperature (TOT), and the exhaust gas oxygen sensor (O2S) in order to determine when conditions are achieved for closed-loop operation.

Default Mode

The default mode is engaged when the PCM detects a problem that appears serious enough to cause damage. In general, default mode shuts down some electronic operations and limits others, allowing the vehicle to continue to be driven, but at reduced capacity.

A PCM operating in the default mode may restrict transmission operation to a single gear—no upshifts or downshifts. The operating gears of a transmission in default mode vary among manufacturers and can be identified using a shift solenoid application chart (figure 9-8). The default gear will be the one that can be achieved without any electronic signals—all solenoids OFF.

It's important to note that many modern systems are able to function "around" minor problems to maintain effective performance. In such cases the PCM may override or ignore a faulty signal, calculate a new value, replace the faulty signal with a value stored in memory, or substitute a different signal from another sensor. In some cases, the con-

	GEAR	SHIFT SOLENOIDS	
		SS1	SS2
ⒹRANGE	4	ON	ON
	3	OFF	ON
	2	OFF	OFF
	1	ON	OFF
D RANGE	3	OFF	ON
	2	OFF	OFF
	1	ON	OFF
1 RANGE	2	OFF	OFF
	1	ON	OFF
R, P, N RANGE	–	ON	OFF

Figure 9-8. Solenoid application chart—Ford AODE.

trol system can provide such a high level of self-correction that the driver is not even aware there is a problem. In most of these cases the PCM will illuminate the Service Engine Soon (SES) or Check Engine lamp.

SENSORS

A sensor is a device that provides an electrical signal to a control module to indicate certain physical conditions such as temperature, movement, position, or speed. Electronic control systems, including systems used in the control of automatic transmissions, use a variety of sensors to monitor different parameters and operating conditions.

Switches

A switch is the simplest kind of sensor. A switch opens or closes an input circuit to provide the control module with a high or low voltage signal. Some common uses of switches include the following:

- Brake pedal position switch—An input to tell the module when the

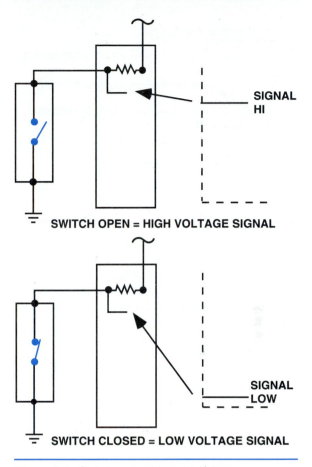

SWITCH OPEN = HIGH VOLTAGE SIGNAL

SIGNAL HI

SIGNAL LOW

SWITCH CLOSED = LOW VOLTAGE SIGNAL

Figure 9-9. Switches provide module input.

brake pedal is applied. This input affects TCC lockup. Lockup is disengaged during brake applications.
- Power steering pressure switch—An input that alerts the PCM to high hydraulic pressure conditions in the power steering system. The PCM uses this input to compensate for additional engine loads during parking maneuvers by adjusting the idle speed and transmission line pressure.
- Gear position switch—This input informs the PCM of the gearshift position.

Switches can be either normally OPEN or normally CLOSED; and most are installed on the ground side of the circuit. Referring to figure 9-9, when the switch is OPEN, the module sees a HIGH voltage signal; when the switch is CLOSED, the module sees a LOW voltage signal.

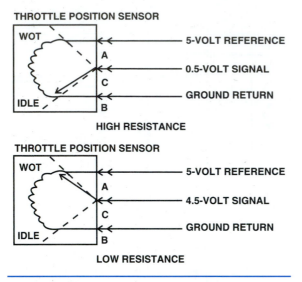

Figure 9-10. Potentiometer—throttle position sensor.

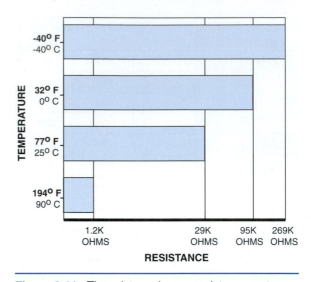

Figure 9-11. Thermistors change resistance as temperature changes.

Potentiometers

Potentiometers are variable resistors that sense motion or position. A potentiometer has three terminals used for the following connections:

- **Reference voltage**
- Signal voltage
- Ground return

The module applies a reference voltage (typically 5 volts) to the terminal at one end of a resistor. The terminal at the opposite end of the resistor connects to ground and provides a return path. The third terminal, located between the other two, attaches to a movable wiper that sweeps back and forth across the resistor. This terminal sends a variable voltage signal back to the PCM as an input. The wiper mechanically attaches to the device to be sensed, such as throttle linkage.

The signal voltage from the potentiometer will be high or low, depending on whether the movable wiper is near the supply end or ground end of the resistor. Most potentiometer sensors install so the linkage they are sensing holds the wiper in a low-voltage, or high-resistance, position. Using a throttle position sensor as an example, signal voltage will be at its lowest when the throttle is closed (figure 9-10). Move the throttle to a wide-open position and signal voltage will rise to its highest possible reading.

Constant current through the potentiometer resistor maintains constant temperature, so resistance does not change due to temperature variation. This ensures a constant, uniform voltage drop across the entire resistor. The return signal voltage varies only in relation to movement of the wiper.

Thermistors

A **thermistor** is a solid-state variable resistor, usually with two connector terminals. The resistance of a thermistor changes as temperature changes (figure 9-11). The module applies a reference voltage through a pull-up resistor to the thermistor. The computer then monitors the voltage drop across the pull-up resistor and interprets any change in voltage as a signal of changing temperature.

When exposed to cold temperatures the resistance is high, so it drops most of the reference voltage. Therefore, the signal voltage, which is measured ahead of the thermistor, will be high. An increase in temperature causes resistance across the thermistor to decrease, causing the signal voltage to drop as well (figure 9-12).

The variable resistance curve of a thermistor throughout its operating range makes it an ideal analog temperature sensor. Different sensing element designs allow thermistors to gauge the temperature of various substances. A typical automotive sys-

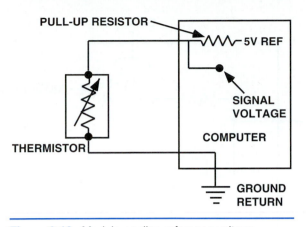

Figure 9-12. Module applies reference voltage.

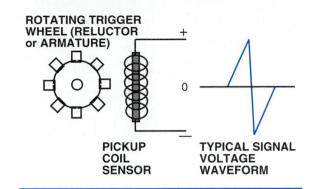

Figure 9-13. Typical magnetic pulse generator.

tem uses thermistors for the engine coolant temperature (ECT) sensor, intake air temperature (IAT) sensor, and transmission oil temperature (TOT) sensor.

Voltage-Generating Sensors

Voltage-generating sensors are active devices that produce their own voltage and do not depend on a reference voltage from the module. This type of sensor typically monitors rotational speed. There are several types of voltage-generating sensors, including the following:

- **Magnetic pulse generator**
- **Hall-effect switch**
- **Galvanic battery**

Magnetic Pulse Generator

A magnetic pulse generator has many names: magnetic pickup, pickup coil, reluctance sensor, and permanent magnet generator. Regardless of what you call them, they are voltage-generating devices and they all work like the earliest pickup coils in electronic distributors.

The pickup coil is wound around a permanent magnet. As the teeth of a rotating trigger wheel pass by the magnet, the magnetic field expands and collapses to generate an alternating-current voltage in the pickup coil (figure 9-13). This current is sent as a digital input signal to the PCM. The frequency of the signal pulse varies in proportion to the speed of the rotor, but voltage can

only be either high or low. Many transmission shaft speed sensors are the magnetic pulse generator type. Pickup coils may also be used to provide an engine speed (RPM) signal, crankshaft position (CKP) signal, camshaft position (CMP) signal, vehicle speed signal, and wheel speed signals for antilock brake systems (ABS).

Hall-Effect Device

A Hall-effect switch also produces a digital signal voltage and may be used as a timing or speed sensor. However, a Hall-effect switch requires input voltage and current in order to produce an output voltage signal.

With a Hall-effect switch, the module applies current through the Hall element, which is a small semiconductor chip. A magnet positioned at a right angle to the chip surface creates a magnetic field, and a rotating shutter wheel induces voltage pulses within the element (figure 9-14). The frequency of the voltage signal varies with the speed of the shutter wheel, but voltage is either high or low.

Galvanic Battery (Oxygen Sensor)

A galvanic battery generates an analog voltage signal through a chemical reaction. An O2S is a galvanic battery made of zirconium dioxide (zirconia). An O2S can generate an output voltage up to approximately 1 volt, with a usable signal range from about 0.1 to 0.9 volt (100 to 900 mV). The difference in the amount of oxygen in the exhaust compared to the amount of oxygen

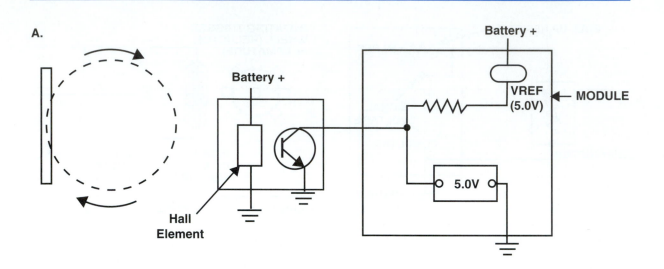

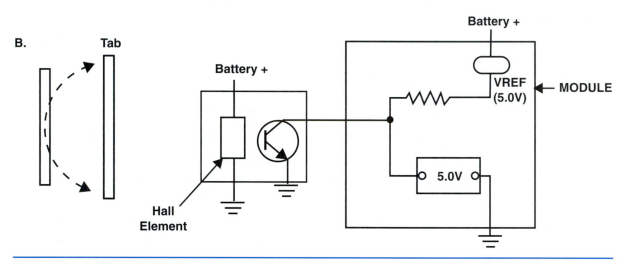

Figure 9-14. Typical Hall-Effect device.

in the outside air generates the signal voltage (figure 9-15).

When exhaust oxygen content is high, there is little difference between the oxygen in the exhaust and oxygen in the outside air. Therefore, sensor voltage is low (100 to 450mV). This is equivalent to a lean mixture, or lean exhaust condition. When exhaust oxygen content is low, there is a large difference between the oxygen in the exhaust and oxygen in the outside air. Therefore, sensor voltage is high (450 to 900mV). This is equivalent to a rich mixture, or rich exhaust, condition.

A zirconia oxygen sensor must warm to at least 300° C (572° F) before it will generate a valid signal. Remember, the O2S is one of

the primary signals the PCM uses to regulate loop control. Engine and transmission control system operations may be impaired if the PCM cannot enter closed-loop due to an O2S fault.

Pressure Measurement Sensors

Many systems measure pressure changes using a **piezoelectric** sensor. This type of sensor takes advantage of the special electrical properties of piezoelectric crystals. When pressure is applied to a piezoelectric crystal, the crystal produces a voltage signal.

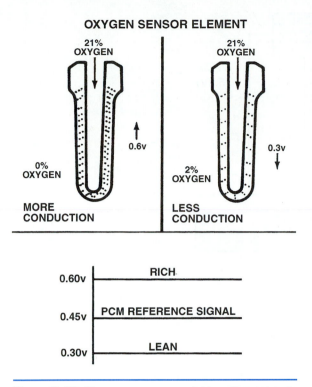

OXYGEN SENSOR ELEMENT

21% OXYGEN	21% OXYGEN
0.6v	0.3v
0% OXYGEN	2% OXYGEN
MORE CONDUCTION	LESS CONDUCTION

0.60v — RICH

0.45v — PCM REFERENCE SIGNAL

0.30v — LEAN

Figure 9-15. Oxygen sensor—variable voltage signal.

Piezoelectric sensors act like microphones and perform as knock sensors (KS) in many engine control systems to detect detonation (figure 9-16).

ACTUATORS

After the module processes input signals and calculates the required response, it sends the necessary output to devices called actuators. An actuator converts electrical signals into mechanical actions to perform the physical control tasks demanded by the module. A transistorized output driver inside the module regulates the movement of the actuators through electronic signaling. These output drivers are switches that open or close the ground side of the actuator circuit (figure 9-17).

Most actuators contain some kind of induction coil, and all actuators have a minimum resistance specification. If the resistance is too low, excess current flows through the device and this additional power is dissipated as heat by the actuator and module. Low resistance can overheat

and destroy both the actuator and its output driver.

In automotive applications, actuators can be relays, stepper motors, or solenoids. A transmission control system uses several varieties of solenoids to carry out the commands of the module.

Solenoids

A solenoid is an electromechanical device that uses magnetism to move an iron core. The core provides mechanical motion to some other system part. Therefore, a solenoid changes electrical voltage and current into mechanical movement. Solenoids operate like a switch that either energizes or de-energizes when it receives a voltage signal from the module. A solenoid is a digital device because it can be in only one of two states: ON or OFF. With electronic automatic transmissions, solenoids operate the TCC, develop governor and throttle pressure, toggle shift valves, and modify transmission line pressure.

Solenoids can operate in one of two ways: switch on or off and remain that way for a length of time, or rapidly pulse on and off at a given rate. These two methods of control are known as ON/OFF switching and **pulse-width modulation (PWM)**, respectively. Typically, shift solenoids are ON/OFF switching units while pressure regulating solenoids are PWM. Both types are used for the TCC solenoid, but most modern designs use a PWM signal for more precise control of converter clutch application.

Pulse-Width Modulation (PWM) Duty Cycle

All solenoids are direct-current electrical devices that can only be either fully on or fully off. However, if electrical current to a solenoid rapidly cycles on and off, the solenoid can be made to regulate motion or pressure as if it were capable of maintaining a position somewhere between fully on and

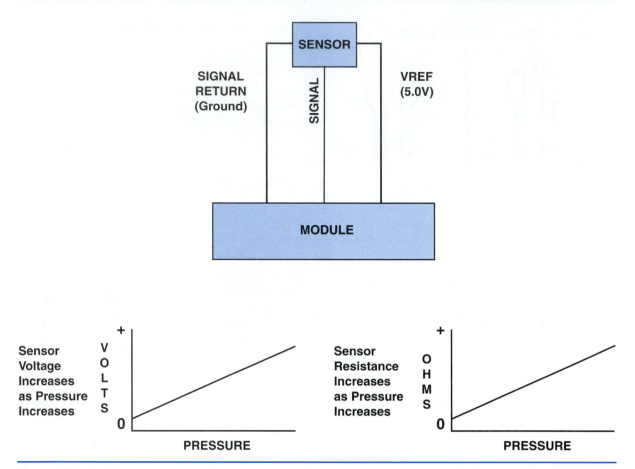

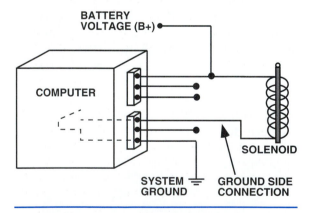

Figure 9-16. Pressure sensor operation.

Figure 9-17. Module control of actuators.

fully off. This type of control, known as PWM, is commonly used to regulate TCC applications and mainline pressure on modern automatic transmissions.

To be effective, the module must precisely regulate current to the solenoid as it switches on and off rapidly at a specific number of cycles per second, or **hertz** (Hz).

The complete operating cycle of a pulsed solenoid is the sequence from OFF to ON and back OFF again. Depending on its design and use, an actuator solenoid can operate at any number of cycles per second. For example, the TCC solenoid of a Hydra-Matic 4T80-E operates at 32 hertz, whereas the pressure control solenoid on the same transmission operates at 292.5 hertz. This means that whenever the engine is running the TCC cycles OFF-ON-OFF 32 times every second, whereas the pressure control solenoid cycles almost 300 times per second. These are simple examples; some solenoids switch faster, and some slower. In general, the higher the number of cycles per second, the more precisely a solenoid can control pressure or motion.

With a PWM solenoid, the total cycle time is the time the solenoid is ON in addition to the time the solenoid is OFF. The time it takes to complete the cycle is the period of the cycle, and the number of times per second the cycle occurs is the **frequency**. The percentage of time the solenoid is energized, or ON, compared to the total cycle time is called the **duty cycle**. Pulse width is the amount of time a solenoid is energized, or the ON part of the cycle, and is usually measured in milliseconds (ms). Pulse-width modulation allows a module to obtain a very smooth, near-analog response from a digital device.

ONBOARD DIAGNOSTICS

All electronic automatic transmission control systems are designed with fully self-diagnostic capabilities that run system and component tests at start-up, then monitor system operations continuously during vehicle operation. The onboard diagnostics also have technician-activated programs for testing and troubleshooting the control system.

Typically, the PCM runs a series of initialization tests when it first energizes at start-up. The first test checks internal PCM circuits and memory to ensure the PCM itself is working correctly. Next, the PCM applies power to the remainder of the control system and performs initialization tests on the sensors and actuators. All this happens so rapidly the driver does not even notice. Once the PCM verifies the controls are functional, it allows the engine to start. With the engine running, the PCM begins monitoring electronic feedback signals.

During vehicle operation some PCM programs continuously run self-test routines, while others run them at intervals. Each system sensor and actuator has a valid operating range. As part of self-test strategy, the PCM monitors these devices to ensure they are operating within normal limits. Typically, the PCM looks for input and output signals that are bad, missing, or out-of-limits according to the lookup tables and program maps.

Should the PCM detect any minor problems during the start-up or monitor testing, it logs a record of them in memory.

Figure 9-18. Malfunction indicator lamp (MIL).

Depending on the fault, the PCM may or may not set a **diagnostic trouble code (DTC)**. For faults of a more serious nature, the PCM sets a DTC and flashes, or illuminates, the **malfunction indicator lamp** (MIL) to notify the driver, figure 9-18. In the event of a severe failure, the PCM enters default strategy and disables electronic operations.

Diagnostic Trouble Codes (DTCs)

Diagnostic trouble codes are multiple-digit characters that reflect the general types and locations of circuit problems. They are designed to assist a technician in troubleshooting the system by directing attention to likely problem areas. Most codes are set by electrical problems, but some mechanical and hydraulic problems can also set a DTC. Although a DTC cannot identify the exact cause, nature, or location of a failure, it can identify which circuit has the problem.

Early self-diagnostic programs offered only a limited number of possible codes typically associated with circuit opens or shorts. Modern onboard diagnostic programs have the ability to send test signals to check circuit operations, operate system components to check feedback response, and continuously perform self-tests during normal operation. In addition, modern systems allow a technician to command the PCM and test specific components. The latest OBD-II systems even monitor system *efficiency*. Diagnostic trouble codes on these sophisticated programs provide some fairly specific information on circuit activity, such as the following:

- Erratic signal
- Absent signal
- Improbable signal
- Out-of-Range signal

The PCM retains a record of some codes until a technician retrieves them, repairs the source of the fault, and clears the PCM memory. Other codes may automatically erase after a certain length of time, number of drive cycles, or number of engine starts. Some codes can also be displaced by another DTC that represents a higher priority failure.

A DTC may be categorized as either a hard or soft code depending upon the type of failure it represents. When a DTC sets because of complete failure in a component or circuit, the DTC is known as a hard code. DTCs that set due to momentary signal problems resulting from brief interruptions or intermittent malfunctions that correct themselves are known as soft codes. Although manufacturers use different terms to describe code types, the concept of hard and soft codes applies to all systems.

Hard Codes

This type of DTC indicates a permanent failure. In other words, the problem is present whenever the PCM sends out a test signal or looks for a feedback response. Hard codes indicate ongoing problems that require attention, and most illuminate the MIL.

To compensate for a hard code failure, the PCM will typically ignore the signal from the faulty circuit and substitute a lookup table value. If the failures compromise the integrity of the control system, the PCM typically enters a default mode.

Soft Codes

Soft codes indicate intermittent problems that occur randomly, infrequently, or only once. This type of DTC is often the result of a poor connection or some type of electrical interference. Generally, a PCM notes the problem as it occurs, maintains a record of the fault in volatile memory, and sets a DTC.

Often, the DTC will automatically erase if the setting conditions do not re-occur within an established time. Should the failure occur more frequently, the DTC may change to a hard code. For some soft codes, the MIL may flash briefly when a code sets, then go out. Other intermittent problems may set a DTC without illuminating the MIL at all.

OBD-II

The California Air Resources Board (CARB) began regulating On-Board Diagnostic (OBD) systems on vehicles sold in California beginning with the 1988 model year. The initial requirements included identifying likely areas of malfunctions with respect to the fuel metering system, Exhaust Gas Recirculation (EGR) system, and other emission-related components including the PCM. A Malfunction Indicator Lamp (MIL) labeled "Check Engine" or "Service Engine Soon" was also required to illuminate to alert the driver of such malfunctions. Finally, diagnostic trouble codes (DTCs) were required to assist the technician in diagnosing the faults.

The CARB, along with the federal Environmental Protection Agency (EPA), mandated enhanced OBD systems, known as OBD-II, in 1994. The objectives of OBD-II are to improve air quality by reducing emissions caused by emission-related malfunctions, reducing the time between the occurrence of a malfunction and its detection and repair, and assisting in the diagnosis and repair of emission-related concerns. As of 1996, all passenger cars and trucks (up to 14,000 lb GVWR for California and 8500-lb GVWR for all other states) are required to comply with either CARB OBD-II or EPA OBD-II requirements.

The OBD-II system monitors vehicle systems for malfunctions. Some component operations are monitored continuously, regardless of driving mode; others are monitored non-continuously, once per drive cycle during specific drive modes. When faults are detected, DTCs are stored in the PCMs Keep Alive Memory (KAM). In most cases, the MIL is illuminated after two consecutive drive cycles with the malfunction present. Once the MIL is illuminated, three consecutive drive cycles without a malfunction detected are required to extinguish the MIL.

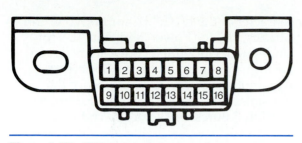

Figure 9-19. OBD-II data link connector.

The DTC is erased from the PCM's memory after 40 engine warm-up cycles without the MIL illuminated.

In addition to specifying and standardizing much of the diagnostics and MIL operation, OBD-II calls for the standardization of a vehicle's:

- Data Link Connector (DLC) (figure 9-19)—Standardization is with respect to the configuration of the DLC for purposes of interfacing with scan tools; also with respect to its location on the vehicle.
- Communication protocols—PCMs are required to communicate with a variety of scan tool devices, not just those developed by the specific manufacturer.
- DTCs—All manufacturers are required to use standard five-character formatted DTCs.

Other OBD-II standards include a common glossary of terms, standard procedures for clearing DTCs, standards for monitoring emissions, and standards associated with **freeze-frame data**.

OBD-II Monitor Systems

OBD-II vehicles may be equipped with up to nine diagnostic monitors, as follows:

- Comprehensive Component Monitor—Monitors for malfunctions in any powertrain electronic component or circuit that provides input or output signals to the PCM that can affect emissions and is not monitored by another OBD-II monitor.
- Misfire Detection Monitor—This monitor detects if there is a lack of combustion in a cylinder resulting in a misfire. The misfire monitor is designed to

identify the cylinder that experienced the misfire. There are two types of misfires: "A" and "B."

A type "A" misfire is one that can cause catalyst damage and is the most severe type of misfire. Upon detecting a type "A" misfire, the PCM will cause the MIL to blink once per second during the actual misfire, and a DTC will be stored.

A type "B" misfire is one that will cause excessive emissions or cause a vehicle to fail an Inspection/ Maintenance (IM) emissions test. The MIL will illuminate and a DTC will be stored.

- Thermostat Monitor—This monitor is executed once per drive cycle following a two-hour engine-off soak period. It is used to ensure that the engine is operating within normal temperature parameters.
- Catalyst Efficiency Monitor—Uses two oxygen sensors (one before the catalyst and one after the catalyst) and infers catalyst efficiency based on the oxygen storage capacity of the catalyst.
- EGR System Monitor—Tests the integrity and flow characteristics of the EGR system.
- Fuel System Monitor—Monitors the fuel trim system to ensure the proper air/fuel ratio is maintained during closed-loop operation.
- HO2S Monitor—This monitor checks the voltage output and switching rate of the heated oxygen sensors.
- Secondary Air Injection System Monitor—This monitor uses the HO2S sensors to test the function of the electric air pump and the integrity of the Secondary Air Injection System, on vehicles so equipped.
- Evaporative Emissions Leak Check Monitor—Checks for leaks from openings in the evaporative emission system equal to or greater than 1.016 mm (0.040 inch).

The extent to which concerns detected by these monitor systems affect vehicle performance, including automatic transmission functions, depends upon the nature of the concern and the severity of the concern. However, that any concern severe enough to illuminate the MIL and cause a DTC to be stored is a concern that *must* be addressed before pursuing any further diagnostic or service operations.

OBD-II Drive Cycles

An OBD-II drive cycle is a method for driving a vehicle that allows the OBD-II monitors to execute and complete. A drive cycle should be performed as part of the repair verification process. Generally speaking, a drive cycle begins by allowing the vehicle to idle for a prescribed period of time, allowing the engine to reach normal operating temperature. The process continues by driving the vehicle in stop-and-go conditions as well as steady-state cruise conditions, each for a prescribed period of time and at various speeds. The manufacturer's service manual outlines specific procedures to follow in driving the vehicle to successfully execute and complete the monitors. It is very important to follow these driving procedures exactly as stated. Failure to follow the prescribed driving method may cause one or more monitors not to execute or complete.

OBD-II DTCS

OBD-II DTCs follow a five-character alphanumeric format. The first character, a letter, defines the system where the code was set. The second character, a number, reveals whether the code is OBD-II-required or manufacturer-defined. The remaining three characters, all numbers, describe the nature of the malfunction (figure 9-20).

Base System
There are four letters currently assigned for system recognition to be used as the first

character of the DTC: "B" for Body, "C" for Chassis, "P" for Powertrain, and "U" for Undefined. Undefined codes are reserved for future assignment by the Society of Automotive Engineers (SAE). Since the transmission is part of the powertrain, transmission failures will set a "P" code.

Code Type
The second character of the DTC will be either a "0," "1," "2," or "3." A zero in this position indicates a malfunction that is defined by OBD-II; the number one is a code defined by the vehicle manufacturer. The numerals two and three are designated for future use and both are reserved for SAE assignment in powertrain codes.

Vehicle System
The third character of a powertrain DTC indicates the system where the fault occurred. Transmission control problems are indicated by either a "7" or "8" in this position. Other numbers assignments are: "1" and "2" for fuel or air metering problems, "3" for an ignition malfunction or engine misfire, "4" is the auxiliary emission control system, "5" is either the vehicle or idle speed control system, and "6" is for PCM faults. The numerals "9" and "0" are reserved for future use.

Fault Definition
The remaining two digits of the DTC tell you the exact condition that triggered the code. Different sensors, actuators, and circuits are assigned blocks of numbers. The lowest numeral of the block indicates a general malfunction in the monitored circuit. This is the "generic" DTC. Ascending numbers in the block provide more specific information, such as low or high circuit voltage, slow response, or out-of-range signal, known as enhanced OBD-II codes. Multiple codes are not allowed, so if the system has the capability, an enhanced code will take precedence over a generic code (figure 9-21).

SUMMARY

The engine and transmission control modules used in electronic control systems are

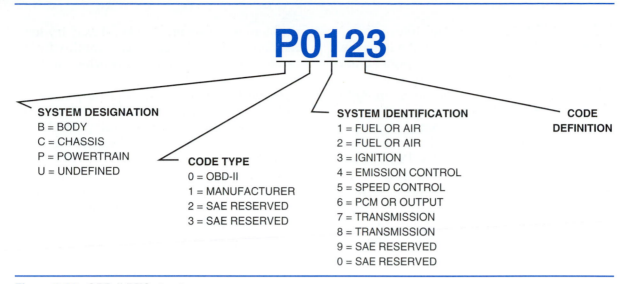

Figure 9-20. OBD-II DTC structure.

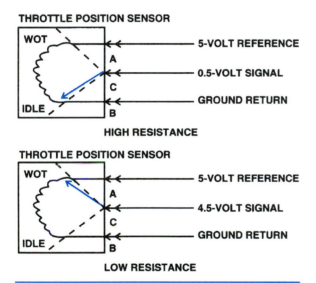

Figure 9-21. OBD-II transmission-related DTCs—SAE-defined.

onboard vehicle computers. Current industry practice is to include engine and transmission control in a single unit called a powertrain control module (PCM).

Computer operations can be classified into four basic functions: input, processing, storage, and output. The PCM receives inputs from sensors as voltage or current signals and processes them according to the programs and data stored in its memory. The PCM implements control decisions by sending output voltage or current signals to system actuators.

A PCM often receives analog input signals from the system sensors, but it can only use digital signals internally. Special PCM circuits condition and convert these analog signals to digital signals before they are processed.

Sensors throughout the vehicle provide information about engine and transmission operating parameters such as temperatures, pressures, and component positions. The sensor types used in automotive control systems include switches, thermistors, potentiometers, Hall-effect switches, magnetic pickups, and piezoelectric devices.

A PCM uses different types of memory it to store data: read-only memory, or ROM, is programmed by the manufacturer and stores permanent data and program instructions that cannot be erased. The programmable read-only memory, or PROM, is a special type of ROM that stores data particular to a certain vehicle that is collected by engine mapping. The random-access memory, or RAM, can be changed and updated by the PCM and is used to store and retrieve temporary data and information.

A control system has two general operating modes: open-loop or closed-loop. In open-loop, the PCM ignores feedback signals and uses predetermined data for system control. In closed-loop, the PCM can respond to feedback signals, allowing it to judge the results of previous commands and readjust its output if necessary. Closed-loop operation provides better output control.

Late-model control systems have an adaptive learning capability that allows the PCM to learn about system components and operating conditions as the vehicle is driven. If necessary, the PCM adjusts its memory to accommodate any short-term operating changes or long-term component wear.

Modern control systems also have certain self-diagnostic capabilities. The PCM monitors system components and operations continuously and can store a diagnostic trouble code (DTC) if it notes a problem. If the problem is severe, the PCM may switch to a default mode to prevent damage. If the problem is not severe, the PCM may try to restore or improve vehicle driveability by recalculating, replacing, or ignoring faulty signals.

Powertrain Control Module output control actions are implemented by system actuators, such as solenoids, relays, and motors. Actuators convert electrical signals into physical actions. A PCM may control the actuator using a pulse-width modulated (PWM) duty signal. Pulse-width modulation rapidly cycles the solenoid on and off and enables the PCM to achieve very smooth and precise control.

Review Questions

Choose the single most correct answer. Compare your answers to the correct answers on page 213.

1. Technician A says electronic transmissions use electronic components to replace many mechanical devices.
   Technician B says electronic components are reliable because there are no moving parts to wear out.
   Who is right?
   a. A only
   b. B only
   c. Both A and B
   d. Neither A nor B

2. Technician A says modern electronic control systems use a single module to control engine and transmission operations.
   Technician B says all electronic control systems use separate modules to control engine and transmission operations.
   Who is right?
   a. A only
   b. B only
   c. Both A and B
   d. Neither A nor B

3. The basic functions of a computer control system are
   a. Input, processing, storage, and output
   b. Input, processing, storage, and conditioning
   c. Input, processing, translating, and output
   d. Input, processing, translating, and storage

4. Technician A says system input signals may require conditioning before a PCM can use them.
   Technician B says a PCM contains circuits to convert digital input signals into analog computer signals.
   Who is right?
   a. A only
   b. B only
   c. Both A and B
   d. Neither A nor B

5. Technician A says analog signals take on a range of possible signal values as they vary.
   Technician B says digital signals have only two possible values.
   Who is right?
   a. A only
   b. B only
   c. Both A and B
   d. Neither A nor B

6. Some of the basic functions and operations controlled by a vehicle control system may include
   a. Fuel metering and ignition timing
   b. Idle speed control and air injection control
   c. Transmission gear shifts and shift timing
   d. All of the above

7. Technician A says a PCM uses programs, instructions, and data to determine how to process system input signals.

   Technician B says programs, instructions, and data are stored in computer memory in different locations.

   Who is right?
   a. A only
   b. B only
   c. Both A and B
   d. Neither A nor B

8. Diagnostic trouble codes (DTCs) are:
   a. Single-digit characters that identify general circuit and component concerns
   b. Two-digit characters that identify general circuit and component concerns
   c. Multiple-digit characters that identify general circuit and component concerns
   d. Multiple-digit characters that identify transmission fault conditions only

9. Technician A says that an objective of OBD-II is to improve air quality.

   Technician B says an objective of OBD-II is to reduce the time between the occurrence of an emission-related malfunction and its detection and repair.

   Who is right?
   a. A only
   b. B only
   c. Both A and B
   d. Neither A nor B

10. Technician A says that OBD-II involves the standardization of DTCs.

    Technician B says that manufacturers may use different terms to decribe the same things.

    Who is right?
    a. A only
    b. B only
    c. Both A and B
    d. Neither A nor B

11. A type "A" misfire is
    a. Less severe than a type "B" misfire
    b. More severe than a type "B" misfire
    c. More severe than a type "C" misfire
    d. Less severe than a type "C" misfire

12. Technician A says a control system uses feedback to determine how effective its output control has been.

    Technician B says a control system uses feedback to determine how the system inputs have been changed by output commands.

    Who is right?
    a. A only
    b. B only
    c. Both A and B
    d. Neither A nor B

13. Technician A says a control system uses feedback when it enters open-loop mode.

    Technician B says a control system uses feedback when it enters closed-loop mode.

    Who is right?
    a. A only
    b. B only
    c. Both A and B
    d. Neither A nor B

14. The following are examples of OBD-II monitors:
    a. Comprehensive Component, Fuel System, Catalyst Efficiency
    b. Throttle Position, Evaporative Emissions, HO2S
    c. Engine Speed, Secondary Air Injection, EGR
    d. Misfire Detection, Thermostat, Shift Points

15. Technician A says that an OBD-II drive cycle is performed only for emission testing purposes.

    Technician B says that it is necessary to perform an OBD-II drive cycle to retrieve DTCs.

    Who is right?
    a. A only
    b. B only
    c. Both A and B
    d. Neither A nor B

16. With the OBD-II DTC P0123, the following is true:
    a. The "P" indicates this is a code associated with the powertrain.
    b. The "0" indicates that the code is manufacturer-specific.
    c. Both A and B
    d. Neither A nor B

17. Technician A says some sensor types require a fixed reference voltage signal that is provided by the PCM.

    Technician B says a potentiometer, used as a sensor, modifies a reference voltage signal to provide the sensor input.

    Who is right?
    a. A only
    b. B only
    c. Both A and B
    d. Neither A nor B

18. Technician A says most switches used as system sensors provide an analog input signal.

    Technician B says most switches used as system sensors are installed on the ground side of a circuit.

    Who is right?
    a. A only
    b. B only
    c. Both A and B
    d. Neither A nor B

19. Technician A says a magnetic pulse generator is one type of voltage generator sensor.

    Technician B says a Hall-effect switch is one type of voltage generator sensor.

    Who is right?
    a. A only
    b. B only
    c. Both A and B
    d. Neither A nor B

20. Technician A says actuators are a different type of system sensor the PCM uses to collect input information.

    Technician B says actuators are mechanical output devices the PCM uses to convert electric output signals into command actions.

    Who is right?
    a. A only
    b. B only
    c. Both A and B
    d. Neither A nor B

10

Electronic Control Systems

In years past, automatic transmissions were operated by mechanical and hydraulic actions. The driver selected a gear range by moving the shift lever. In response, mechanical linkage positioned the manual valve in the valve body. Gearshifts were regulated by governor and throttle pressure interacting with the shift valves. Torque converter lockup in these early units was achieved by hydraulic means. Later units used simple electrical and vacuum circuits that applied and released the converter clutch.

Today, almost all automatic transmissions use electronic systems to manage shifting, converter clutch operation, and hydraulic pressure. This chapter covers modern methods of electronic operation.

ELECTRONIC CONTROL FUNCTIONS

Basic transmission theory is the same today as in previous generations. However, the advent of electronic controls has changed transmission operation. Electronics manage hydraulic pressures more precisely, providing smoother operation of apply devices and overall better shift characteristics over a wider range of operating conditions.

Through the use of electronic controls, a number of internal components have been eliminated or simplified. This results in lighter, more compact transmission assemblies that produce more torque. Some designs eliminate the overrunning clutch and reduce the number of valves and hydraulic circuits. Other designs rely entirely on clutches and do not use bands and servos (figure 10-1).

Control System Test Characteristics

Technicians can communicate with electronic control systems by using a **scan tool**

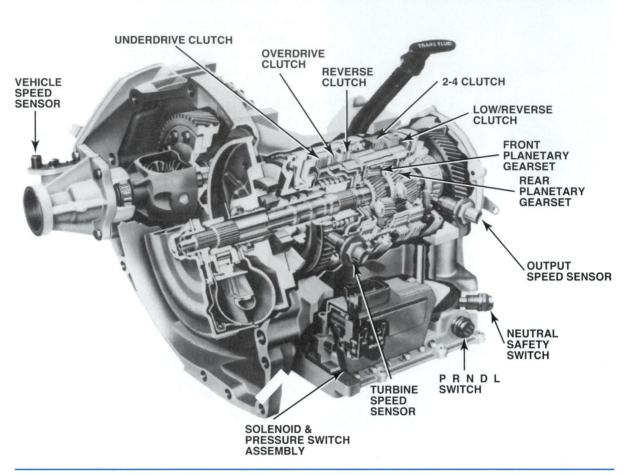

UNDERDRIVE CLUTCH

OVERDRIVE CLUTCH

REVERSE CLUTCH

2-4 CLUTCH

VEHICLE SPEED SENSOR

LOW/REVERSE CLUTCH

FRONT PLANETARY GEARSET

REAR PLANETARY GEARSET

OUTPUT SPEED SENSOR

NEUTRAL SAFETY SWITCH

P R N D L SWITCH

TURBINE SPEED SENSOR

SOLENOID & PRESSURE SWITCH ASSEMBLY

Figure 10-1. Chrysler 41TE transaxle—four forward and one reverse gear provided entirely by clutches. Daimler Chrysler Corporation

(figure 10-2) . The procedures for using a scan tool are covered in more detail in the accompanying *Shop Manual*. In general, scan tools provide an interface with electronic systems to retrieve diagnostic trouble codes (DTCs) and to initiate diagnostic sequences.

Transmission Control System Inputs

The powertrain control module (PCM) uses input signals from several sensors to determine torque converter clutch (TCC) lockup and shift points. There are three primary input sources: engine-related, driver demand, and transmission sensors.

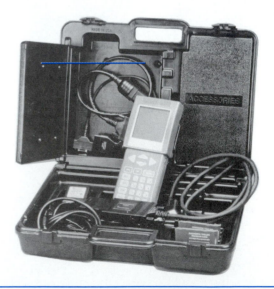

Figure 10-2. Typical scan tool device.

Engine-Related Inputs
Engine-related input signals provide engine operating information such as speed, load,

timing, and temperature. To efficiently operate the transmission, the TCM considers signals from these engine sensors:

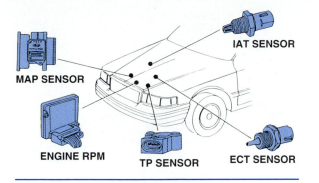

Figure 10-3. Typical engine-related input sensors.

- Mass air flow (MAF)
- Intake air temperature (IAT)
- Manifold absolute pressure (MAP)
- Crankshaft position (CKP)
- Engine coolant temperature (ECT)

These signals, or data parameters, reflect basic engine operating conditions (figure 10-3).

Driver Demand Inputs

Driver demand inputs provide the PCM with information about driver preferences, selections, and operating conditions. Typical driver demand sensors include the following:

- Transmission range (TR) sensor
- Throttle position (TP) sensor
- Brake ON/OFF (BOO) switch
- Overdrive cancel switch (OCS)

Transmission Range Sensor
The TR sensor translates the gear selection made by the driver into an electrical signal used by the PCM. This sensor often contains the neutral safety and backup lamp switches (figure 10-4).

Throttle Position Sensor
The PCM determines how much torque and acceleration the driver is demanding based on TP sensor voltage. The TP is typically connected to the throttle plates (figure 10-5). TP sensor voltage varies in proportion to the motion of the throttle. An electronic transmission uses the TP sensor signal in place of hydraulic throttle pressure to effect gear shifts.

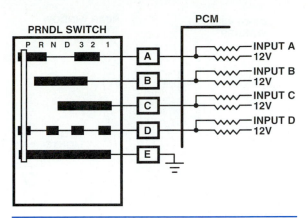

Figure 10-4. TR sensor informs PCM of driver-selected gear range.

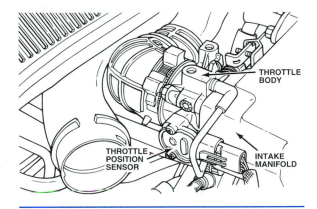

Figure 10-5. TP sensor provides PCM with throttle-opening input to help determine shift points.

Brake ON/OFF Switch
The brake ON/OFF switch informs the PCM when the driver is applying the brakes. This input is used by the PCM to disengage the TCC to prevent shudder and stalling as the vehicle comes to a stop.

Overdrive Cancel Switch
Some vehicles have a driver-controlled switch to cancel overdrive operation (figure 10-6). Pressing the switch with the vehicle operating in fourth gear causes the transmission to make a 4-3 downshift. If activated in a lower gear, the transmission will not make a 3-4 upshift.

Transmission Sensors

Transmission-related sensors provide operating information and feedback signals about internal transmission conditions, such

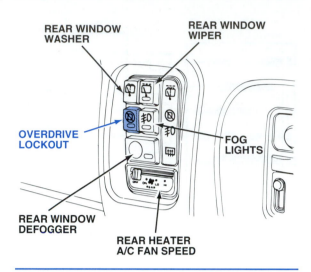

Figure 10-6. Driver-activated overdrive cancel switch disables fourth gear.

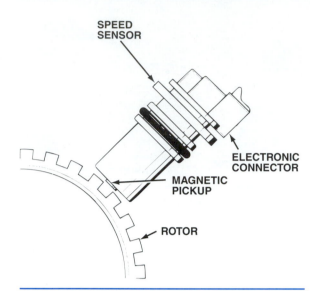

Figure 10-7. Turbine speed sensor (TSS)—typically a magnetic-pickup type sensor.

as shaft speeds, fluid temperature, and gear selection. The type and number of sensors used varies by transmission. Following is a brief description of some common transmission sensors.

Transmission Fluid Temperature (TFT) Sensor
This is a thermistor-type sensor that is usually located on the valve body or in the solenoid assembly. When the sensor signal indicates that temperature is below the normal operating range, the PCM adopts a "cold start" shift schedule. This schedule shifts gears at lower engine speeds to compensate for decreased powertrain efficiency during cold operation. TCC engagement is also prevented when the transmission fluid is cold.

The TCM also uses the TFT signal to monitor fluid temperature for signs of overheating. Exactly how a system reacts to an overheat condition varies by transmission. When fluid temperature first begins to rise above the normal operating range, the PCM generally locks the converter clutch. This eliminates slippage and lowers fluid temperature because the converter is the primary source of heat generation in a transmission. In the event of severe overheating, the PCM sets a DTC, disables the TCC, substitutes a default signal for that of the TFT sensor, and possibly enters a limited operating strategy.

Turbine Speed Sensor (TSS)
The PCM needs to know the speed of the torque converter turbine to determine engine-transmission operating ratio and torque converter slip rate. Turbine speed, also referred to as input speed, is determined in one of two ways: either with a direct-reading turbine speed sensor (TSS) or mathematically calculated as an internal PCM function.

When a TSS is used, it will generally be a magnetic-pickup type sensor (figure 10-7). Speed cannot be directly read off of the turbine because it is rotating inside the torque converter (which is also rotating), and there is no way to run an electrical circuit through these moving parts. Therefore, the TSS signal must be taken from a separate component that rotates at the same speed as the turbine. Typically, the TSS signal is triggered by an exciter wheel on the turbine shaft or input shaft of an automatic transaxle or off the input shell on a RWD transmission.

To compute turbine speed using mathematical formulas, the PCM uses transmission output shaft speed, engine speed, shift solenoid, and switch position signals. Through engine mapping, converter slip rate and other operating factors are programmed into the PCM lookup tables. The PCM calculates turbine speed by compar-

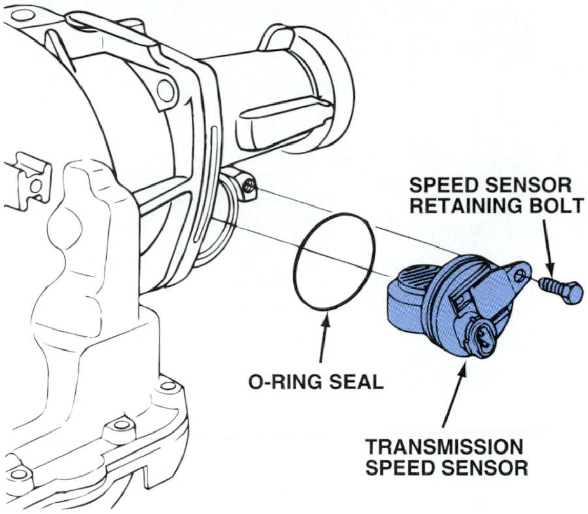

Figure 10-8. Output shaft speed (OSS) sensor.

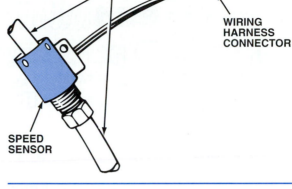

Figure 10-9. Early Chrysler VSS works off speedometer cable.

ing live data readings to lookup table information.

Output Shaft Speed (OSS) Sensor
This speed sensor is direct-reading and transmits transmission output shaft RPM to the TPM. Most output shaft speed (OSS) sensors are magnetic-pickup types (figure 10-8). Signal voltage frequency varies in proportion to the speed of output shaft rotation. The PCM relies on the OSS sensor signal to determine gear ratio, shift points, TCC lockup, and hydraulic pressure.

Fully electronic transmissions use the OSS sensor in place of the governor. Governor pressure is speed-related; the PCM knows the exact transmission output speed and can quickly calculate exactly how much pressure is needed at any given moment. A PWM solenoid delivers the required pressure to oppose throttle pressure and shift gears. Response is faster and more accurate than is possible with a mechanical governor.

Vehicle Speed Sensor (VSS)
The vehicle speed sensor (VSS) transmits a voltage signal in proportion to vehicle speed. The sensor may be located on the transmission case, on the differential housing, or in the speedometer assembly (figure 10-9). The PCM uses the VSS signal as an additional speed input to verify OSS signals

and modify shift scheduling. Generally, the OSS provides the main vehicle speed signal for transmission control and the VSS signal is used as backup.

Transmission Pressure Switches
Many transmissions use internal oil pressure switches to inform the PCM as to which hydraulic circuits are pressurized. Using switch signals, the PCM can determine what gear the transmission is operating. The switches provide information as to which bands and clutches are applied. This feedback information verifies gear selection and solenoid operation.

ELECTRONIC SHIFT CONTROLS

Toyota was the first vehicle manufacturer to introduce an automatic transmission with electronic shift control. Chrysler, Ford, General Motors, and other manufacturers soon followed suit with transmission designs that electronically controlled shifting and TCC lockup. Several factors led to the development of electronic transmission control.

Valve bodies were becoming increasingly complex as manufacturers introduced

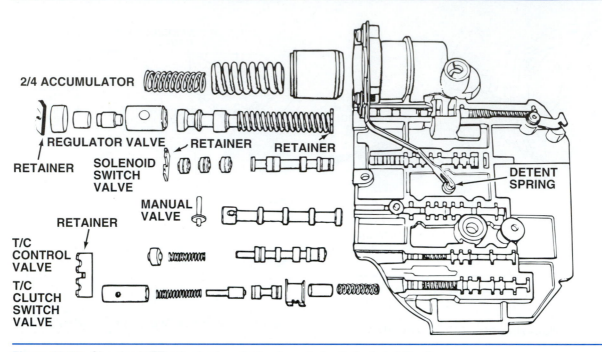

Figure 10-10. Chrysler 41TE valve body—electronic controls eliminated shift valves.

4-speed transmissions with lockup torque converters to improve fuel economy. These castings were expensive to design and manufacture. In addition, the many spool valves, springs, check balls, and orifices were prone to clogging and sticking. Electronic solenoids and ball valves replace many of these valve body parts on late-model transmissions (figure 10-10). Electronic shift controls are less expensive, more efficient, and more reliable than their predecessors.

Basic Shift Control Principles

Figure 10-11 provides a simplified illustration of how a generic four-speed electronic automatic transmission shift system operates. Although actual electronic shift controls are more complex, this simplified design is helpful in learning how the solenoids control shift operations.

In this generic application, pressure to apply the clutches is routed from the manual valve through several passages to the shift control valve. Spring force acts on the left end of the shift control valve and mainline pressure acts on the right end of the

valve. The mainline pressure circuit includes solenoids that direct pressure flow.

Mainline pressure must pass through a restricting orifice before reaching the shift control valve. This ensures that *all* of the pressure acting on the valve will exhaust when both solenoids are open. With only one of the solenoids open, *part* of the pressure vents—how much depends on which solenoid is open. Solenoid #1 has a smaller bleed opening; therefore, it releases less pressure than solenoid #2.

To engage first gear the PCM opens solenoid #1 to exhaust a small portion of the pressure acting on the right end of the shift control valve (figure 10-11A). This enables spring force to move the valve a specific distance to the right, such that pressure flows through the valve and into the forward clutch circuit. This applies the forward clutch and the transmission operates in first gear.

To cause a second gear upshift, the PCM opens solenoid #2 to exhaust a greater portion of the mainline pressure acting on the shift control valve (figure 10-11B). Again, spring force acting on the opposite end of the shift control valve moves it a specific distance farther to the right. A wide valley in

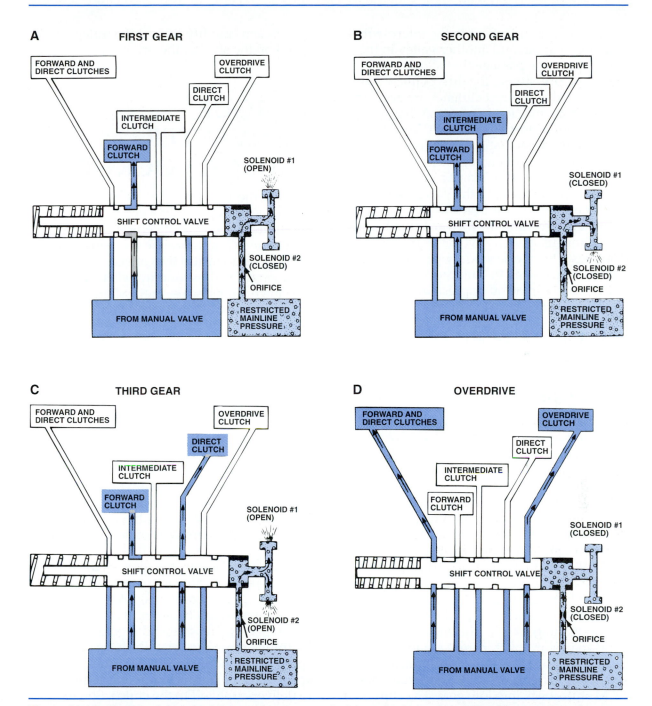

Figure 10-11. Generic electronic shift control system—a single spool valve and two solenoids operating a four-speed transmission.

the valve permits the forward clutch to remain applied while another valley opens a passage to route hydraulic pressure to the intermediate clutch. With the forward and intermediate clutches applied, the transmission operates in second gear.

For third gear, the PCM opens both solenoids to exhaust all of the pressure acting on the shift control valve. Without any pressure to overcome, spring force moves the valve fully to the right and it bottoms in the bore (figure 10-11C). The wide valley again maintains pressure in the forward clutch circuit.

However, hydraulic flow to the intermediate clutch is shut off, and another valley in the valve opens the passage that allows hydraulic pressure to the direct clutch. Now, the forward and direct clutches are applied and the transmission operates in third gear.

To achieve fourth gear, the PCM closes both solenoids so that full mainline pressure can act on the right end of the shift control valve (figure 10-11D). Mainline pressure exceeds spring force, so the valve moves left until it bottoms in the bore. This closes the wide valley feeding the forward clutch, but simultaneously opens two other hydraulic channels. One is a secondary passage that maintains pressure to both the forward and direct clutches; the other pressurizes the overdrive clutch circuit. With forward, direct, and overdrive clutches applied, the transmission operates in fourth gear.

Shift Control Options

An advantage of electronic shift control is that it allows shift options that are not possible or practical with a purely hydraulic system. These options give the driver more control over transmission operation and offer improved vehicle driveability. In modern transmissions, smooth shifts are made possible by reducing engine torque during gear changes and applying the proper amount of oil pressure to gently engage clutches and bands. Electronic designs reduce *shift shock* to a low level.

To reduce vehicle creep when the vehicle is stopped in gear with the engine idling, the PCM may shift the transmission into second gear. As soon as the TP sensor indicates that the driver is depressing the accelerator, the PCM shifts back into low gear. The shift is so well regulated that it goes relatively unnoticed by the driver.

Some systems permit the driver to lock the transmission in a selected gear. This *hold* or *lockout* feature gives the driver manual shift capability at the press of a button. The purpose is to provide added traction when starting off on a slippery surface. Many systems permit the driver to choose between sport and economy drive programs by operating a selector switch. Sophisticated adaptive systems modify their shift strategies based on the style of the driver.

TORQUE CONVERTER CLUTCH LOCKUP

Locking the TCC provides a direct 1:1 mechanical coupling between the engine and transmission. Most vehicles lock the converter clutch hydraulically using a large piston located inside the converter housing between the turbine and impeller. To apply the clutch, oil passages in the shaft route hydraulic pressure between the turbine and clutch piston. Hydraulic apply pressure moves the piston and holds it tightly against the inside of the converter housing. This effectively locks the turbine to the impeller, providing better fuel economy and lower operating temperatures.

Automatic transmissions may use hydraulically or electronically controlled valves to regulate clutch apply pressure and fluid flow direction. These valves are known by many names, such as **converter clutch control valve**, **lockup control valve**, or **clutch apply valve**. They all have a common purpose: to deliver apply oil to the clutch piston.

Electric and electronic controls direct fluid flow to hydraulically apply the converter clutches. On most systems, solenoids and spool valves work together to move the clutch piston. The solenoid regulates a hydraulic pressure signal that acts on the spool valve and moves it in its bore. The spool valve performs like a hydraulic relay to deliver apply oil to the clutch. Some systems use release pressure, or release oil, directed between the converter housing and the clutch piston to deliver a quick release and prevent unwanted engagement.

Previous generations used electric solenoids that received one or two simple switch inputs to determine when to engage the clutch (figure 10-12). With today's modern electronic systems, the PCM analyzes a number of different sensor inputs to regulate TCC operation (figure 10-13).

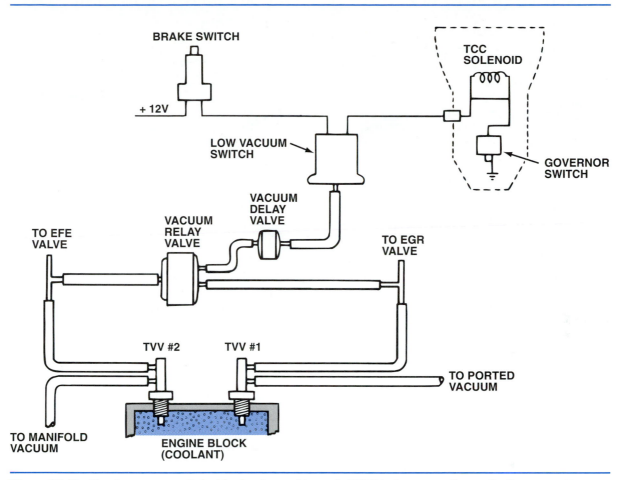

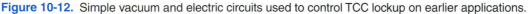

Figure 10-12. Simple vacuum and electric circuits used to control TCC lockup on earlier applications.

TCC Apply Conditions

The TCC applies only under certain operating conditions. These include (1) engine temperature warm enough to handle the extra load without stumbling or stalling and (2) vehicle speed fast enough to provide for smooth power transfer. Closely matched transmission and engine speeds are also needed to prevent shuddering or surging during engagement. The throttle must be partially open, and engine manifold vacuum must be in a certain range.

A locked TCC must release when vehicle speed drops in order to prevent the engine from stalling when the vehicle comes to a stop. The TCC also releases whenever torque multiplication is needed for acceleration. On systems where TCC lockup is available in more than one gear, the clutch unlocks during gearshifts for smooth power flow. The

TCC also releases during closed-throttle deceleration to reduce emissions, improve fuel economy, and relieve excess engine load should manifold vacuum drop too low.

TCC Break-In

A TCC must allow a certain amount of slippage, even when lockup is fully engaged. On a Chrysler electronically modulated converter clutch, for example, the slip rate gradually decreases to a fixed point over the first 1500 miles of operation. This variable slip rate information is part of the PCM's programming and prevents TCC application for the first 500 miles. From 500 to 1500 miles, the PCM gradually reduces the amount of slip allowed from 200 to 60 rpm. At that point the TCC becomes fully functional and can achieve full lockup.

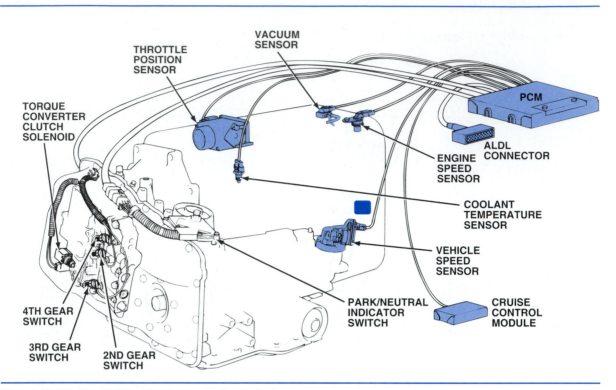

Figure 10-13. The PCM and sensors used on today's modern electronic control systems.

Partial Lockup Torque Converters

Earlier generations of lockup torque converters operated in one of two operating states: locked or unlocked. Late-model control systems added a partial lockup feature. Partial lockup allows a regulated amount of slippage at the TCC. The slip rate is regulated by a pulse-width modulation (PWM) solenoid. Partial lockup offers improved fuel economy, the ability to isolate the drivetrain from engine pulses, and a smoother transition to full TCC lockup.

The TCC connects the main components of the hydraulic converter, pump, and turbine to reduce power loss due to slippage. To maximize efficiency, it is necessary to lock the clutch as often as possible. On the other hand, the torque converter is an important element in the prevention of unwanted powertrain vibrations. Therefore, lockup is always a compromise between low fuel consumption and high driving comfort. Partial lockup makes the most of this compromise, as it gains some of the fuel economy benefits of a locked

clutch and makes transitions from engaged to disengaged that go unnoticed by the driver.

To prevent powertrain vibrations, the TCC opens during closed-throttle coasting. This practice uses the torque converter to dampen vibrations. In some applications, the clutch momentarily releases during gear changes for improved shift comfort. Early versions allowed partial lockup only in third and fourth gears, while most newer designs allow partial lockup in second gear as well. In all cases, the lockup sequence for an upshift is unlocked converter, partially locked converter, and fully locked converter (figure 10–14). All manufacturers now use partial lockup torque converters.

ELECTRONIC SYSTEMS

Following are descriptions of the operating characteristics of a few electronic transmis-

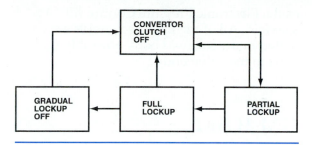

Figure 10-14. Gradual lockup and release improves driveability and efficiency.

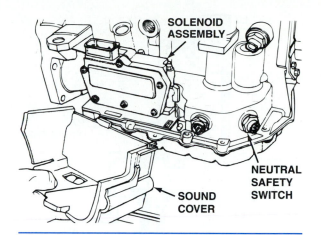

Figure 10-15. Chrysler 41TE solenoid assembly.

sion systems. When servicing any transmission, always refer to the appropriate manufacturer's service information for procedures and specifications.

Chrysler 41TE and 42LE Systems

The Chrysler electronic four-speed transaxle, originally termed the A604 Ultradrive, simplified the internal components of a standard transaxle by eliminating mechanical components, such as the overrunning clutch, bands, and servos. Instead, multiple-disc clutches provide all of the gear ranges. Two variations of the A604 transaxle are in use: 41TE and 42LE. The 41TE is configured for applications with a transverse engine, and the 42LE is for longitudinal engine installations. The operation and construction of both units are similar.

Torque converter lockup function is similar to other Chrysler converters, but the electronic controls are different. Clutch lockup is regulated by the PCM and applied hydraulically by the solenoid assembly and valve body. The solenoid assembly and valve body also operate the multiple-disc clutches to control gear changes.

Shift and clutch solenoids are contained in the solenoid assembly, which also houses the three pressure switches that feed gear selection inputs to the PCM (figure 10-15). The PCM controls power to the solenoid assembly through the transmission control relay; the relay controls the transaxle default mode. If the PCM identifies a failure that

may prevent safe transaxle operation, the PCM shuts off power to the relay, which de-energizes all transaxle solenoids. In default, the transmission operates only in reverse and second gear.

Hydraulic pressure to the TCC is routed by two valves: torque converter control and lockup switch. The torque converter control valve directs mainline pressure from the regulator to the converter clutch. Pressure is reduced as it passes through the valve, and then is directed to the front, or OFF, side of the clutch piston, through the lockup switch valve. To engage the clutch, the lockup switch valve moves in response to the solenoid signal and redirects apply pressure from the torque converter control valve to the back, or ON, side of the piston (figure 10-16).

A PWM solenoid is used so that the PCM can vary TCC apply pressure between zero and mainline pressure. This allows for a regulated amount of clutch slip, known as partial lockup, to ensure a smooth transition between gears. Originally, partial lockup was only available in third and fourth gears. However, newer versions of this transmission allow partial lockup in second gear as well.

Ford AX4S and E4OD

The AX4S (formerly known as the AXOD) and E4OD transmissions allow converter

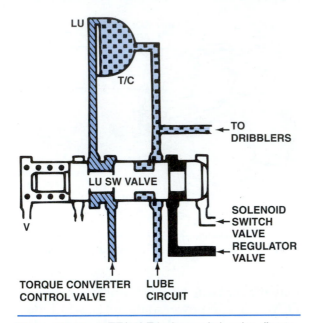

Figure 10-16. 41TE/42LE lockup switch valve directs pressure to lock and unlock the TCC.

clutch lockup in third and fourth gear when certain vehicle operating conditions are met, such as coolant temperature, throttle position, and vehicle speed. The electronic control system adjusts TCC application to provide good driveability, efficient operation, and adequate power.

In third gear, the TCC can apply when the throttle opening conditions are satisfied. Lockup can occur at speeds as low as 27 mph (43 km/h) if the throttle opening is small. At larger throttle openings, lockup is delayed to ensure adequate power for acceleration. In fourth gear, TCC application is permitted when the throttle opening is between 5 and 45 percent. The clutch may engage at vehicle speeds as low as 35 mph (56 kph) if the throttle opening is small and constant.

To prevent repeated TCC locking and unlocking during short-duration throttle openings, the PCM is programmed to delay any change in lockup status for a short period of time after a significant change in throttle position. The 3-2 and 4-3 pressure switches signal the PCM to de-energize the TCC solenoid and unlock the TCC during upshifts and downshifts.

The E4OD regulates shifting and pressure with an electronically controlled variable force solenoid (VFS), which Ford designates as the Electronic Pressure Control (EPC) solenoid. All of the E4OD solenoids are contained in the solenoid body assembly that bolts to the valve body.

GM 4L80-E

The 4L80-E, introduced in 1991, was the first fully electronic automatic transmission from General Motors. Based on the Turbo Hydra-Matic (THM) 400, the 4L80-E adds an overdrive assembly to gain a fourth speed and incorporates an electronic control system to regulate operations. A PCM controls engine and transmission operations.

The control system uses two shift solenoids to engage gears, a variable force motor (VFM) to regulate mainline pressure, and a PWM solenoid to control TCC operation. The PWM solenoid is used with the converter clutch shift valve and TCC enable valve to direct modulated hydraulic pressure to the converter clutch apply circuit. A fluid pressure switch assembly supplies a feedback signal to the PCM, which it uses to judge how well the transmission and control system are functioning (figure 10-17).

GM 4T60-E

General Motors also introduced the 4T60-E transaxle in 1991. The 4T60-E uses two solenoids, the TCC solenoid and the PWM solenoid, to control converter clutch operation (figure 10-18). To achieve lockup the PCM energizes the TCC solenoid, which allows hydraulic pressure to move the converter clutch valve and apply the converter clutch. At the same time, the PWM solenoid modulates the clutch apply pressure for maximum efficiency and a smooth transition. In effect, the TCC solenoid applies and releases the clutch, and the PWM solenoid regulates the pressure and feel of clutch application. Like the 4L80-E, the 4T60-E uses two shift solenoids to control transaxle shifts. The 4T60-E also uses a vacuum modulator to help regulate the hydraulic pressure in the transaxle.

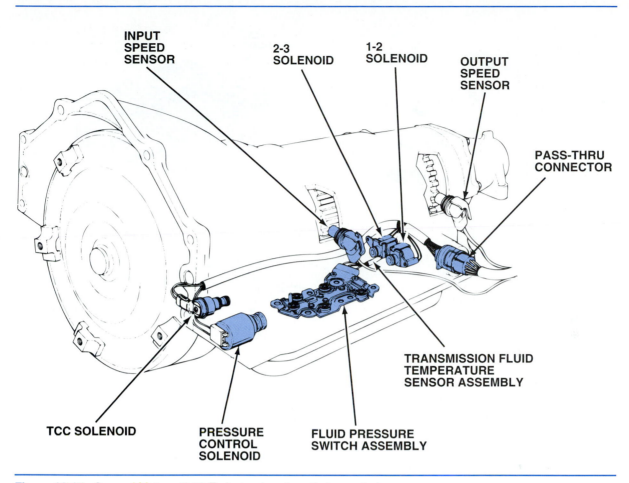

Figure 10-17. General Motors 4L80-E electronic automatic transmission.
General Motors Corporation, Service and Parts Operations

Allison 1000 (M74)

The Allison 1000 (M74), new in 2001, is an electronically controlled automatic five-speed transmission used on GM applications equipped with either the L18 or LB7 engines. It has one reverse and five forward gears, which include a direct-drive fourth gear and an overdrive fifth gear (figure 10-19).

Unlike most other GM electronically controlled transmissions, the Allison 1000 uses a *separate* transmission control module (TCM), not the PCM, to control transmission operations. However, the TCM and PCM do communicate through a Class 2 data line. The TCM, performs diagnostic tests for the transmission. Failed tests result in stored DTCs and may cause MIL illumination. Certain DTCs will cause the range indicator to flash. That flash occurs when the TCM

stores a DTC that requires operating in a default gear.

This transmission uses six solenoids to control shifting and TCC operation. One solenoid is used for the TCC. There are three shift solenoids and two **shift trim solenoids**. Unlike other GM transmissions, the Allison does not have a main pressure control solenoid.

The control valve assembly attaches to the bottom of the gearbox module, is enclosed by the oil pan, and consists of the following components:

- Main valve body—Contains the trim valves, TCC valve, exhaust backfill valve, and the control main relief valve
- Shift valve body—Contains the shift valves, control main pressure valve, and the manual selector valve.

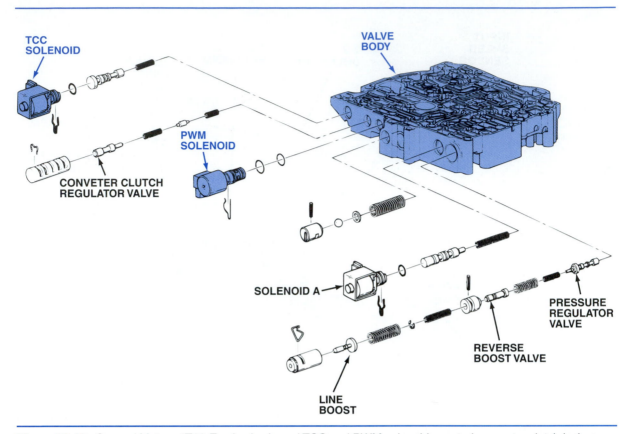

Figure 10-18. General Motors 4T60-E valve body and TCC and PWM solenoids control converter clutch lockup. General Motors Corporation, Service and Parts Operations

Several torque converters are available to match a variety of diesel and gasoline engines. At higher speeds the TCC is automatically engaged to provide direct drive from the engine to the transmission. Hydraulic fluid for converter charging pressure comes from the sump and is supplied by the input pump.

Gears one through five are provided in the overdrive range. Selecting other drive ranges limits the number of shifts. Because the selector does not have a drive 4 position, fourth gear cannot be manually selected (figure 10-20). However, limited use of fourth gear is available in the tow/haul mode.

The planetary gear train includes three constant-mesh planetary gearsets containing helical gears. Five clutches (two rotating and three stationary) direct power flow through the transmission. All range clutches are hydraulically actuated and spring-released.

SUMMARY

Input devices, or sensors, tell the PCM about operating conditions throughout the vehicle. The PCM analyzes information from all input devices using the control logic and program instructions stored in its memory. It then makes control decisions and provides the necessary signals to the appropriate output devices. The output devices convert the electric signals from the PCM into physical actions that regulate the transmission, engine, and other systems to meet vehicle and driver demands.

Electronic shift control increases shift-programming flexibility, reduces valve body complexity, and provides the driver with shift control options such as selective shift schedules. Input devices provide the PCM with signals that it analyzes and compares to the shift schedules and torque curves stored in memory. The PCM controls transmission shift actions by switching on the

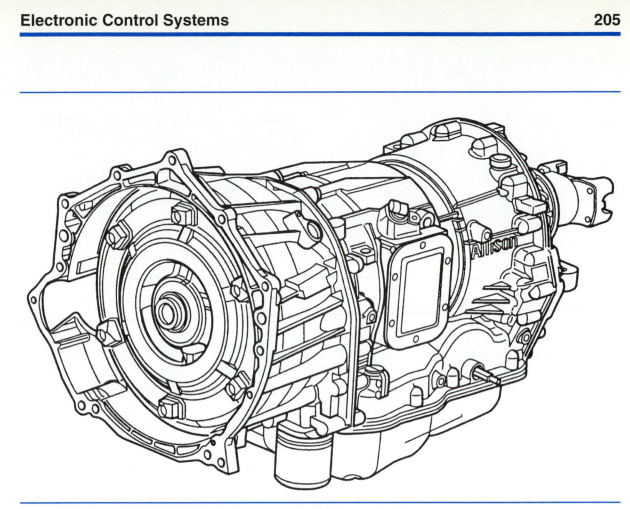

Figure 10-19. Allison 1000 five-speed automatic transmission.

Selected Range	Reverse Gear	First Gear	Second Gear	Third Gear	Fourth Gear	Fifth Gear
R	x					
D		x	x	x	x	x
3		x	x	x		
2		x	x			
1		x				
Gear Ratio	4.49:1	3.10:1	1.81:1	1.41:1	1.00:1	0.71:1

Figure 10-20. Allison 1000 gear ranges.

correct combination of electric shift solenoids needed to direct hydraulic pressure to the apply devices that hold gearset members and produce the required gear ratio.

Electronic transmission controls regulate TCC operation. These controls have the ability to consider important operating factors outside the transmission in the decision to lock or unlock the converter clutch. A TCC remains unlocked until the engine is warm enough to handle the extra load, vehicle speed is high enough to allow a smooth power transfer, and the engine and transmission speeds are close enough to prevent lockup from causing a shudder or surge. The TCC unlocks during downshifts, when torque multiplication is needed for acceleration, and whenever the vehicle brakes are applied. A solenoid locks and unlocks the clutch by routing a pressure signal to reposition one or more spool valves. The valves direct mainline pressure to one side of the clutch plate to lock it and the opposite side to release it.

Electronic pressure regulation and partial TCC lockup are managed using a pulse-width modulated solenoid; PWM switches the solenoid on and off quickly to regulate and precisely control pressure.

Review Questions

Choose the single most correct answer. Compare your answers to the correct answers on page 213.

1. Technician A says electric and electronic converter clutch controls are used with hydraulically applied torque converters.
   Technician B says the solenoids that regulate converter clutch lockup are mechanically controlled.
   Who is right?
   a. A only
   b. B only
   c. Both A and B
   d. Neither A nor B

2. Technician A says applying the vehicle brakes will unlock a torque converter clutch.
   Technician B says if vehicle speed drops below some minimum level the torque converter clutch will unlock.
   Who is right?
   a. A only
   b. B only
   c. Both A and B
   d. Neither A nor B

3. Technician A says most late-model control systems allow the system to communicate with diagnostic test equipment.
   Technician B says most late-model control systems can run pre-programmed system diagnostics and generate trouble codes.
   Who is right?
   a. A only
   b. B only
   c. Both A and B
   d. Neither A nor B

4. Technician A says a transmission control system may respond to inputs from transmission-related sensors.
   Technician B says a transmission control system does *not* respond to inputs from engine-related sensors.
   Who is right?
   a. A only
   b. B only
   c. Both A and B
   d. Neither A nor B

5. Advantages of a partial lockup torque converter clutch include
   a. Improved fuel economy
   b. Ability to isolate the drivetrain from engine pulses
   c. A smoother transition to full lockup
   d. All of the above

6. Technician A says partial TCC slippage is regulated by a pulse-width modulated solenoid.
   Technician B says pulse-width modulation is used to vary the duty cycle of the solenoid control signal.
   Who is right?
   a. A only
   b. B only
   c. Both A and B
   d. Neither A nor B

7. Technician A says GM electronic control systems control TCC lockup by grounding the TCC solenoid through the PCM instead of a governor switch.

    Technician B says GM electronic control systems eliminated the TCC solenoid, and they control TCC lockup by energizing the PCM.

    Who is right?
    a. A only
    b. B only
    c. Both A and B
    d. Neither A nor B

8. Technician A says electronic shift controls complicate valve body design by adding extra solenoid ball valves.

    Technician B says electronic transmissions use a throttle position sensor signal as the electronic equivalent of a hydraulic throttle pressure signal.

    Who is right?
    a. A only
    b. B only
    c. Both A and B
    d. Neither A nor B

9. Technician A says electronic transmissions control shifts by directing the shift solenoid output pressure to the bands and clutches.

    Technician B says electronic transmissions control shifts by directing the shift solenoid output pressure to the shift valves.

    Who is right?
    a. A only
    b. B only
    c. Both A and B
    d. Neither A nor B

10. Which of the following groups contains *only* driver-related inputs?
    a. TRS, TPS, VSS, OCS
    b. TPS, BOO, MAF, VSS
    c. VSS, MAP, BOO, OCS
    d. TRS, TPS, BOO, OCS

11. A TFT sensor is a
    a. Potentiometer
    b. Thermistor
    c. Switch
    d. Voltage Generator

12. On Chrysler 41TE and 42LE transmissions, the shift solenoids are mounted on the _____ assembly.
    a. Valve body
    b. Torque converter
    c. Case
    d. Solenoid

13. Technician A says that vehicle speed and load are determining factors for TCC lockup in most transmissions.

    Technician B says that vehicle speed and load are NOT factors for determining the 1-2 shift point in most transmissions.

    Who is right?
    a. A only
    b. B only
    c. Both A and B
    d. Neither A nor B

14. Technician A says that the TCC can apply on Ford AX4S and E4OD transmissions in third gear.

    Technician B says that only the shift solenoids of an E4OD transmission are attached to the solenoid body and bolted to the valve body assembly.

    Who is right?
    a. A only
    b. B only
    c. Both A and B
    d. Neither A nor B

GLOSSARY OF TECHNICAL TERMS

Accumulator: A device that absorbs the shock of sudden pressure surges within a hydraulic system. Accumulators are used in transmission hydraulic systems to control shift quality.

Actuator: A device that translates hydraulic pressure or a computer output voltage signal into mechanical energy.

Adaptive memory: A feature of computer memory that allows the microprocessor to adjust its memory for computing output response based on changes in vehicle operating conditions.

Analog signal: A voltage signal or processing action that is continuously variable relative to the operation being measured or controlled.

Apply devices: Hydraulically operated bands, multi-disc clutches, and mechanically operated one-way clutches that drive or hold the members of a planetary gearset.

Axial motion: Movement along, or parallel to, the centerline (axis) of a shaft. A dynamic seal is required to contain fluids where axial motion is present.

Axial play: Movement along, or parallel to, the centerline (axis) of a shaft. Also called end thrust or endplay.

Axis: The centerline around which a gear, wheel, or shaft rotates.

Belleville spring: A diaphragm-type spring used to help apply and release a multiple-disc clutch.

Bevel gear: A gear with teeth cut at an angle on its outer surface. Bevel gears often transmit motion between two shafts at an angle to each other.

Binary: A mathematical system, consisting of only two digits (0 and 1), that allows a digital computer to read and process input voltage signals.

Boost valve: A device that works against a pressure regulator valve to increase mainline pressure when needed.

Bus: An electrical conductor, or conductors, serving as a common connection for three or more circuits.

Bushing: A cylindrical metal sleeve that inserts into a machined bore to reduce the effect of friction on moving parts or decrease the diameter of the hole.

Cantilever: A lever that is anchored and supported at one end by its fulcrum and provides an opposing force at its opposite end.

Centrifugal force: The natural tendency of objects, when forced to move in a curved path, to move away from the center of rotation.

Check ball: A type of hydraulic valve, consisting of a ball, that seals an orifice when it is seated and can be unseated to open the orifice.

Clutch drum: A component of a clutch assembly that usually houses the clutch discs and pressure plate. A band often closes around the outside diameter of a clutch drum.

Clutch pack: The assembly of clutch and pressure plates that provides the friction surfaces in a multiple-disc clutch.

Clutch plate: A generic term for the friction and steel discs used in a multiple-disc clutch.

Coefficient of friction: A numerical value expressing the amount of friction between two surfaces. It is obtained by dividing the force required to slide the surfaces across one another by the pressure holding the surfaces together.

Compound planetary gearset: A gearset that contains more than just the three basic members of a simple planetary gearset.

Compressibility: The ability of a gasket to conform to surface irregularities. "Soft" gaskets are more compressible than "hard" gaskets.

Copolymer: A substance made of giant molecules formed from the smaller molecules of two or more unlike substances.

Coupling phase: The period of torque converter operation when there is no torque multiplication, and rotary flow causes the stator to unlock and rotate with the impeller and turbine at approximately the same speed.

Depth filter: A filter that traps contaminants within the matrix of the filter material. A felt filter is a type of depth filter.

Detent: A valve that controls downshifting by boosting throttle pressure.

Diagnostic Trouble Code (DTC): Alpha-numeric identifier for a fault condition.

Differential: The assembly of a carrier and spider gears that allows the drive axles to rotate at different rates of speed as the car turns a corner.

Digital signal: A voltage signal or processing function that has only two levels: on/off or high/low.

Diode: An electronic device that allows current to flow in one direction and be blocked in the other.

Direct drive: A 1:1 gear ratio in which the engine, transmission, and driveshaft (on RWD vehicles) all turn at the same speed.

Downshift valve: An auxiliary shift valve that increases throttle pressure to force a downshift under high driveline loads; also called a kickdown or detent valve.

Duty cycle: The percentage of the total time that a solenoid is energized during pulse-width modulation as determined by a timed voltage pulse from the computer.

Dynamic friction: The coefficient of friction between two surfaces that have relative motion between them. Also called kinetic friction.

Dynamic seal: A seal that prevents fluid passage between two parts that are in motion relative to each other.

Elastomer: A synthetic polymer or copolymer that has elastic properties similar to those of rubber.

Electronic automatic transmission: An automatic transmission with computer-controlled pressure regulation that gives precise control of shift scheduling and rapid response to changing conditions.

Endplay: The total amount of axial play in an automatic transmission. Endplay is typically measured at the input shaft.

External gear: A gear with teeth on its outside surface.

Feedback: The return of a portion of the output (actuator) to the input (computer), used to maintain an output device within predetermined limits.

Final drive: The last set of reduction gears the powerflow passes through on its way to the drive axles.

Flame point: The lowest temperature at which a volatile oil will ignite and burn when exposed to a flame.

Flash point: The lowest temperature at which the vapor of a volatile oil will ignite with a flash.

Flexplate: The thin metal plate, used in place of a flywheel, that joins the engine crankshaft to the fluid coupling or torque converter.

Force: A push or pull acting on an object, usually measured in pounds or Newtons.

Frequency: The number of periodic voltage oscillations, or waves, occurring in a given unit of time, usually expressed as cycles per second or Hertz.

Friction modifiers: Additives used to alter the friction coefficient of an ATF blend.

Galvanic battery: A direct current voltage source generated by the chemical action of an electrolyte.

Gear pump: A positive-displacement pump that uses an inner drive gear and an outer driven gear, separated on one side by a crescent, to produce oil flow. Gear pumps may use either helical or spur gears and are sometimes called gear-and-crescent pumps.

Gear ratio: The number of turns, or revolutions, made by a drive gear compared to the number of turns made by a driven gear. For example, if the drive gear turns three times for one revolution of the driven gear, the gear ratio is three, 3 to 1, or 3:1. Also, the ratio between the number of teeth on two gears.

Gear reduction: A condition in which the drive gear rotates faster than the driven gear. Output speed of the driven gear is reduced, while output torque is increased. A gear ratio of 3:1 is a gear reduction ratio.

Geartrain: A series of two or more gears meshed together so that power is transmitted among them.

Governor: A hydraulic pressure signal that indicates vehicle road speed.

Governor pressure: The transmission hydraulic pressure that is directly related to vehicle speed. Governor pressure increases with vehicle speed and is one of the principle pressures used to control shift points.

Governor valve: The valve that regulates governor pressure in relation to vehicle road speed.

Hall-effect switch: A signal-generating switch that develops a transverse voltage across a current-carrying semiconductor when subjected to a magnetic field.

Helical gear: A gear on which the teeth are at an angle to the gear's axis of rotation.

Hertz: A unit of frequency equal to one cycle per second.

Hydraulic lever: A means to multiply force using additional stages of mechanical leverage.

Hydraulics: The study of liquids and their use to transmit force and motion.

Hypoid gear: The combination of a ring gear and pinion gear in which the pinion meshes with the ring gear below the centerline of the ring gear. Commonly used in automotive final drives.

Hysteresis bands: The areas between two curves on a graph that indicate when a torque converter clutch locks and when it unlocks. Hysteresis bands also exist between graph curves that indicate when a transmission upshifts and when it downshifts between two gears.

Idler gear: A gear that transmits movement between the drive and driven gears, but does not affect the speed relationship of those gears.

Impeller: A rotor or rotor blade used to force a gas or liquid in a certain direction under pressure.

Incompressible: A volume of liquid that remains the same under pressure.

Input member: The drive member of a planetary gearset.

Integrated circuit: An electronic circuit containing many interconnected amplifying devices and elements formed on a single body, or chip, of semiconductor material.

Internal ring gear: A gear with teeth on its inside circumference.

Lands: Areas of a spool valve that control the opening and closing of hydraulic passages.

Lookup tables: Part of a computer program, or instructions. One set of lookup tables is common to all microprocessors of a specific group. Another set of lookup tables is used for specific engine calibrations and is located in the PROM.

Magnetic pulse generator: A signal-generating switch that creates a voltage pulse as magnetic flux changes around a pickup coil.

Mainline pressure: The pressure developed from the fluid output of the pump and controlled by the pressure regulator valve. Mainline pressure operates the apply devices in the transmission and is the source of all other pressures in the hydraulic system.

Malfunction Indicator Lamp (MIL): Warning light to alert driver of a fault that can affect emissions or powertrain performance.

Manual valve: The valve that is moved manually, through the shift linkage, to select the transmission drive range. The manual valve directs and blocks fluid flow to various hydraulic circuits.

Miscibility: The property that allows one fluid to blend with other fluids.

Multiple-disc clutch: A clutch that consists of alternating friction and steel discs that are forced together hydraulically to lock one transmission part to another.

On-Board Diagnostic (OBD): A feature of the powertrain control module to test itself, sensors, and actuators as well as store information about malfunctions.

One-way clutch: A mechanical holding device that prevents rotation in one direction, but overruns to allow it in the other. One-way clutches are either roller or sprag clutches.

One-way sprag clutch: A device that consists of a hub and drum separated by a number of sprags.

One-way valve: A type of switching valve that allows fluid to pass in one direction and only when the pressure is sufficient to unseat the valve.

Orifice: A small opening or restriction, in a line or passage, that is used to regulate pressure and flow.

Output member: The driven member of a planetary gearset.

Overdrive: A condition in which the drive gear rotates slower than the driven gear. Output speed of the driven gear is increased, while output torque is reduced. A gear ratio of 0.70:1 is an overdrive gear ratio.

Oxidation: The process in which one element of a compound is combined with oxygen in a chemical process that produces another compound.

Piezoelectric: Voltage caused by physical pressure applied to the faces of certain crystals.

Piezoresistive: A sensor whose resistance varies in relation to pressure or force applied to it. A piezoresistive sensor receives a constant reference voltage and returns a variable signal in relation to its varying resistance.

Pinion gear: A smaller gear that meshes with a larger gearwheel or toothed rack.

Piston: A small cylinder fitted inside a hollow cylinder which moves back and forth by fluid pressure to transmit reciprocating motion.

Planet carrier assembly: One of the members of a planetary gearset. The carrier, or bracket, on which the planet pinions are mounted.

Planetary gearset: A system of gears consisting of a sun gear, internal ring gear, and planet carrier with planet pinion gears.

Polymer: A substance made of giant molecules formed from smaller molecules of the same substance.

Poppet valve: A valve that plugs and unplugs its opening by axial motion.

Positive-displacement pump: A pump that delivers the same amount of fluid for reach revolution of the pump.

Potentiometer: A variable resistor with three terminals. Return signal voltage is taken from a terminal attached to a movable contact that passes over the resistor.

Power: The rate at which work is done or force is applied. In mechanics, power is measured as torque times speed and expressed in units such as horsepower or kilowatts.

Powertrain: All of the vehicle components that contribute to the generation, transmission, and distribution of drive torque to the wheels.

Pressure: Force applied to a specific area, usually measured in pounds-per-square inch or kilo-Pascals.

Pressure plate: A reaction plate used in clutch packs to adjust their clearance.

Pressure regulator valve: A spool valve and spring combination that regulates the main hydraulic pressure.

Pressure relief valve: A valve in any hydraulic component that opens to bleed excess pressure when fluid pressure is excessively high. In a power steering system, a pressure relief valve may be used in the pump and/or the steering gear.

Programmable read-only memory (PROM): An integrated circuit chip installed in a computer that contains appropriate operating instructions and database information for a particular application.

Pulse-width modulation (PWM): The continuous on/off cycling of a solenoid a fixed number of times per second.

Pump: A device that creates or increases fluid flow. Most oil pumps are mounted directly behind the torque converter and usually driven by the converter drive hub.

Radial play: Movement at a right angle to the axis of rotation of a shaft, or along the radius of a circle or shaft. Also called side thrust or side play.

Radio frequency interference (RFI): A form of electromagnetic interference created in the ignition secondary circuit which disrupts radio and television transmission.

Random-access memory (RAM): Temporary short-term or long-term computer memory that can be read and changed but is lost whenever power is shut off to the computer.

Ravigneaux gearset: A compound planetary gear system consisting of two sun gears and two sets of planet pinions that share a common ring gear.

Reaction member: The member of a planetary gearset that is held in order to produce an output motion. Other members react against the stationary, held member.

Read-only memory (ROM): The permanent part of a computer's memory storage function. ROM can be read, but not changed, and is retained when power is shut off to the computer.

Reference voltage: A constant voltage signal (below battery voltage) applied to a sensor by the computer. The sensor alters the voltage according to engine operating conditions and returns it as a variable input signal to the computer, which adjusts system operation accordingly.

Resultant force: The combined force and oil flow direction produced by rotary and vortex flow in a fluid coupling or torque converter.

Ring gear: The outermost member of the gearset which has teeth in the inside circumference.

Rotary flow: The oil flow path, in a fluid coupling or torque converter, that is in the same circular direction as the rotation of the impeller.

Rotational motion: Movement that occurs when a shaft turns (rotates) on its axis. A dynamic seal is required to contain fluids where rotational motion is present.

Rotor pump: A positive-displacement pump that uses an inner drive rotor and outer driven rotor to produce oil flow. Lobes on the rotors create fluid chambers of varying volumes and eliminate the need for a crescent as used in a gear pump.

Scan Tool: Device that communicates with a computer through an electrical connection.

Sensor: A device that provides an electric signal to a control unit to indicate a certain physical condition.

Servo: A hydraulic piston and cylinder assembly that controls the application and release of a transmission band.

Shift valve: A spool valve acted on by throttle and governor pressure to time transmission shifts. Also called a "snap" valve or timing valve.

Simpson gearset: A compound planetary gear system consisting of two ring gears and two planet carrier assemblies that share a common sun gear.

Solenoid: An electromagnetic actuator consisting of a moveable iron core with a wire coil surrounding it. When electrical current is applied to the coil, the core moves to convert electrical energy to mechanical energy.

Speed ratio: The number of revolutions made by the turbine for each revolution of the impeller. Turbine (output) speed is divided by impeller (input) speed and expressed as a percentage.

Spool valve: A type of hydraulic valve, consisting of lands and valleys that resembles a spool for thread. The lands seal orifices and the valleys open them.

Sprag: A figure-eight-shaped locking element of a one-way sprag clutch.

Spur gear: A gear on which the teeth are parallel with the gear's axis of rotation.

Stall speed: The maximum possible engine and torque converter impeller speed, measured in rpm, with the turbine held stationary and the engine throttle wide open.

Static friction: The coefficient of friction between two surfaces that are at rest, or have no motion between them.

Static seal: A seal that prevents fluid passage between two parts that are in fixed positions relative to each other.

Stator: A reaction member of a torque converter mounted on a one-way clutch. Stators multiply torque by redirecting fluid flow from the turbine back to the impeller.

Strut: A device that transfers servo apply force to the transmission band. A strut may be located either between the servo or lever and band, or between the anchor and band.

Sump: The oil pan, or reservoir, that contains a supply of fluid for the transmission hydraulic system.

Sun gear: The central gear of a planetary gearset around which the other gears rotate.

Surface filter: A filter that traps contaminants on its surface. Screen and paper filters are types of surface filters.

Thermistor: An electronic component whose resistance to electric current changes rapidly and predictably as its temperature changes.

Throttle pressure: The transmission hydraulic pressure that is directly related to engine load. Throttle pressure, which increases with throttle opening and engine torque output, is one of the principle pressures used to control shift points.

Throttle valve: The valve that regulates throttle pressure based on throttle butterfly opening or intake manifold vacuum.

Torque: A twisting or rotating force that measures the amount of work that can be done; usually expressed in foot-pounds, inch-pounds, or Newton-meters.

Torque converter: A type of fluid coupling used to connect the engine crankshaft to the automatic transmission input shaft. Torque converters multiply the available

engine torque under certain operating conditions.

Torque converter capacity: The ability of a torque converter to absorb and transmit engine torque in relation to the amount of slippage in the converter.

Torque converter clutch (TCC): Similar to a clutch in a manual transmission, a torque converter clutch uses a friction disc, operated by a hydraulic piston, to mechanically couple the turbine to the impeller.

Torque curve: A graphic depiction of the amount of torque available at different engine speeds.

Torque multiplication phase: The period of torque converter operation when the vortex flow is redirected through the stator to accelerate impeller flow to the turbine and increase engine torque.

Transistor: A three-element semiconductor device that transfers electrical signals across a resistance.

Transmission band: A flexible steel band lined with friction material that is clamped around a circular drum to hold it from turning.

Turbine: A driven member that connects to the transmission input shaft and provides torque input to the planetary gearset.

Vacuum pump: A mechanically or electrically driven pump that provides a source of vacuum. Vacuum pumps are commonly used with Diesel engines which have little or no intake manifold vacuum.

Valve: A device that regulates, restricts, or directs the pressure and flow of transmission fluid.

Valve body: The casting that contains most of the valves in a transmission hydraulic system. The valve body also has passages for the flow of hydraulic fluid.

Vane pump: A pump that uses a slotted rotor and sliding vanes to produce oil flow. The vane pumps used in automatic transmissions are variable-displacement pumps.

Variable-displacement pump: A pump that automatically regulates output volume of fluid based on the needs of the transmission.

Viscosity: The tendency of a liquid, such as an oil or hydraulic fluid, to resist flowing. The more viscous a fluid or oil is, the thicker it is, and the less it tends to flow.

Viscous converter clutch (VCC): A torque converter clutch that uses a silicone fluid to transfer and multiply torque, the silicone absorbs shock and dampens engine vibration during clutch application.

Vortex flow: The oil flow path, in a fluid coupling or torque converter, that is at a right angle to the rotation of the impeller and rotary flow.

Work: The transfer of energy from one system to another, particularly through the application of force.

Worm gear: A gear that is shaped like a shaft with gear teeth cut in a continuous spiral around its outer surface. A worm gear changes the axis of rotation when it turns another gear.

ANSWERS TO REVIEW QUESTIONS

Chapter 1: Introduction to Automatic Transmissions and Transaxles
1-D 2-C 3-A 4-C 5-C 6-B 7-C
8-A 9-D 10-A 11-C 12-B 13-C
14-C 15-D 16-A 17-C 18-C
19-A 20-D

Chapter 2: Gears and Gearsets
1-C 2-B 3-C 4-B 5-C 6-C 7-A
8-D 9-D 10-A 11-C 12-B 13-B
14-A 15-C 16-D 17-A 18-B
19-D 20-C

Chapter 3: Hydraulic Fundamentals
1-C 2-D 3-C 4-A 5-B 6-B 7-C
8-A 9-C 10-B 11-B 12-D 13-A
14-D 15-C 16-C 17-C 18-D
19-A 20-C

Chapter 4: Transmission Hydraulic Systems
1-A 2-A 3-C 4-C 5-C 6-D
7-C 8-A 9-B 10-D 11-C 12-A
13-D 14-B 15-B 16-C 17-C
18-D 19-A 20-C

Chapter 5: Fluid Couplings and Torque Converters
1-A 2-C 3-D 4-C 5-C 6-D
7-D 8-C 9-B 10-A 11-D 12-C
13-A 14-A 15-C 16-B 17-A
18-B 19-B 20-D

Chapter 6: Apply Devices
1-D 2-B 3-C 4-A 5-C 6-A 7-A
8-D 9-B 10-D 11-D 12-C 13-A
14-D 15-B 16-C 17-A 18-C
19-B 20-D

Chapter 7: Transmission Fluids, Filters, and Coolers
1-C 2-C 3-A 4-D 5-C 6-C 7-A
8-B 9-D 10-D 11-C 12-D 13-C
14-D 15-D 16-C 17-D

Chapter 8: Gaskets, Seals, Bushings, Bearings, Washers, and Snaprings
1-D 2-A 3-C 4-A 5-C 6-B 7-C
8-A 9-A 10-C 11-C 12-B 13-D
14-B 15-B 16-D 17-C 18-A
19-A 20-B

Chapter 9: Basic Computer and Electronic Controls
1-C 2-A 3-A 4-A 5-C 6-D
7-C 8-C 9-C 10-A 11-B 12-C
13-B 14-A 15-D 16-A 17-C
18-B 19-C 20-B

Chapter 10: Electronic Control Systems
1-A 2-C 3-C 4-A 5-D 6-C
7-A 8-B 9-C 10-D 11-B 12-D
13-A 14-A

INDEX

Note: Boldface numbers indicate illustrations.